THE

PATCH

THE PEOPLE, PIPELINES, AND
POLITICS OF THE OIL SANDS

CHRIS TURNER

PUBLISHED BY SIMON & SCHUSTER

NEW YORK   LONDON   TORONTO   SYDNEY   NEW DELHI

SIMON &
SCHUSTER
CANADA

Simon & Schuster Canada
A Division of Simon & Schuster, Inc.
166 King Street East, Suite 300
Toronto, Ontario M5A 1J3

This Simon & Schuster Canada edition September 2017

SIMON & SCHUSTER CANADA and colophon are
registered trademarks of Simon & Schuster, Inc.

For information about special discounts for bulk purchases,
please contact Simon & Schuster Special Sales at 1-800-268-3216
or CustomerService@simonandschuster.ca.

Library and Archives Canada Cataloguing in Publication

Turner, Chris, 1973–, author
The Patch : the people, pipelines and politics of the oil sands / Chris Turner.
Issued in print and electronic formats.
ISBN 978-1-5011-1509-7 (hardcover)
ISBN 978-1-5011-1511-0 (ebook)
1. Oil sands industry—Social aspects—Canada. 2. Oil sands
industry—Political aspects—Canada. 3. Environmentalism—Canada.
I. Title.
HD9574.C22T87 2017 333.8'2320971 C2017-901922-8
C2017-901923-6

Manufactured in the United States of America

10 9 8 7 6 5 4 3 2 1

ISBN 978-1-5011-1509-7
ISBN 978-1-5011-1511-0 (ebook)

For Sloane and Alexander,
two children of Alberta

The fifth freedom, the Freedom of Individual Enterprise, is the keystone of the arch on which the other Four Freedoms rest. This is what freedom means.

—Nicholas Murray Butler,
President of Columbia University, 1943

There are strange things done in the midnight sun
  By the men who moil for gold

—Robert W. Service,
"The Cremation of Sam McGee" (1907)

CONTENTS

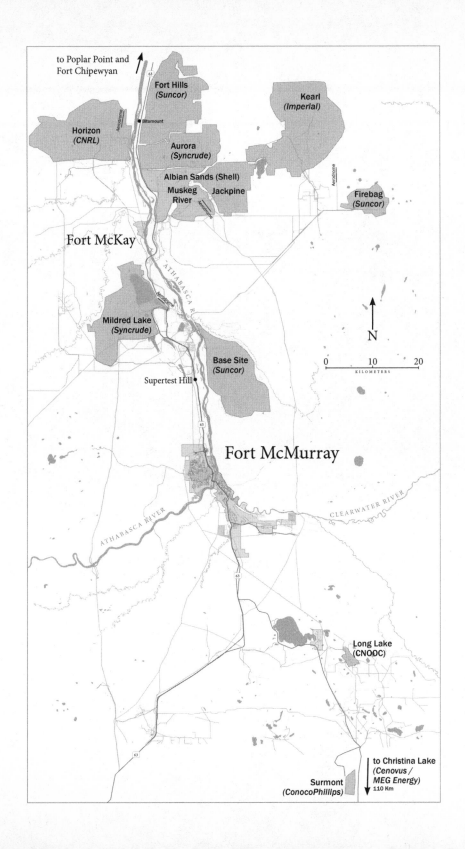

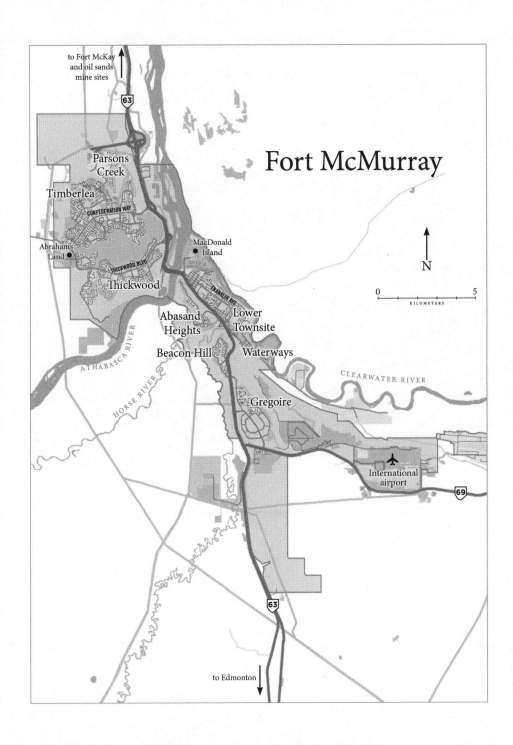

to Fort McKay
and oil sands
mine sites

63

Fort McMurray

Parsons
Creek

Timberlea

CONFEDERATION WAY

MacDonald
Island

Abraham's
Land

THICKWOOD BLVD

SNYE R.

N

0   5
KILOMETERS

Thickwood

FRANKLIN AVE

Abasand
Heights

Lower
Townsite

ATHABASCA RIVER

Beacon Hill

Waterways

CLEARWATER RIVER

HORSE RIVER

Gregoire

International
airport

69

63

to Edmonton

DUCKS ON A POND

The North American Central Flyway exists primarily as a collective in-stinct in the minds of millions of migratory birds. Whooping cranes and piping plovers, bald eagles and brown pelicans, mallard ducks and Canada geese—in twos and fours, in dozens and scores and vast flocks of thousands, all of them follow the same general path from winter nest to summer breeding grounds and back again each spring and fall.

The flyway is a vestige of the last Ice Age, when glaciers spread far south over the wide flat centre of the North American continent. The ice sheet isolated birds to the east and west, where they developed migratory routes on either side. When the glaciers retreated, they carved thousands of ponds and lakes into the prairie. Waterfowl and other migratory birds soon returned to the region, following food and sanctuary north and south along this newly thawed route. It stretches today from the Gulf of Mexico in the south to the Mackenzie Delta on the Arctic Ocean in the north, and it provides habitat and sustenance for millions of birds.

In April 2008, obeying those ancient instincts, in response to spring warmth and melting ice, ducks took flight from ponds across North America's broad plains. They had wintered in North Dakota and Minnesota, on frigid but unfrozen bodies of water in southern Saskatchewan and British Columbia and on rivers like the North Saskatchewan that cut across central Alberta. They flew north hard and fast, stopping at newly thawed open water along the way to feed. They flew as fast as sixty miles per hour at times, perhaps a thousand feet in the air. In less than a week, thousands of them had reached Alberta's boreal forest, bound likely as not for the nesting and feeding grounds of the Peace-Athabasca Delta, a waterfowl habitat as bounteous and expansive as the Mississippi.

The flyway had been there before there were roads and rails below, before there were cities and towns, before there was industry. The ducks followed a path older than the farms beneath them in southern Saskatchewan, older than the coal mines they passed over in Alberta's Badlands. Their route predated the internal combustion engine, the pumpjack, and the ingenious two-cone rotary rock drill bit. It was there before the Cree moved west to find fur for trade, before the peoples of the Peace-Athabasca Delta named their homeland Denendeh, perhaps before any *Homo sapien* had crossed from Asia onto the American land mass. Each spring, as day's light stretched into evening and the breeze turned warm, the ducks came north, alighting on thawed ponds to rest and eat before proceeding farther north to the delta to find mates and make nests. And then there would be more ducks to repeat the flight, year upon year, until the ice sheet's return—an eventuality well beyond the ken of any duck.

On April 20, 2008, as sometimes happens in the boreal forests of northern Alberta in spring, snow began to fall. Along the banks where the great Athabasca River makes its final hard turn north toward the delta, the snow that day fell in a formidable blizzard. It stormed for three days, and nearly half a metre blanketed the river banks and the forests of pine and spruce and the lakes and ponds strewn across the landscape east and west of the river.

The weather troubled the ducks. The low cloud made it hard to navigate, and the new snow and cold air made open water scarce and harder to spot. Sometime in the evening of April 27 or in the warming dawn of April 28, many flocks of them—mallards, mostly, but also quite a few mergansers, a smattering of other breeds—found a pond in the middle of a broad stretch of treeless ground. They came in one after the other, each chasing the next down onto the dark calm surface of the water. And one after another, they discovered a strange substance floating on the pond's surface, a thick dark goo the likes of which they had never encountered before. It was native to the region, but it belonged properly to the hidden depths of soil and sand deep beneath the boreal forest floor. It had no place in the flyway's ponds a thousand years ago, and it was scarce enough even ten years back that no flock of ducks had ever collided with it in such numbers.

Because a duck has never needed to see what is immediately in front of it as it descends upon a pond—or far less need, at least, than it has for seeing distant predators after it lands—its eyes are on either side of its head. Its forward vision thus limited, it isn't likely to notice its cousins flailing in distress until it too has landed. Landing on a pond is, in any case, the very essence of a duck's routine. There has never been any need for caution. The ducks flying low over the boreal forest north of Fort McMurray in this disorienting spring snowstorm were concerned only with finding open water. The pond below was an escape, an oasis, a temporary home.

This is how 1,611 ducks came to land on a settling basin at Syncrude Canada Ltd.'s Aurora oil sands mine, a body of water and many other superfluous substances produced during the separation of bitumen from raw oil sands ore. It is better known as a tailings pond.

A duck's feathers are coated in an oily substance secreted by its uropygial gland, which renders the feathers water resistant. A duck floats on water in part because it has a hollow skeleton but also because the uropygial oil prevents it from becoming waterlogged and heavy when it alights on water. If the feathers become coated in petroleum, however, the duck's defences are neutralized. A bird born to float on water can sink.

Because an oil sands tailings pond contains not just water but also residual bitumen, boreal dirt, heavy metals, and a slow-settling slurry of oil-processing chemicals and fine clays, its surface melts faster than a natural lake. And because this phenomenon is well understood by oil sands producers, tailings ponds are routinely ringed each spring with radar-triggered, propane-fired sound cannons. Even if a mallard duck might not know quite what a propane-fired cannon is, or for that matter *why* it is, it surely knows to hightail it elsewhere when faced with a sporadic barrage of loud explosions. At Syncrude Aurora, though, the blizzard had slowed down the cannon deployment process. The piles of snow had made it especially difficult to get crews out to the tailings pond, and then the rapid switch back to warm spring temperatures after the snow stopped had turned access roads and the pond's wide earthen dike walls into a mess of mud and snowmelt. The air around the tailings pond was silent on that April morning.

Like any other crude oil, bitumen floats to a pond's surface at low temperatures. It flows into a tailings pond "frothed"—aerated as part of the separation process. The bitumen froth won't mix with water, but it clings eagerly to anything else it encounters, including more of itself. It forms broad mats on the surface of the tailings pond. It's hard to imagine a more fervent mating of complementary materials than sticky bitumen froth and duck feathers. To the 1,611 ducks on the Syncrude Aurora tailings pond that morning, it must have seemed like the pond itself was rising up to snatch them. And refusing, inexplicably, to let go.

Ducks were still landing on the Aurora tailings pond when a Syncrude heavy equipment operator named Robert Colson came upon the scene at nine in the morning on April 28. Colson could see oddly shaped lumps out among the bitumen mats on the pond. He reported what he'd seen to his boss by radio. Later that morning, an anonymous caller—not

Colson—reported the incident to the Fort McMurray office of the Alberta government's Ministry of Sustainable Resource Development.

Todd Powell, the area wildlife biologist in the ministry office, had started his career in the Yukon. The land there could feel barely settled, the population sparse, the wild and rugged landscape remarkably close. The Yukon is a place where even the busiest downtown thoroughfares are sometimes shared with bears, and you meet office workers proficient in the field dressing of moose carcasses. Powell found there was never any question of the value of wildlife or the merit of his work protecting animals from human encroachment.

He took a job in wildlife management for the Alberta government in 2007 and relocated with his wife to Fort McMurray. The wildlife was nearby there as well, but he found people's attention was mostly elsewhere. The pace of life was faster, the money easier, your average resident far more likely than a Yukoner to be a recent arrival, having little direct experience with the wildlife of the Canadian North. There didn't seem to be much interest in conservation, population management, species at risk. The city existed to dig oil from underneath the forest. The forest's inhabitants were an afterthought at best.

Powell was out of his office the morning of April 28, but he returned just after lunch to find a voice mail message from an anonymous worker at the Syncrude Aurora site. It described hundreds of ducks mired in the toxic muck of a tailings pond.

"This isn't right," the caller said. "You need to get up here and do something about this."

Powell called Syncrude's environmental representative and arranged to meet at the Aurora mine.

In April 2008 Fort McMurray was the epicentre of the greatest oil boom in Canadian history, and the boom was just then reaching its zenith. The city's population had nearly doubled over the preceding decade and was still growing beyond anyone's reckoning. Which is to say that traffic was its usual mess as Powell crossed the two-lane bridge north out of downtown in his white Alberta government pickup truck, and the traffic

remained heavy as ever on Highway 63 as he drove the seventy-five kilometres north to Syncrude's Aurora site. Then there were security protocols
at the plant gate, a briefing with the Syncrude reps who met him there,
all the usual hoops to bounce through. It was early evening by the time he
arrived at the tailings pond.

Powell had been on the job with the Alberta government for only a
year, but he was already familiar with the destructive relationship between
duck feathers and bitumen froth. The environmental reps at Shell Canada's new Albian Sands mine were particularly fastidious, calling Powell
every time a duck or two landed on their tailings pond and got mired in
the petrochemical muck. It gunked up their wings, and as they struggled
to flap free, they would only become more deeply enmeshed. Sometimes
the trapped birds could be plucked out and sent to a rehabilitation centre
in Edmonton for cleaning, and sometimes there was nothing more to be
done other than put them out of their misery. It was an ugly business,
but on an industrial site of such scale, a certain amount of damage was
inevitable.

None of these previous incidents had prepared Todd Powell for what
he encountered at the Aurora pond that evening. There was a large pool of
bitumen some distance from the pond's edge—far enough away that not
every detail was clear, near enough for Powell to raise his camera and begin documenting the situation. The frothy black mat was alive with churning lumps, hundreds of them, which Powell immediately understood were
trapped ducks. They were fighting and struggling in vain to regain flight.
They would poke at the oil with their heads, searching for a way under
it, and when they pulled back up, the gooey bitumen hung from their
beaks like cold molasses. Ravens, relentless opportunists of the boreal forest, swooped down from time to time to pluck at their eyes. There was
nothing to be done that evening. Powell took photos, shot some video, and
left, with plans to return once Syncrude had organized its rescue effort.

He arrived at the pond the next day to find a robust salvage operation
set up in a warehouse building nearby. Syncrude had organized a couple
of dozen volunteers from the mine's massive workforce, directed by one of

the company's environmental monitoring representatives. Powell, like the Syncrude crew, had been anticipating a frenzied rescue scene, a place of triage and first aid, wounded birds by the score to be readied for airlift to a rehab facility in Edmonton. By early afternoon, Powell had mustered a boat and steered out to the edge of the bitumen mat, intending to pull out ducks and ferry them in for cleaning. But few of the birds remained at the surface. Aside from a handful who'd managed somehow to pull themselves from the froth and crawl out onto the muddy wall of the dike, there were none left to be rescued.

The trajectory of their fate had been mercilessly slow but inevitable. In ones and twos or by the dozen, they were swallowed whole by the froth. They had been trapped, and then the weight of the bitumen pulled them below the surface, and then they died. Weeks later, their bloated carcasses began to resurface, often stripped of skin and feathers by chemicals in the murky tailings below the pond's surface. In all, the pond claimed 1,606 ducks—all but five of the flock that had come to land on it.

Powell took pictures of the few ducks that crawled out onto the dike. In the end, just three birds—two mallards and a bufflehead—were evacuated from the site and airlifted aboard a Syncrude corporate jet to the Wildlife Rehabilitation Society of Edmonton. On April 29 Syncrude issued a press release noting that it was "working closely with Alberta Fish and Wildlife and Alberta Environment to coordinate recovery efforts relating to a large flock of ducks that landed on Syncrude's Aurora Settling Basin on Monday, April 28th." Powell passed his photos along to his bosses. There was little else, at the moment, to be done.

The story was picked up by the Canadian Press later that day. The initial report suggested that approximately five hundred ducks had been killed. In a province where hunters shoot and kill more than three hundred thousand waterfowl each year, on a continent home to ten million breeding mallards, the difference between five hundred and sixteen hundred is akin to a rounding error, the statistical definition of a nonstory. The incident was cruel and avoidable, but in greater ecological terms, it meant nothing beyond the gates of the Aurora mine.

There was something, though, about Powell's pictures and videos, which were on file with the provincial government when the media came calling. The piteous way the beached birds struggled to shake themselves loose of the gluey black bitumen. The way it resonated for an audience primed by larger catastrophes—particularly the 1989 *Exxon Valdez* oil spill, in which millions of gallons of oil spilled into the ocean off the coast of Alaska, killing hundreds of thousands of seabirds—to empathize with the dying wildlife, to immediately wonder at its potential scope, to imagine years or even decades of recovery. That the Syncrude disaster posed no such larger or lingering threats was lost in this resonance.

The Syncrude tailings pond incident was a top national story in Canada the following day. CBC's flagship nightly newscast, *The National*, framed its coverage that night with a simple, damning headline: "Dead Ducks." International media outlets started to pick up on the story the day after that. And Powell's documentary point-and-shoot pictures of migrating mallards soaked in bitumen were soon reprinted in newspapers around the world.

For untold millions of people, this was their first real introduction to the colossal industrial project operating in Alberta's boreal forest and their first encounter with a thick, energy-rich petroleum goo that was often referred to colloquially as "tar sands" (although the industry was vehement in its use of the term "oil sands"). It was, by either name, cast in this story primarily if not exclusively as a producer of toxic sludge that gathered in ponds the size of small lakes and killed innocent ducks. Even for many Canadians, well familiar with the vast oil deposits of northern Alberta and the explosive economic boom that had been felt nationwide over the preceding decade, the images of dead ducks provided the most intimate glimpse they had seen of the daily operation of an oil sands mine.

Both the provincial and federal governments eventually charged Syncrude with neglect under their respective environmental protection regulations. In 2010, after a trial at which Todd Powell was a key witness, a provincial court judge found the company guilty of a provincial charge of failing to prevent the tailings from coming into contact with wildlife and a federal charge of storing a substance in a manner harmful to migratory birds. Syncrude was ordered to pay a $3-million fine. It was the largest environmental fine ever levied in Alberta, but a shrug of a punishment in terms of Syncrude's bottom line—less than an hour's work for a company producing nearly three hundred thousand barrels of oil each day worth $90 apiece. The full cost of the 1,606 deceased ducks, however, would not be measured merely in immediate material terms. In some sense, it is still being paid by Syncrude and the rest of Alberta's oil patch today.

This, then, was the lesson the ducks taught the industry, even if it wasn't understood right away: in a twenty-first-century media environment, you have rapidly diminishing control over how you are perceived in the energy game. None whatsoever, sometimes, over scale and proportion. A few hundred ducks could become the whole world's ecological decline. By the same process, a single bitumen pipeline can be transformed into the conduit for the entire climate crisis, the fuse leading to a carbon bomb that, if detonated, would be the breaking point for the whole project of civilization. It matters little if these assertions are largely unfounded or their sense of proportion wildly out of whack. In today's energy business, this is no longer a marginal conversation, the crisis of a single news cycle to be managed and spun. It is central, existential. Years later, the dead ducks will still haunt you.

As a central character in the broader narrative of the global energy industry in the age of climate change, the story of the oil patch that arose over the last fifty years in Alberta's oil sands—*the Patch*, for short—began with those slain ducks. The birds and the tailings pond became a proxy for a wider polluted world in conflict, and in short order the whole industry became the embodiment of climate change itself, the poster child for the whole sinful age of fossil fuels, the face of an invisible global catastrophe. Sixteen hundred birds landed on a tailings pond, a collision of ecological disaster and economic necessity, and, in some sense, the fate of the world's oil industry—and certainly of Alberta's oil sands project—has come to rest on its ability to reconcile that conflict with the planet's energy demands. It remains an open question whether the industry is able to do so.

The conflict now underway in the Patch is not just of incongruous energy and climate policies but of competing world views. Alberta's oil sands industry emerged out of the High Modern ideal of progress that defined the twentieth century, that trust in bigger machines and better technology to fuel the good life. The industry's opposition is an extension of a new definition of progress, one native to the twenty-first century, born out of the emerging necessities of the Anthropocene epoch—that new chapter in geological time created by human hands in a time defined by climate change. The Anthropocene ideal aims for balance and sets as its highest priority the rapid reduction in greenhouse gas emissions created by burning fossil fuels.

The High Modern and Anthropocene world views have collided head-on in the oil sands. This book is a record of the collision and its aftermath, and a survey of that reconciliation project. It is also the story of how the pond came to be along the ducks' ancient migratory flight path in the first place, and how one of the most colossally scaled engineering projects in human history sprung into being deep in the boreal forest of northern Alberta. And it is finally the story of how the industry that built the pond became the first major battleground in a global conflict over the future of energy in the Anthropocene epoch.

The twenty-first century will be defined by how civilization reconciles its powerful hunger for energy with the toll taken on the planet's basic equilibrium. The trial run in that long contest—the first skirmish of proxies in that much larger war—is underway today in the Patch.

ONE

RUSH HOUR

ANY GIVEN DAY IN THE PATCH

On any given day, well before dawn in the interminable boreal winter and long after the sun has risen on the longest days of the bright boreal summer, the traffic in Fort McMurray streams out onto Highway 63. The flow is heaviest by far in the northbound lanes, heading to the big oil sands mining sites north of town that employ workers by the thousands. There are oil sands projects south of the city as well, but those are drilling operations for in situ oil sands deposits, deeply buried bitumen seams extracted by drilling operations that require far fewer workers than the mines. Twelve-hour shifts are the norm here, fourteen-hour shifts not uncommon. And though the traffic, like the industry itself, goes around the clock, it is heaviest during the morning and evening shift changes, just before six in the morning and after six in the evening. Every day.

The industry's footprint in the region stretches from mining sites ninety kilometres north of Fort McMurray to in situ projects more than two hundred kilometres south, but there is a company town's sense of unified purpose throughout. The traffic scatters north and south and veers off to this mine or that well pad. But everyone is bound for a single destination. In the national imagination, in political speeches and corporate brochures, on protest signs, this is the oil sands. The vast oil patch of northeastern Alberta. The Patch.

Out on Highway 63, the twin lanes heading north have filled with a steady rush of vehicles by six in the morning. There are smatterings of the commuter cars common in other cities, little Honda Civics and Toyota Camrys and those ubiquitous crossover SUVs—the station wagons of twenty-first-century suburbia—but they are in the minority. This is prime habitat for trucks. Beyond Fort McMurray's tidy suburban avenues, this is a world of muddy ruts and heavy snowpack, dirt parking lots and gravel side roads. It is a workplace of tradespeople, skilled technicians and engineers, where office spaces are often set in the midst of vast industrial operations and even the white-collar workers have job titles that speak of intimacy with raw earth: geologists and geophysicists, chemists and reservoir engineers. These are workers who go to site in bright-white half-ton pickup trucks caked with boreal dirt. These are parents who drive to school and the grocery store in meticulously maintained 4x4 trucks—GMC Sierras, Chevy Silverado Z71s, Dodge Ram 1500 5.7L HEMIs and Ford F-150 FX4s, some of them jacked up high above the slop on oversized tires and elongated shock absorbers and struts via the status symbol of a lift kit. These are families who celebrate weekends and holidays by latching campers and cargo trailers to their lifted pickups and loading them full of ATVs and snowmobiles and dragging the whole motorized circus to campsites down long backwoods roads thick with mud and snow where four-wheel drive is a legitimate necessity.

This is a land of trucks, built by trucks for trucks to mine more fuel for all those trucks. And there they all are in the Alberta predawn on Highway 63, headed north to the site. At times the traffic seems composed of almost nothing but those generic white work-site pickups, big F-350s and

Ram 2500s with the names of oil companies and oil-field service firms stencilled on the door. Suncor and Syncrude and Shell, Aecon and Schlumberger and Halliburton, local welding and electrical and pipefitting contractors. And then there are much larger trucks. Service trucks and dump trucks, cement mixers and tanker trucks. Trucks with built-in elaborate industrial gear for cleaning and fixing oil-field equipment. Flatbeds topped with huge pipes and massive hunks of fabricated steel. Eighteen-wheelers hauling sea containers or double trailers. There's so much heavy trucking traffic, it can seem as though there must be some kind of major emergency project in need of resupply out there in the woods. Such is the daily traffic flow in the Patch.

There is a steady, resolute uniformity to this truck-dense traffic, an air of solidarity, almost. There is even an ersatz national flag, an oil sands battle standard. This flag flies from the flatbed of almost every pickup truck. It's most often mounted on a flexible pole two metres long. The flag is usually made of fine-weave all-weather nylon mesh, a half oval of high-visibility orange with a Day-Glo yellow X on it. The flags and their poles are known locally as "buggy whips," and they are mounted on the back of big half-ton and full-ton pickups to alert the drivers of much larger work vehicles on oil sands sites to their presence there in that land of true giants. Off-site, the buggy whips can be bent over in a semicircular half-mast and fastened to the side of the truck bed, but many weary and bleary oil sands workers don't bother, so they flap in the morning breeze by the score on the drive out to the site, a united truck army headed north under these banners of alert and safety. There are surely few places on earth with more sheer trucking volume, and seemingly nowhere else where the banner of *Safety First* is more ubiquitous.

Amid all the jacked-up 4x4s and eighteen-wheelers hauling gear, there is also a convoy of big white buses, high-riding luxury coaches with smoked windows and "Diversified" printed in red down the side. A tagline—"Driven by Safety"—appears next to the company name in smaller italic script. Diversified Transportation Ltd. runs much of the private mass transit service that ferries thousands of workers from Fort McMurray to site and back again. And any given day, there's Raheel Joseph behind the wheel of one of those big Diversified coaches.

Joseph is 33 years old in 2015, a Pakistani immigrant who landed in Fort McMurray in 2007 just like the hundreds of others arriving each month from every point on the compass. He arrived with no training, no plan and no hard notion of why he had come aside from a friend's enticement. Joseph's friend was a fellow Pakistani immigrant, a guy he'd known back in Islamabad. Joseph lived in Mississauga, a Toronto suburb, at the time, and the friend was somewhere in Quebec. Neither had been in Canada very long, but both were finding it more difficult than they'd expected. Certainly much harder than the perception back in Pakistan, which was that getting to Canada was the challenging part, that once you arrived, it was "a paradise where you pluck the money from trees," as Joseph recalled years later.

His sister ran a salon in Brampton, so he went to cosmetology school. What man would imagine such a thing in Islamabad? This is how it looks now from the northbound lanes of Highway 63—a ridiculous concept, an absurd fever dream long faded—but his sister said this was the way to get ahead in Canada, and Joseph was in no position to argue. So he studied cosmetology, got his diploma, and was just setting to work in the salon when this old friend got in touch and said he was heading to Fort McMurray. That's where the real opportunity was, his friend assured him.

Joseph could not have found the place on a map. He knew Brampton and the CN Tower in Toronto, and he knew Niagara Falls, because every Canadian newcomer knows Niagara Falls. He knew less than nothing, which was probably for the best, because even a Pakistani immigrant who has made it through Toronto's winter knows nothing of what awaits him in the subarctic boreal forest. Still, it held more promise than working for his sister in a salon. "The reason why I came here," he recalled later, "is with the ambition to do something in life. To be successful."

In November 2007, Joseph and the friend from Quebec and two other guys they knew piled into a car together and drove across the country to Fort McMurray, dreaming of a new kind of life.

There's likely never been a boom like the one that convulsed Fort McMurray circa 2007. Perhaps the Klondike gold rush itself, but even Dawson City didn't have multiple $5-billion industrial expansion projects simultaneously on the go. And Dawson City was never fed by fleets of pickup trucks and roaring luxury coaches and a vast network of chartered planes, bringing in thousands more from every city in Canada to work twenty straight days before getting four or maybe six days off to go home and try to keep the family together—or else drive a new 4x4 into Fort McMurray and raise hell like the whole town was Dan McGrew's Malamute Saloon in a twenty-first-century riff on old Robert Service, the bard of the Klondike.

The city existed in a perpetual state of growth and agitation. Numbers were murky at the peak of the boom—no one could get a clear count of the "shadow population" living in work camps and other short-term arrangements—but safe to say there were many hundreds like Raheel Joseph arriving each month. Hundreds and hundreds of young people, young men especially, who'd come from somewhere far away because here was a place where the full scale of opportunity a person could grasp all at once was still an open question. And so there were too many people and there was too much money and there was not enough of anything else in Fort McMurray in 2007. A little snow or a single stalled truck, and traffic on Highway 63 was pure gridlocked chaos. You went to Walmart, and no one was stocking shelves—they couldn't afford the wages to pay someone to do it, and there was no time. They just put the groceries or housewares or work clothes or whatever new stuff had made it to the boomtown that week out on pallets, and the pallets would be empty within hours. This was really how things went, day in and day out. Any warm body could find a job, but try to get a table at a restaurant, try to get a coffee at Tim Hortons in less than half an hour, try to find a bed to sleep in. Good luck with that.

Fort McMurray had doubled in size between 1999 and 2007. The provincial unemployment rate was 3.4 percent, which in Fort McMurray amounted to a statistical placeholder for less than zero. The length of the line at the Tim Hortons drive-thru just off Highway 63 became internationally famous, and you could earn $16 an hour (twice the provincial minimum wage) handing coffee and donuts out the window—if you were willing to do such a menial job in a city of boundless employment opportunities. One local restaurant couldn't attract a single applicant in town for its vacant jobs, so it had started offering a free plane ticket to Fort McMurray as a sort of signing bonus.

This was the calamitous land of opportunity that presented itself to Raheel Joseph, barely a year departed from Islamabad, in the northwestern woods of Canada that madcap year of 2007.

Joseph's friend from Quebec had an uncle in town, also from Pakistan, who was pulling in $40 an hour as a security guard. So they all got jobs in security and bunked down with the uncle for a couple of weeks while they figured out how to navigate the boomtown. They started with a safety course—no matter what your work was in the Patch, you needed safety certification before you could do a thing—and they met some Indian guys in the course who had found an apartment, which verged on miraculous at the time. It was a three-bedroom apartment with just one bathroom. Arrangements were summarily made—with Joseph and the three friends who'd come west with him now included, there were thirteen young men living in it. They were making crazy money in their new security jobs and sleeping in shifts in seemingly less space than you'd expect even in a Karachi slum. If you wanted to lay down your head atop a twenty-first-century gusher, then a pillow and a place to put it came at a wildly high premium.

Joseph didn't much like the work as a security guard. You did nothing but sit for twelve hours straight out at the site, minding some post, checking ID badges at the shift changes and studying the middle distance the rest of the time. Who would like this job? Still, this was how you waited on the next opportunity, the next rung on the ladder to the good life. Or so he hoped. Joseph spent a year at Suncor's new Fort Hills mine and then two more at the company's base site closer to the city. He went back to Pakistan to get married—his family had arranged it, per the Pakistani norm—and brought his wife to the boreal forest of northern Canada, and he watched the trees fill with snow and then melt, the days grow deliriously long and then impossibly short. He contracted diabetes, and he was sure that sitting there motionless twelve hours a day had brought it on. He waited out the short hiccup of a bust after the financial crisis in 2009, and then, two years later, as Fort McMurray was returning to its lunatic boomtown stride, Joseph landed a plum job as a bus driver with Diversified.

Joseph's day starts even earlier than the Patch's usual. He reports to the Diversified shop in the industrial park just off Highway 63 at five in the morning. Next comes the requisite forty-five minutes of maintenance and safety, and then he hits the road.

Diversified's routes wind through every suburb in Fort McMurray, scooping up oil sands workers at the city's municipal bus stops like the most extensive and efficient mass transit system a city of eighty thousand ever had. Diversified drivers bid on routes by the month, with the most senior guys getting their choices met first; they tend to snatch up the shortest ones with the fewest number of stops and tight turns. Like every other job in the Patch, each particular route comes with a work schedule attached, a certain number of days on and then a certain number of days off. Different bids also include three or even four routes a day instead of just two, which leads to more hours and more overtime and more money. Folks in Fort McMurray rattle off their work schedules like sports scores: twenty-and-ten or fourteen-and-six or ten-and-four. Everyone chases more overtime. What's the point of riding a boom's wild waves if not to soak up every possible chance to do more, make more, push further ahead? Everyone seems to have vague plans to cash out, too, a date or bank balance or property value that serves as a finish line. Who knows how many ever hit such targets or stick to them?

Like a lot of Diversified drivers, Joseph prefers a twenty-one-and-seven: three straight weeks of work on the same routes and then a solid week off. He's been at it long enough by 2015 that he's settled on preferred routes.

When he could, for example, he would bid on Suncor Route 13—a tidy little loop of a dozen or so stops laced along wide roads in the suburb of Timberlea on the north edge of town, then a quick run out to the main Suncor site closest to the city. There are more plant workers than the norm on Route 13—office types, not tradespeople—and Joseph found them a little more polite, less likely to gripe. But he didn't have real complaints about any route, about any of it at all. It was a good steady job and he had a wife and a new baby, barely a year old. Instead of sitting in a guardhouse counting the minutes, he could see a long, prosperous life stretched out ahead of him like a bustling highway. There he was every morning in the thick of that flow of waving buggy-whip flags, a cog in the great machine, making fantastic money just like everyone else, including all those bleary-eyed guys he scooped up along his route in the predawn rush. By shortly after six in the morning, you could imagine him content as he navigated that northbound traffic on Highway 63.

LOCKED IN

The city of Fort McMurray, like the region it anchors, is defined by its rivers. The Clearwater River comes from the east, flowing gently down a broad, forested canyon of remarkably pleasant aspect—"beautifully mean-dering," the Scottish explorer Alexander Mackenzie wrote of it on his 1792 journey, and "displaying a most delightful mixture of wood and lawn." The river begins to zigzag in a series of tight S-curves as it turns northward just upriver from Fort McMurray. The community of Waterways, formerly the terminus of North America's northernmost railroad when the Alberta and Great Waterways Railway was completed in 1921, sits in one of the curves. Beyond Waterways, the Clearwater carries on to the northwest in a widen-ing valley, with a broad floodplain on its western bank.

The Athabasca River arrives from the west, nearing the end of a 1,200-kilometre journey from the Columbia Glacier high in the Rocky Mountains. It runs slow along a flat riverbed with low, steep bluffs to either side. The two rivers meet in an inverted V as the Athabasca veers north, the Clearwater flowing from the southeast into the larger Athabasca through a main channel as well as a small secondary channel just south of it called the Snye. Downtown Fort McMurray sits in the crook of this V, on the Clearwater's floodplain. As the city rapidly outgrew its original town site in the years after commercial oil sands operations began in 1967, it spread in a series of suburban subdivisions: Abasand Heights and Beacon Hill, south of the Athabasca, in the 1970s and 1980s; and then Thickwood and Timberlea, north of the river, since the 1990s. More than fifty-four thousand current residents—fully 65 percent of the total urban population of eighty-two thousand, as of the 2015 municipal census—live in the neighbourhoods north of the Athabasca, which have continued to expand west and north as the city booms.

The rivers define the city, its location on the map and its general layout. But the city's backbone, the conduit of its daily life, is Highway 63. The artery runs north and south along the western edge of the original downtown, crosses the Athabasca just before its confluence with the Clearwater on a pair of two-lane bridges, and then points straight north at the series of mining operations known locally as "the site." The term is used generically to refer to any one of the major mine sites. There are eight in all, starting with the original Suncor and Syncrude sites twenty-five kilometres north of town, with a half-dozen more projects—all built in a flurry of construction over the last fifteen years—sprawling across vast excavations on either side of the next forty-odd kilometres of highway: Syncrude's Aurora and Suncor's Steepbank, Shell's two Albian Sands operations, Imperial Oil Ltd.'s Kearl Lake and Canadian Natural Resources Ltd.'s Horizon. But the same term also loosely describes the entire operation north of town along Highway 63. Thousands of oil sands workers travel "out to the site"—or often just "out to site" in the local lingo—and "back from site" on the highway, and McMurrayites speak of happenings "out at site," regardless of which specific site they are describing.

The full scale of the oil sands project extends far beyond the ribbon of Highway 63 north of Fort McMurray. South of the city, down a long side road paved only recently (Highway 881), there are more than twenty other oil sands extraction operations that are either running or under development. To the north, much of the extraction is surface mining, vast open pits where bitumen is carved from the earth by mammoth truck-and-shovel operations. To the south, all the projects are in situ operations, with the bitumen extracted by drilling rigs and horizontal wells, most often by a process known as steam-assisted gravity drainage. SAGD injects hot steam through one well to melt the bitumen and get it flowing downward to a second well, from which it is pumped to the surface.

At Christina Lake, 150 kilometres southwest of Fort McMurray, MEG Energy produces 70,000 barrels of oil per day (bpd) using SAGD technology, and Cenovus Energy extracts another 150,000 bpd from the same deposit. A further 150,000 comes from two SAGD sites operated by CNRL. Devon Energy Corporation pumps 66,000 bpd from its Jackfish Lake project, and the Chinese oil company CNOOC (China National Offshore Oil Corporation) Ltd. produces 38,000 at the Long Lake plant it took over when it bought a Canadian company called Nexen a few years back. ConocoPhillips Company generates 25,000 at Surmont, and so on down the list to small test operations run by Pengrowth Energy Corporation and Japan Canada Oil Sands (JACOS) Limited and Osum Oil Sands Corp. North of the city, Suncor's Firebag SAGD project produces 187,000 bpd.

All told, a slim majority of the oil pumped from Alberta's oil sands has come from these in situ operations since 2012. The big mines, meanwhile, produce oil the old-fashioned way in six-figure daily quantities, from 325,000 at Suncor's base site to 110,000 at Shell's Jackpine mine. They all operate around the clock, through long winter nights and the near-permanent sunlight of summer's longest days and every day in between. Roughly 1.1 million barrels of oil per day are extracted at mine sites, and about 1.3 million barrels per day come from in situ deposits.

In 2015, oil companies produced a total of 869.3 million barrels of oil from all of Alberta's oil sands operations. Production peaked at a record level of nearly 2.6 million bpd in July, but in other months, production dipped as low as 2.2 million bpd. New projects came online during 2015, while others proved uneconomical and shut down. Technological tweaks to this mine or that drilling operation nudged the production rate upward; other innovations proved not to be worth their cost and bumped it downward. Production rates ebbed and flowed along with supply and demand, and persistently low prices convinced major oil sands players to spend more time on maintenance than they had in previous years. But on a typical day in 2015, the industry produced about 2.4 million barrels of oil.

In the industry's parlance, this is the "locked-in" production. This is the solid state. This is what was dug or pumped from the earth each day. This is what was shipped by pipeline to waiting storage tanks or loaded onto railcars for delivery to refineries. Whether the price rose or fell that day or that week, whether a small company failed or a large one announced a new investment, whether cars filled the highways for a holiday weekend or stayed close to home, the world's oil supply, which averaged about 91.7 million bpd in 2015, included 2.4 million barrels of Alberta bitumen.

This is how the oil sands flow. Twenty-four hours a day, seven days a week. Any given day.

THE AGE OF OIL

This, then, is the Patch: 2.4 million bpd, an industrial cluster and the communities built to serve it. The daily production is drawn from a total proven reserve of 166 billion barrels—third only to Saudi Arabia and Venezuela, as boosters never tire of noting—supplying two-thirds of the oil industry's total output nationwide, which accounts for 3 percent of Canada's GDP and 14 percent of its total exports.

It is one oil patch, but in truth there are many. Alberta's Patch is part of a worldwide wave of expansion that emerged in the past quarter century as the global oil industry raced to keep up with relentlessly skyrocketing demand. Conventional fields like the ones scattered across the Arabian Peninsula continue to produce the lion's share of the world's oil, as they have since the rise of oil as the dominant fuel source of the industrial age in the early nineteen hundreds. Much of the industry's constant hustle for new sources, however, has moved to the margins—to long-shots and risky plays, new technologies and complex, high-cost extraction techniques. Deepwater wells far out to sea, hydraulic fracturing in prairie shale beds, oil sands in the boreal forest. The shift is mirrored in the other fossil fuel industries: coal seams in the most remote wilderness of China and Australia, mountaintop-removal coal mining in the Appalachian Mountains of the eastern United States, natural gas fracking from Pennsylvania to Poland. More than 85 percent of the world's primary energy comes from fossil fuels—oil, coal and natural gas—and the demand for all three rose precipitously through the last decades of the twentieth century. The gas pump, electricity meter and basement furnace may not have betrayed a revolutionary shift in how all that energy was procured, but a whole new industrial world had emerged by the turn of the century to keep the engines humming, the lights on and the house warm.

In the Gulf of Mexico, 200 miles south of the Louisiana coast, Shell's Stones project pumps oil from 26,500 feet below sea level in water nearly 10,000 feet deep, using a converted oil tanker as a floating production and storage vessel. Elsewhere in the Gulf, ConocoPhilips operates a drilling platform more than twice the height of the CN Tower. Off the coast of Brazil, drilling rigs reach down through a mile of ocean and then a mile of shifting salt to reach pockets of crude. From North Dakota to West Texas, subterranean injections of water and chemicals under enormous pressure pulverize ancient layers of shale, a porous sedimentary rock full of tiny pockets that yield oil and natural gas for extraction. And in pursuit of the same manic need for more fuel, there came to be a bustling modern city of more than 80,000 in the boreal forest of northern Alberta, where not too long ago a small, stagnant outpost of the fur trade once stood. One more arm of a vast global enterprise—drilling rigs and pumpjacks, sprawling refineries and rows of gargantuan storage tanks, massive offshore drilling platforms and an armada of colossal tanker ships, millions of miles of pipe snaking across the continents and along the sea floors—all of it to fill and deliver those 91.7 million barrels each and every day.

There are oil fields and frontier towns that few outside the industry have ever heard of, from booming Khanty-Mansiysk in Siberia and Yasuni National Park in the Ecuadorian Amazon to rigs hundreds of kilometres offshore in the North Atlantic Ocean and in the disputed waters of the South China Sea. In each of these and dozens more oil patches around the world, thousands or millions of barrels are extracted each day.

The story of Alberta's Patch is different—and singular—because it did not remain obscure. It expanded beyond the industry's internal lore, its bitumen-derived fuel coming to stand as a symbol for a global crisis—for the entire oil industry; for the global fossil fuel extraction enterprise; for the complex technocratic, energy-thirsty world it powers; and for the whole planet's climate, which has been fundamentally altered by the greenhouse gases pumped into the atmosphere by all those burning hydrocarbons. The extraordinary industrial project of the oil sands, the final triumphal effort by which sludgy bitumen was finally transformed into valuable fuel feeding the global flow, had been understood during the latter years of the twentieth century as an engineering marvel and a monument to progress. But in the early years of the twenty-first century, another idea of progress emerged, one that places the planet's ecology at the highest rung on the priority list and sees a stable climate as the ultimate goal of human enterprise. From this point of view, the oil sands were recast instead as the worst culprit in a global regime causing the greatest environmental catastrophe civilization has ever known.

The oil sands of northern Alberta became the first major battleground between the economic necessity of oil production and the ecological necessity of reducing greenhouse gas emissions. And as the position of oil in the world undergoes a seismic shift from vital fuel source to necessary evil, it has become a defining story of the twenty-first-century energy business. Competing definitions of progress, tracing narrative arcs across very different cultural terrain over the past fifty years, have collided first and most decisively in the oil sands, the opening act in a worldwide debate that will determine the global economy's future energy basis and the planet's long-term environmental health. This is the defining economic and political challenge of our time—and it has reached its first profound inflection point in Alberta's Patch.

In the story of the oil age, the conflict in the Patch is primarily about investment and risk in a world where the industry's product remains in greater demand than ever but with less certainty regarding its future than it has seen in generations. "Never before has humanity faced such a challenging outlook for energy and the planet," wrote Royal Dutch Shell CEO Jeroen van der Veer in the introduction to the company's 2008 report *Shell Energy Scenarios to 2050*. "This can be summed up in five words: 'more energy, less carbon dioxide.'"

For years, Shell has employed a team of "scenario planners" to study broad global trends of all kinds and develop plausible visions of the future, around which to plan the company's long-term strategy. In the 2008 report, the scenario planners delineated three "hard truths" guiding the years to come: (1) a "step change" upward in energy demand owing to development and economic growth in China and India; (2) a struggle for energy producers trying to keep up; and (3) steadily increasing "environmental stresses."

The report outlined two future visions of civilization's collective response to climate change. The first, which the planners named "Scramble," would be characterized by a "focus on national energy security," where short-term political calculations and the growing influence of fossil fuel companies would drive a frenzied worldwide hunt for the last of the planet's fossil fuel supplies, triggering booms in the coal business, biofuels and unconventional oil. The Scramble scenario would also see mounting damage from climate change and a "political backlash" against the energy industries.

The second scenario, "Blueprint," envisioned a "critical mass of positive responses" to climate change that, in time, would propel a globally coordinated transition away from fossil fuel dependency. Fossil fuels—especially oil—would still account for a substantial amount of the world's energy, but their use and the influence of the industries that extract them would steadily decline.

When Shell's CEO introduced the report at the World Economic Forum in Davos, Switzerland, in January 2008, he indicated the company's preference for the orderly Blueprint scenario, with its potential to avert the worst climate change impacts. But just weeks later, when Shell bid more than $2 billion for drilling leases in the warming Arctic Ocean, it suggested that the oil giant saw the Scramble as being at least as likely an outcome. For unconventional oil developments like Alberta's oil sands, even the near collapse of the global financial system later in 2008 represented barely a moment's pause in a long boom. The record year for capital expenditures in the oil sands was 2014, when oil companies and energy investors around the world spent $34 billion. Gazing into the future from Fort McMurray in the years after Shell's report, it was easier to see the world of the Scramble than that of the Blueprint dawning on the horizon.

Still, even if it was not recognized in many boardrooms in Calgary or anywhere else in the industry, oil's dominance could no longer be taken for granted. Climate change was not readily managed like the sludge in a single tailings pond or contained like the mess from a single pipeline spill. This was a more profound challenge to the industry's story of progress—perhaps an existential one. In the years after Shell unveiled its two scenarios, environmental activists began to stand in opposition to one new fossil fuel project after another, and bankers and investors started to ask industry executives tough questions about whether their reserves represented future profits or "stranded assets." And starting with the proposed Keystone XL project, a major new pipeline that intended to carry Alberta's bitumen from a storage terminal on the prairie south of Fort McMurray to the Gulf of Mexico, the oil sands became the front line in this larger conflict. In the story of progress being told with climate change at its centre, the world had no choice but to move as quickly as possible toward an economy free of greenhouse gas emissions. For a variety of reasons connected only tangentially to the daily operation of an oil sands site—American political considerations and universal symbolic impact, in particular—the elimination of the Patch's daily ration of the world's oil supply came to be seen as the essential first step in this decarbonization process.

To put it in the blunt terms of America's polarized politics, this was *Drill Baby Drill!* versus *Keep It in the Ground!* And by 2015, the conflict's global epicentre was Alberta's oil sands. In 2015 the US Congress passed a bill ordering the State Department to approve the Keystone XL pipeline. President Barack Obama vetoed it, and later in the year, he announced that he was denying TransCanada PipeLines Ltd. its application to build the pipeline. Also in 2015 the Federal Bureau of Investigation (FBI) called environmental activists in Idaho, Washington and Oregon to question them about their opposition to "megaload" equipment shipments headed for the Patch. In 2015, with low oil prices slowing growth in the oil business province-wide to a standstill and the Alberta economy plunging into recession, Albertans voted out the Progressive Conservatives for the first time in forty-four years, replacing them with a left-leaning New Democratic Party government that vowed both to get pipeline projects approved *and* to get serious about climate change. A few months later, Canadians replaced a federal Conservative government that had been brayingly boosterish about the oil sands for a decade with a new Liberal government promising, like Alberta's NDP, to deepen the country's climate change action and get pipelines built. As oil prices slumped below $50 per barrel month after month, the Illinois-based manufacturing company Caterpillar, which had boomed making huge trucks and other outsized equipment for oil sands operations and other energy projects, laid off hundreds of workers at factories in Decatur and Peoria. The coal industry buckled under low prices and competition from clean energy sources as well in 2015, and investors and financial analysts around the world began to openly question the longstanding assumption that energy demand would continue to increase for decades to come, the way it had in the decades just passed. In the last weeks of the year, the world's political leadership met in Paris and arrived at the broadest agreement yet on climate change action. The fossil fuel business reeled, climate activists celebrated, and Shell's Blueprint scenario seemed ascendant for the very first time.

Still, with all of this hanging in the balance and the global spotlight shining in as never before, the Patch carried on in 2015 with the daily grind of producing 2.4 million barrels of oil.

OUT TO SITE

North of Fort McMurray, the highway follows the Athabasca River. About twenty kilometres out of town, there is a long, steep uphill grade the locals call Supertest Hill because of the challenge it presents to flatbed trucks carrying superheavy loads. At Supertest's crest, on a clear day, the two original oil sands mines come into view on either side of the highway. Syncrude's Mildred Lake mine, which started operating in 1978, is on the left, west of the highway. The Suncor base site, which began as the Great Canadian Oil Sands mine in 1967 but now stretches well beyond the original lease area across multiple mining sites, is on the right.

The Suncor base site, like all the oil sands mining sites, is a sprawling industrial city all its own—a gated, tightly monitored, self-contained universe. It hums nonstop, grinding bitumen from the ground and turning it into crude oil, 24 hours a day and 365 days a year. It is the oldest commercial oil sands site and remains the largest, producing 327,000 barrels of oil per day on average in 2015.

The mining complex has its own exit on Highway 63, so when Raheel Joseph arrives around half past six, he pilots his Diversified bus down a dedicated off-ramp that gives way to an access road, winding past three massive workforce accommodation complexes—"lodges" assembled from stacks and rows of narrow modular office trailers—to the main gate. Beyond the gate, the road skirts around a small tailings pond, with a flat, grassy plain dotted with scrub trees (the early stages of a reclaimed tailings pond) to the right. As Joseph steers his bus northward again, the industrial city's central business district comes into view.

The main plant at Suncor base site is a complicated array of towers and smokestacks, twisting pipe and scaffold, midrise buildings in green and yellow and raw grey concrete. The myriad instruments of bitumen upgrading and oil refining form a dense skyline, like a modern metropolis built at half scale. Billowing clouds of steam and smoke pour from some of the towers, and others are topped with fierce flames like enormous torches. At night, the main plant of an oil sands mine looks from a distance like a glittering city on fire. The plant's outskirts are covered in low, aluminum-sided administrative buildings, scatterings of the Patch's ubiquitous ATCO-brand office trailers with their distinctive yellow top stripe, and tidy rows of enormous concrete storage tanks. Pipes of various sizes snake everywhere. The site's hard-packed dirt roads are busy with white work trucks, bulldozers and backhoes, plus the yellow school buses that serve as on-site shuttles for Suncor workers, all of them trailing away to the gaping open mines and bitumen processing facilities in the distance to the south and east.

Joseph started his career at Diversified driving one of those shuttles, running workers from one corner of the vast plant to the other with long, dreary stretches spent waiting in between. But now he simply pulls up to the primary plant's main bus stop in his luxury coach to let off his passengers and pick up workers coming off shift.

The departing workers are in no kind of lockstep as they unload from Joseph's bus, much more a loose group of self-contained work assignments shuffling in the same general direction than a united workforce. But there is a clear sense of solidarity. The jobs on an oil sands mining site range from routine maintenance and garbage pickup to operating heavy equipment of colossal size to wildly advanced engineering and technical supervision, where days are spent in front of banks of computer monitors. But there is a rough uniformity to the oil sands workers' dress and deportment nevertheless. There is near-zero formal business attire. Heavy scuffed work boots with steel toes are worn by a broad swath of the workforce, regardless of gender or place in the mine's work hierarchy. The most common work uniform is full-length blue coveralls filigreed with high-visibility stripes in neon yellow and reflective silver. For those not in coveralls, the norm tends toward hooded sweatshirts, heavy flannel shirts, jeans and white running shoes, sometimes with a bright orange or yellow safety vest worn over the hoodie or flannel. Nearly everyone carries a large daypack, a big nylon bag with multiple zippered pockets, hanging heavy with its load of gear and provisions for a twelve-hour shift. Often these daypacks are emblazoned with the logos of oil companies and references to byzantine safety records at some recent project. Nylon shell jackets, usually black and manufactured by a company called Stormtech and often adorned with similar logos and safety records, are also common. In the winter, everyone wears a heavy parka.

Off they go, putting in another twelve-hour day in their fourteen-and-four or twenty-and-ten, pulling in overtime every chance they get. For all its fast-money boomtown veneer, Fort McMurray is a workaholic's town, and this is a focused, professional, punctual crowd. By seven in the morning, Joseph has collected all the workers coming off the night shift and sets off to navigate the whole route in reverse.

A thousand minor variations on Raheel Joseph's commute are duplicated the full length and breadth of the Patch. From above, the whole oil sands project seems nearly like a single unbroken whole, a tidy chain up and down the length of Highway 63. It extends from Suncor's new Fort Hills mine—the northernmost project, still under construction—south through Fort McMurray, and then veers off to the southeast down Highway 881, just beyond the city's airport, ending in the half-dozen SAGD operations scattered around the First Nations village of Conklin, 155 kilometres south of the city. Look at the whole thing on Google Earth, and even the wide stretches of boreal forest seem tethered together by a vast web of orderly lines cut from the wilderness—access roads and pipeline rights-of-way, arrow-straight and sharp-angled, the lines meeting at the little round nodes of clearing where SAGD drill pads stand, resembling a circuit board.

In addition to the steady traffic north and south out of Fort McMurray, there are scores of work camps scattered throughout the region—more than forty in all—with enough beds to accommodate 75,000 or more workers. The common term harkens back to a time when the facilities were simpler affairs, rugged camps for temporary construction crews, but today they are much more elaborate and permanent structures. Some are "closed" camps, built to house workers on a specific project. These tend to be smaller facilities, with just a couple of hundred beds, though Shell's Albian Village—the closed camp for the workforce on its Albian Sands mines—can house up to 2,500. Rooms at the remaining "open" camps can be booked by any oil sands contractor or visitor, and these open camps are often much larger. Most open camps start around 500 rooms and range all the way up to the massive Wapasu Creek Lodge—situated roughly equidistant from Imperial's Kearl mine, Suncor's Firebag SAGD operation and Shell's Albian Sands—which has rooms for more than 5,000 workers. All told, as many as 60,000 mobile workers, the vast majority bunking in one of the camps, could be at work in the Patch at any given time, the total varying with the seasons, the rise and fall of oil prices, and the volume of new investment and new construction in the Patch.

The first open camp ever built in the Patch was Creeburn Lake Lodge, which opened in April 2008 just off Highway 63 on the outskirts of Fort McKay, about sixty-five kilometres north of Fort McMurray. It was a sort of monument to the scale, sophistication and boundless ambition of the booming industry. Creeburn Lake Lodge was not a temporary work camp for a mine's construction or on-site lodging for a couple of hundred staff; it was a permanent apartment-hotel at the epicentre of the expanded industry. It had been constructed by ATCO, the predominant builder of prefab work camps and temporary offices in the Patch, in barely six months. The residential rooms are stacked rows of the vinyl-sided trailers with the yellow stripe on top that are ubiquitous in industrial Alberta, but the overall structure is more like a rural resort lodge than anything ATCO had ever built before. The entry area is a multistorey vaulted lobby with timber trusses. In addition to the requisite cafeteria, there are lounges, a fitness centre, conference rooms, and a driving range for golfers. The five hundred rooms have large-screen TVs, individual climate control and wireless internet. The Fort McKay First Nation partnered with ATCO on the construction and runs the facility not with the utilitarian bluntness of a company camp but with the friendly professionalism of the hospitality industry. This was a building for a radically different kind of oil enterprise from the one that gave rise to ATCO more than a half century earlier.

ATCO's arc of growth and expansion across the decades is a microcosm of Alberta's. The company began as Alberta Trailer Hire in 1947, just as the first major conventional oil discoveries were made in central Alberta. Ron Southern was a teenager bound for university with $2,000 he'd earned as a busboy at the glamorous Banff Springs Hotel, and his father threw in $2,000 more from the mustering-out money he'd received at the end of the Second World War. Together they bought ten U-Haul type trailers to rent to the new oil business. They charged $2 a day and hoped to earn enough money to cover Southern's university costs. But then Shell Oil came calling, looking for mobile bunkhouses for its workforce on a drilling site up north. Southern decided to build the whole installation himself, and the ATCO trailer was born.

As Alberta's oil and gas industry grew in the years and decades thereafter, ATCO expanded along with it—first across Alberta and then around the world. ATCO trailers found use as battlefield hospitals in Vietnam and research stations in Antarctica. They were used in ICBM missile silo construction and the building of the Alaska pipeline, in Olympic villages and forward operating bases and remote mining sites. ATCO opened manufacturing facilities for its trailers across Canada and in the United States, Saudi Arabia, Australia and Hungary. The company expanded into producing and distributing natural gas and electricity, and the Southern family became Alberta's first homegrown billionaires. And when the Patch exploded out of the boreal forest, ATCO trailers were soon ubiquitous there as well.

By the time Creeburn Lake Lodge opened, ATCO was a diversified multibillion-dollar company with operations and installations around the world. Driving north out of Fort McMurray to the site, you could see the stack of surplus ATCO trailers in an industrial yard at the side of the highway and remind yourself just how far the Patch had come, how deeply dug in the industry was.

By 2015, ATCO and its competitors—a company called Civeo is the main rival—were building such elaborate lodges as the industry standard. Work camps in the Patch now routinely feature a full-service cafeteria, a gymnasium, Wi-Fi and recreational programming. The larger lodges have fitness instructors, yoga classes and floor hockey leagues. Wapasu Creek Lodge has its own Tim Hortons coffee shop. On the shores of Christina Lake—the heartland of SAGD oil sands production south of Fort McMurray—full-time MEG Energy employees bunk at a 150-room lodge called Pirate's Cove, which is equipped with a movie theatre and a gym, as well as an outdoor hockey rink in the winter months and paintball and archery in summer.

Around the same time that Raheel Joseph and his colleagues are getting ready to head out into the suburbs of Fort McMurray to pick up commuters, another fleet of Diversified buses arrives at the work camps to shuttle workers to the various oil sands sites. At Wapasu Creek Lodge, the bus loading area is fenced in and lined on one side by a sort of gate made of work trailers outfitted with multiple evenly spaced doors. Above each door is a signal light. The workers lodged at Wapasu call this Brass Alley, a name borrowed from the working class of another era, when employees were issued brass coins as they passed through turnstiles onto a construction site, a means of keeping tabs on the workforce.

Breakfast starts before five o'clock in the Wapasu Lodge cafeteria. Shortly after five, the morning shift's workers are in the "bag-up" room, assembling brown-bag lunches from the lodge's daily offerings. From there they head out to Brass Alley, lining up tidily in front of the door corresponding to their work crew, standing in blue jumpsuits and high-viz reflective vests, lunches zipped away into their bulging daypacks. At five-twenty the signal light switches from red to green, and the workers file briskly through the doors, swipe their ID badges and tromp out into the loading area, where waiting Diversified buses—sometimes just a handful, other times as many as thirty—wait to ferry them to nearby sites. Within minutes of the first batch of coaches departing, another fleet trucks in, and the Brass Alley ritual repeats itself twice more until the entire Wapasu morning shift is on its way to work, mostly at Imperial Oil's Kearl mine.

The process is similar but less formal at other camps. At Barge Landing Lodge, a 1,500-room open camp near the First Nations community of Fort McKay, there is no Brass Alley. The workers gather instead in loose knots in a dusty clearing next to the lodge access road, like commuters at a busy downtown transit stop, waiting on the arrival of the right bus to take them to their respective sites. The lodge's parking lot, which filled the previous evening with white work-site pickup trucks flying buggy-whip flags, empties out in sporadic bursts alongside the coming and going buses. The nightshift workers arrive back soon after, and by mid-morning, the hallways at Barge Landing have gone quiet again, like a business hotel hosting the same conference day after day.

The traffic comes together in a single bustling early-morning flow out on Highway 63. The trucks and buses and the rest hurry down off-ramps to long dusty access roads and site security gates. And then the workforce scatters across the great brown turned-earth vastness of the oil sands' eight active mines. There are morning safety briefings—nothing commences anywhere in the Patch without a safety briefing—after which on-site shuttles are boarded, and on-site trucks are driven down dirt roads that run parallel with a half-dozen lines of pipe, all of it snaking out around scaffolded storage tanks and industrial-scale conveyor belts toward the mines.

And there, in the gaping tiered pits, the bitumen awaits liberation from the black gummy earth that has held its dense, energy-rich hydrocarbons captive for a hundred million years.

TWO

THE RISE OF
THE PATCH

THE FORMATION

The age of oil would not reach its full stride in northeastern Alberta until the second half of the twentieth century, but it arrived there nearly as early as anywhere else on earth. The major oil strikes that birthed the first oil boomtowns and eventually the whole global oil industry occurred in the mid-1800s—at Titusville, Pennsylvania; Petrolia, Ontario; and Baku, Azerbaijan—and Canadian geologists began to take note of the fossil fuel wealth along the Athabasca River soon after. Cursory studies of the region's geology had been made in the 1840s and 1870s, but Robert Bell of the Geological Survey of Canada conducted the first formal survey of the Athabasca country in the early 1880s, reporting that the bitumen deposits might be so vast as to one day warrant a pipeline to Hudson Bay.

The GSC's R. G. McConnell first used the term "tar sands" to describe the region's oil in an 1894 report. The GSC was by then convinced that the bitumen seeps along the river were residue from a major crude oil reservoir deeper underground, and so drilling equipment was sent from Ontario and exploratory wells were drilled south of the exposed bitumen seams. One of these struck an enormous pocket of natural gas, which was considered essentially worthless in those days and left to blow out the top of the well as waste for more than twenty years. But the region's abundant bitumen deposits failed to lead to a vast pool of crude oil, and so they stayed a mere curiosity as the petroleum industry exploded elsewhere. Meanwhile, one of the world's richest oil strikes remained an afterthought, buried underground as it had been for millions of years.

The bitumen of northern Alberta traces its origins to the Early Cretaceous period, more than 120 million years ago, when an extensive river system ran up the centre of the land mass that would later become North America. It ran roughly south to north from what is now the Gulf of Mexico toward Hudson Bay and the Arctic Ocean. The river system carried silt and sand toward its northern estuary, the debris falling away to the river beds as the flowing water slowed. In time, the cordillera west of the river system rose into a mountain range, redirecting the flow northeastward, and the waters rose. The estuary became a brackish bay and then part of a broad seaway that cleaved the continent in half. A limestone seabed from the Devonian period, formed hundreds of millions of years earlier, rested below the new Cretaceous seaway, and the dynamic interactions of the old river system and the rising sea deposited an especially large amount of sand on the Devonian rock in what would one day be northeastern Alberta.

By about a hundred million years ago, the weather was semitropical even at 57 degrees north latitude—roughly where the Clearwater River now flows into the Athabasca at Fort McMurray—and the sea was teeming with life. It was a region of abundant coral reefs and dense forest. Before the sea inundated the river system, it had been a vast, swampy region overrun with dinosaurs. Creatures great and small lived, died and fell away to the riverbed. Around seventy million years ago, a great dying came—the

Cretaceous-Tertiary, or K-T, extinction event—and the sea floor and its shores grew thicker still with corpses. They were all covered over with sand and silt and rock, which then compacted and hardened over millions upon millions of years. The ancient sea life became energy-dense hydrocarbon matter. Throughout Alberta, these pockets of hydrocarbons flowed together and pooled to form reservoirs of crude oil and natural gas. But in the northeast, in the deep, sandy troughs the rivers had carved in the limestone before the sea rose to cover the whole land, the hydrocarbons were trapped in the pores of much older rock or compacted into hard layers of shale. These oil molecules either seeped up out of the ancient rock into the thick layer of sand or else migrated slowly down out of the shale—the record isn't yet considered conclusive—but in any case, they mixed and bonded there with sand, water and clay. The primary northeastern deposit of the gluey substance that resulted, which would come to be known as the Lower Cretaceous McMurray Formation, contains one of the largest single accumulations of oil anywhere on earth. It settled into a broad, continuous reservoir of sandy petroleum covering 140,000 square kilometres (slightly larger than England, a touch smaller than Florida). The reservoir was up to 200 feet thick and sandwiched between layers of hard shale, and it contained perhaps 1.7 trillion barrels of oil in total. (Along with similar deposits to the south and west, the total deposit is about 2.5 trillion barrels.)

For millions of years, the McMurray Formation remained buried deep underground. The land above churned and weathered away. The continents drifted together into one, erasing the ancient Cretaceous sea. Erosion carried on with its slow, relentless work. And then, at the dawn of the Pleistocene epoch around two and a half million years ago, the land above became covered with snow and ice, advancing and retreating and advancing again, littering the land with stones, carving valleys and lakes. Finally, the glaciers retreated for the last time (to date) twelve thousand years ago. A gentle, verdant climate emerged, and the land above the McMurray Formation bustled again with life. A thick layer of swampy muskeg and trees grew. Great rivers roared down out of the mountains to the west to sculpt deep valleys in the soil and older rock, cutting all the way down to the top layers of bitumen, which oozed into the water in summer.

The wooded land above the McMurray Formation is just one swath of Canada's boreal forest, a wide belt of coniferous trees and wetlands stretching from the Atlantic coast in Labrador to the towering mountain ranges of northern British Columbia, the Yukon and southern Alaska. In Alberta, the boreal band separates the deciduous woodlands and prairie to the south from the Arctic tundra in the far north. Nationwide, Canada's boreal forest contains more wetland terrain than any other ecosystem on earth.

In northeastern Alberta, animals congregated in particular upon a broad delta, just north of the McMurray Formation, where three great rivers intersect. Many millennia hence, these would be named the Peace, Athabasca and Slave, and the region would become known as the Peace-Athabasca Delta, the largest freshwater inland delta on the whole continent. The great rivers and their estuaries and the bogs and fens and lakes all around provided bountiful habitat for enormous herds of caribou and bison, as well as beavers and martens, lynx and wolves, and more than two hundred species of birds.

In time, this profusion of life attracted people. The first ones to cross the Bering Land Bridge from Asia and live in and off this land called themselves simply Dene—"the people"—and named their new home Denendeh, or "the land of our people." The Dene came to live in small communities built on matriarchal kinship, and they were largely self-sufficient. They shared an origin story describing a battle between two giants. One of the giants had been protecting a Dene man, who used an axe with a beaver's tooth blade to fell the stronger giant. Denendeh was the land where the felled giant came to rest. The giant landed with his feet on the shore of the Arctic Ocean, his body sprawled southeastward up the Mackenzie and Slave Rivers, his huge neck and head resting around Lake Athabasca and the delta—a humanoid silhouette in the general shape of the migratory routes of the great caribou herds. The Dene ranged as far as a line of hills southeast of the delta, where the vast river system that drained northwest to the Arctic ended and another system flowing to Hudson Bay began its eastward journey. About twenty kilometres of high ridge and hill country separated the two river systems and served as a natural barrier between civilizations. It would come to be known to European traders and settlers as Methye Portage.

For thousands of years, Denendeh existed north and west of this line almost as its own universe. Some communities followed the caribou, while others concentrated on hunting moose and bison, fishing in the great rivers and lakes, or trapping fur-bearing animals. They wore caribou and moose hides with a distinctive V-shaped flap that hung below the waist in the back. (*Chipewyan*, the name they were given by the Cree, means "men with tails" in the Algonquian languages.) The Dene shared sacred knowledge—*Inkonze*—and developed a common social and cultural fabric based on collaboration and cooperation in the unforgiving climate of Denendeh. Relations with the Cree to the south and the Inuit to the north were largely peaceful, based on friendly trade, notwithstanding the occasional territorial skirmish.

The arrival of European explorers and fur traders in northwestern Canada in the eighteenth century upset this relative balance forever.

For decades before Europeans ventured into Denendeh, the Cree had served as colonial go-betweens in what has been called the "middleman" fur trade. Historically, the Cree nations had lived in the vast boreal woods south and east of Denendeh, but the lucrative fur trade pushed them farther afield, where they acquired what furs they could from the Dene—who had little use for luxury goods and sometimes refused to trade at all in times of plenty—and delivered them to trading posts on Hudson Bay. By the early seventeen hundreds, however, many Cree nations had acquired guns from the newly arrived European colonists, and the decades thereafter would be defined in the boreal northwest by increasingly ferocious and lopsided war between the Dene and Cree.

In 1714 a Cree raiding party presented a Dene woman whom they had taken as a slave to James Knight, the governor of the Hudson's Bay Company (HBC) post at York Factory on Hudson Bay. Her name was Ttha'naltther (Thanadelthur), and she remained at the post for many months. She told Knight stories about the great wealth of Denendeh, its copper and gold and "a Certain Gum or pitch that runs down the river in Such abundance that they cannot land but at certain places." This description, recorded dutifully in Knight's journal, is the first written record of the McMurray Formation's vast oil sands deposits. It was a passing detail to the British governor, irrelevant to his fur trading post. In 1719 a Cree chief called Swan brought a sample of this gummy bitumen to York Factory and presented it to the new governor there, Henry Kelsey. The promise of glittering metals, however, would remain far more interesting to Knight's and Kelsey's kin for many generations to come.

An ambitious American fur trader by the name of Peter Pond was the first settler to traverse the Methye Portage into Denendeh. Pond was one of the loosely associated "Canadian" traders who had begun to challenge HBC supremacy in the Northwest fur trade in the second half of the eighteenth century, and he would become one of the founding partners in the rival North West Company. The traders were called Canadians because they were backed by wealthy families in Montreal as opposed to the British Crown in London, but Pond himself had been born in Connecticut and was a veteran of the colonial army that had helped to take Montreal from the French. He was semiliterate and respected for his skills in the bush, but prone to violent outbursts—he would later be implicated in the murders of two fur trade associates.

Pond crossed the Methye Portage in the summer of 1778, leaving territory ostensibly controlled by the HBC for what the Canadian traders considered an open and untapped market. He journeyed into Denendeh, navigating the glorious Clearwater River to the mighty Athabasca, and passed the winter with the Dene near Lake Athabasca. The following spring, he returned to the other side of the portage with a bounty of furs too great to carry in his small flotilla of canoes. He left the excess stored in caches along the way for later collection. In all, Pond is believed to have hauled more than a hundred thousand beaver skins out of Denendeh that first winter. The promise of riches in the Northwest had been ecstatically confirmed, and the fur trade descended on Denendeh.

The North West Company's Alexander Mackenzie, who navigated and mapped the region extensively in Pond's wake and whose cousin, Roderick, would establish the first permanent European settlement at Fort Chipewyan in 1788, would eventually be the European name most closely associated with the conquest of the Canadian Northwest. Mackenzie's report from his 1789 journey through Denendeh described "bituminous fountains" burbling into the Athabasca River, which were used by his Cree guides to seal their canoes—the first written documentation of the use of oil sands as a resource. (The Dene had little use for canoes at the time.) Centuries later, though, it was not Mackenzie's but Peter Pond's name chosen to adorn a school, park and mall in Fort McMurray. His legacy would be scrubbed of its ugliest details—like many North West Company traders, Pond was coarse and violent in his relations with Indigenous people, beating a Dene man with the flat of a sword for supposed insubordination in one of the few extant reports—and Pond would be reimagined as a tenacious entrepreneur persevering under difficult circumstances.

To the Europeans, the boreal forest and tundra of the harsh Northwest remained on the periphery of affairs for more than a century after Pond's first incursion into Denendeh, except as a steady source of fur. For the Indigenous peoples of the region, however, the fur trade's arrival marked the beginning of a century of cascading cataclysm—a time of disease and death without precedent or evident mercy. The more recent history of the oil sands industry and its relationship with the First Nations of the Athabasca region is impossible to understand without clarity on this history. By the time Canadian government officials started to arrive in Fort McMurray in the 1880s and 1890s to report on the natural resources of the region and induce the First Nations to sign treaties, the world as the Dene and Cree had known it for centuries was in ruin. On the heels of half a century of escalating war fed by European weapons, smallpox had swept through the Northwest along the trade routes of the fur barons from the early 1780s onward with apocalyptic ferocity. Records appear to indicate that the Athapuscow Cree—the Cree tribe that served as the primary middlemen in the Dene fur trade—were wiped out as a distinct entity. A deadly disease vector stabbed northwestward from Peter Pond's trading post at Lac La Ronge on the south side of Methye Portage, killing an estimated 90 percent of what the traders called the Northern Indians, by which they meant the Dene who lived on the land from the portage northwest to Lake Athabasca. Dene communities farther north had long been reluctant to participate in the fur trade and inhabited the land less densely, and so the smallpox epidemic did not spread beyond Great Slave Lake to the river that would eventually be named for Alexander Mackenzie. The boreal forest atop the McMurray Formation, however, was a mass grave. It would be reinhabited in the eighteen hundreds by an almost entirely new mix of peoples, with Dene clans migrating down from the north and Cree and Metis from the south and the east moving in to continue the fur trade. By the end of the nineteenth century, First Nations communities such as Fort McKay and Fort Chipewyan were a mix of relatively recent Metis and Cree migrants living permanently in the shadow of the fort, while Dene families camped nearby seasonally as they carried on their traditional existence throughout the region.

The decades thereafter were no kinder. Waves of disease—whooping cough, tuberculosis, grippe—swept through the Northwest. And then in the 1870s, impossibly, the bison herds collapsed to the verge of extinction across the entire prairie. One of the earth's most abundant food supplies all but vanished in a generation, exterminated in a senseless slaughter by European settlers, with catastrophic ripple effects for the health and peace of Indigenous populations across the Northwest. The ensuing famine would be used by Canada's newborn Dominion government in distant Ottawa to persuade the First Nations of the west to cede their land rights in a series of numbered treaties and relocate to reserves. There were eleven of these treaties in all. In 1899 the Dene and Cree of the Athabasca region signed Treaty 8, the largest land transfer by treaty to that point by a wide margin, covering an area bigger than France. The Dene still lived in small, hereditary groups and had no formal political hierarchy, so the "chiefs" who signed the treaty on their behalf were simply respected elders; they trusted the French priests who served as translators for the negotiations and outlined the terms. The First Nations understood the treaty as an agreement between peoples to share the land, with their own rights of livelihood and use of the land extending, as their oral history of the treaty would put it, "as long as the sun shines, the grass grows and the waters flow." That language did not appear in the final version, and the Canadian government considered the document a direct and unambiguous legal transfer of land ownership. The history of Canada's Indigenous people ever since is in significant measure a history of the tragic consequences of this discrepancy in the meaning of such treaties.

The twentieth century dawned in Denendeh under this fundamental misunderstanding, even as the years to come would be defined by the natural resource that existed in as great an abundance under the lands exchanged in Treaty 8 as it did anywhere else on earth.

PROSPECTORS

Around the same time the Canadian government was persuading the Indigenous peoples of Denendeh to sign away their rights to the land, the oil age was rapidly gathering momentum, and young men of imagination were starting to hunt for the fuel with the zeal of gold prospectors. In the case of the McMurray Formation's first real wildcatter, this was literally the case: Alfred von Hammerstein, a German immigrant who claimed he was a Prussian noble, arrived in Fort McMurray in 1897 en route to the Klondike gold rush in the Yukon. Most of the Klondike's fortune seekers went by Pacific steamer out of Seattle or San Francisco, but a river-borne route via Edmonton and Fort McMurray had begun to attract some Klondikers looking for a shortcut to Dawson City. Von Hammerstein was following that route when, for reasons unknown, he decided to stay in the Athabasca country and hunt for his fortune there instead.

Von Hammerstein had arrived in a place that must have seemed, to the eyes of a German intimately familiar with the scale and sophistication of nineteenth-century European cities, like the forest primeval. Canada's boreal forest stretches nearly coast-to-coast in a band a thousand kilometres wide, encompassing more than three million square kilometres in all—enough wood and bog and lake and fen to hide ten Germanies. By the end of the nineteenth century, the national railway had linked central and southern Alberta to the big cities of the east, and European settlement and intensive agriculture had begun there in earnest. The boreal forest, however, remained an archipelago of fur-trading outposts linked by unmapped waterways. There were more lakes than people. Even today, when the rest of the world imagines Canada as an expansive and largely empty wilderness, they are often thinking of an iconic forest scene in this boreal ecosystem that feels limitless, untamed and inexhaustible. In von Hammerstein's day, it was tethered to the cosmopolitan world he'd come from by the thinnest of strings. Sidney Ells of the federal Department of Mines, describing Fort McMurray as he first encountered it in 1913, wrote, "McMurray consisted of a dozen primitive log cabins, a bug-infested hovel proudly referred to as the 'hotel' and during the summer months many Indian tepees and tents." Mail arrived four times a year, by boat in summer and by dogsled in winter, and the small settlement's scant commercial and cultural life revolved around the fur trade.

Ignoring the ready money to be made in furs, von Hammerstein's passions settled instead on the promise of becoming the first oil baron of the Great Northwest. Local rumours and GSC reports persuaded von Hammerstein that the bitumen along the Athabasca River hid a larger, richer reservoir of free-flowing crude farther below the boreal forest floor. He bought up leases to subsurface resource rights for next to nothing and had drilling equipment shipped to Fort McMurray in 1903. Within a few years, he was drilling wells and forming a syndicate in anticipation of a petroleum fortune soon to come.

The overnight fortunes of the Spindletop oil strike in eastern Texas in 1901—where the young oil industry first heard the term *gusher* and developed much of its wild boomtown strike-it-rich culture and iconography— was surely on von Hammerstein's mind. He soon became a regional legend, addressed as "Count Von Hammerstein" in accordance with his boasts of royal lineage, his travels in and out of Edmonton and Athabasca Landing (a steamboat way station on the great river between Edmonton and Fort McMurray) recorded colourfully in the rudimentary press of the day. By 1907, the *Edmonton Bulletin* was describing him as "the famous explorer of the far north oil fields." Von Hammerstein testified about the McMurray Formation's oil deposits before the Canadian Senate in Ottawa that same year, begging pardon for not divulging precise details of his exploration work for fear of losing his business, surely soon to be booming, to other prospectors.

Drama and rumour swirled around von Hammerstein as he set out time and again into the boreal bush to search for oil. He was accidentally shot in the leg by one of his men on one expedition into the woods. In 1909, newspapers reported breathlessly about his crew's accident on the Horse River, where von Hammerstein's barge capsized in a stretch of rapids and two of his companions drowned; von Hammerstein was found five days later in a deserted shack in the woods by a crew of government mining surveyors, half-naked and desperately hungry. A 1912 report out of Winnipeg, reprinted in many Alberta papers, said the count had been "killed in Paraguay, South America, where he was endeavouring to start a revolution." But von Hammerstein reappeared in Fort McMurray soon after, carrying on with the exploratory work of his Athabasca Oil and Asphalt Company. It would come to nothing, and von Hammerstein's enterprises faded into obscurity. The McMurray Formation was not yet ready to yield its riches. The supposed count's name would live on mainly as a curiosity, an almost absurd figure on horseback in an archival photo, his cavalry hat folded back regally and his baroque moustache carefully waxed into a pair of haughtily upturned points.

BLOOD FROM STONE

Around the time Count von Hammerstein's flailing efforts to turn bitumen into a commodity had begun to wind down, a slower and more systemic campaign of discovery and development emerged in the quiet woods of northeastern Alberta. It began with the aforementioned Sidney Ells, the Department of Mines engineer, who was sent from Ottawa to conduct a full study of the commercial potential of the Athabasca region's oil sands. Ells set out by boat for Fort McMurray from Athabasca Landing in June 1913, recording 247 outcroppings of bitumen on his nine-day journey. The travel and surveying were difficult, beset by natural and logistical challenges, the country a "fly-infested" wilderness in Ells's estimation. But he was a determined and diligent student of bitumen's mysteries. He'd already seen similar deposits in the Caribbean and studied the work at ten plants in the United States that were attempting to process heavy oil into commercial products. Years later, Ells would examine "bituminous sand and bituminous limestone" across Europe, from Spain to Albania.

The Mines Department engineer arrived in the Athabasca region knowing that bitumen had been used in the Middle East in pre-Christian times as a material for paving and waterproofing, and he returned to Fort McMurray in 1914 to take core samples and ship some of the bitumen to Edmonton for further study and testing as a paving substance. That summer, Ells had his crew fill 1,200 sacks with a hundred pounds of bitumen each from sites across the region. They were shipped to Fort McMurray by barge and then carried overland to Edmonton in the subzero depths of winter in early 1915—sixty tons of oil sands in all, the first significant excavation of the substance ever undertaken. War had broken out by then, and Ells enlisted and waited for his orders, carrying on with his study of bitumen in the meantime. He spent two months in New York learning how to operate the proper laboratory equipment for analyzing his samples and then bought gear of his own and had it shipped to his lab in Ottawa. Even as his samples made their slow progress through the woods from Fort McMurray to Edmonton in 1915, Ells travelled to the Mellon Institute of Industrial Research in Pittsburgh to investigate a process for separating oil from sand.

Ells referred to the stuff he'd excavated interchangeably as "oil sand" or "bituminous sand." In Edmonton in the summer of 1915, he built a small processing plant based on techniques he'd studied at the Mellon

Institute and turned his sixty tons of bitumen into asphalt. A sign went up on Kinnaird Street in downtown Edmonton that summer: "Experimental Pavement Laid With Alberta Bituminous Sand." Ells had a crew cover a block of roadway with it. The substance proved resilient in the face of the city's dramatic fluctuations of temperature and moisture, sturdy under ice and snow. "Eminently satisfactory results," Ells concluded. The pavement was still there and holding up fine more than a decade later, when Ells set off in 1927 for Jasper in the Rocky Mountains to pave a whole strip of highway in bitumen-derived pavement. His passion for the subject never wavered the rest of his career. His 1962 technical memoir, *Recollections of the Development of the Athabasca Oil Sands*, continued to prophesy a bright future for the McMurray Formation:

> In 1913, a great and potentially valuable resource in the northern part of the province of Alberta lay dormant and unknown while even the surface of the country was unsurveyed. Yet as a result of investigations in the field and in the laboratory, the outcome may ultimately be reflected in important commercial development. Where now the almost unbroken wilderness holds sway, industrial plants may arise and tall stacks dominate the landscape.

In the intervening decades, however, Ells had been obliged to abandon his bitumen experiments for years at a time in favour of war service and other postwar duties at the Department of Mines back in Ottawa. And so another scientist's name would come to be more closely associated with the transformation of the McMurray Formation from dormant resource to commercial enterprise.

Karl A. Clark of the University of Alberta first took an appointment as a research scientist at the provincial government's newborn Alberta Research Council in 1920. The council assigned him the task of investigating the commercial potential of the oil sands, and it would occupy him off and on for the rest of his life. Unlike Ells, who had to trek in and out of Fort McMurray either by boat or on foot—porters on one of Ells's expeditions died on the journey—Clark rode at least part of the way by train. The railway line, first constructed in 1914, stretched farther northeast on the route from Edmonton each year. The Alberta and Great Waterways Railway finally reached Waterways, the old steamboat port a few kilometres south of Fort McMurray, in 1925. Later on, Clark would often travel by air in and out of the bustling bush-plane hub at Fort McMurray, where First World War aces like Wop May were frequent visitors.

Perhaps due in part to the relative ease of travel, Clark came to see the natural wonders of the boreal wilderness as a joy rather than a burden. His letters to colleagues would make note of having seen the "prettiest mosquitoes" on a field research trip, and at least once he toured prospective investors around the oil sands by dogsled. Building on Ells's research, Clark identified the crux of the oil sands riddle: how to separate hydrocarbon pay dirt from useless sand. Bitumen deposits can be either "water wet" (the sand grains encased in a film of water, with the oil surrounding them) or "oil wet" (the grains surrounded first by oil and then by water). Luckily for Clark, the McMurray Formation's oil sands were water wet, meaning the sand and oil could be separated by treating them with hot water, which would steam off the watery coating and cause the sand to drop away. Ells had already conducted experiments with this "hot water separation" process, and Clark expanded on his work, determining before long that the valuable heavy oil could be skimmed from the sand with considerable ease. As early as 1921, Clark was telling colleagues the separation problem had been virtually solved. Two years later, he set up a lab-scale hot water separation plant in the basement of a building at the University of Alberta to refine the process. He expected he would soon be done making the case for commercial oil sands production.

The 1920s and 1930s were the first of many periods of rapidly alternating enthusiasm for and indifference to the commercial potential of the oil sands on the part of minders in distant capitals. An international oil crisis in the early 1920s deepened interest, spurring Clark's work, which was still focused on turning bitumen more efficiently into asphalt. Ells returned to the scene in 1926, boasting that the oil sands could be a source of liquid fuel as well as pavement, but by then, oil prices had stabilized and the urgency of the project waned. Nevertheless, both the federal government (bankrolling Ells's work) and the Alberta government (backing Clark's) pushed forward with plans for experimental hot water separation plants in the Fort McMurray area. There were vague agreements to work jointly, but mistrust between the two levels of government was always high. Ells and Clark viewed each other to some extent as rivals, working on similar but far from identical techniques for processing bitumen, both chasing the prize of unlocking the McMurray Formation's vast hydrocarbon riches.

Clark's new plant began operations on the Clearwater River in October 1929. Ells, meanwhile, found a private partner, an engineer from Denver named Max Ball, and from 1930 on, the Ells process drove the operations of Abasand Oils Ltd. on the Horse River, a tributary of the Athabasca. With the onset of the Great Depression, the Alberta Research Council disbanded, and Clark occupied himself with other work until the end of the Second World War. Abasand, meanwhile, continued to operate and improve its processing techniques, but it barely stayed afloat and never became profitable. More than a decade after Clark had thought he might have the oil sands' riddle solved, bitumen's potential remained unrealized, its hydrocarbon power still trapped in sand and clay.

Throughout that time, Fort McMurray remained a quiet, muddy little village, a trading post and way station along air and water transport routes fed by the resource wealth of mines and forests farther north. Dogsleds were a more common sight than automobiles on Franklin Avenue, and muskrat pelts were far easier to obtain locally than the newfangled consumer goods of the Roaring Twenties. When bitumen failed to provide steady cargo for the Alberta and Great Waterways Railway, local entrepreneurs turned instead to salt deposits discovered accidentally by oil drillers at the confluence of the Horse and Athabasca Rivers. The Alberta Salt Company set up its first production plant there in 1925, but it soon failed due to high shipping costs; a second plant opened in 1937 and operated profitably until the early 1950s.

Yet still the wildcatting dreamers came, a steady trickle of would-be oil barons determined to poke holes in the boreal forest floor and hatch grand business plans. None did so more ambitiously or tenaciously than one Robert C. Fitzsimmons, a Maritimer born and raised on Prince Edward Island who came west—first to Spokane, Washington, then to Fort Mc-Murray—as a real estate speculator. Like Count von Hammerstein before him, Fitzsimmons became convinced that a lucrative crude oil reservoir lingered somewhere beneath the bitumen, and he established the International Bitumen Company in 1923 to hunt it down and turn it to liquid gold.

When his gusher failed to materialize, Fitzsimmons looked for ways to make bitumen pay on its own. He found a site more than eighty kilometres north of Fort McMurray on the eastern bank of the Athabasca River, a fat, exposed seam of oil sands that turned into such a soft, mushy, asphalt-like sludge in the summer sun that you could tear off pieces with your bare hands like pulling apart taffy. This was oil, after a fashion, and Fitzsimmons was sure it had to be worth something to a world powered by more and more of the stuff with each passing year. He named his site Bitumount, and he had a copy of Karl Clark's bitumen processing plant built there in 1930 to produce waterproof roofing materials for sale in hardware stores. But the plant operated only until 1932, its prospects deflated by the Great Depression.

Fitzsimmons, undeterred by his stalled business and the crippling economics of the time, pushed on with his Bitumount dream, convinced the oil sands could be transformed not just into building materials but into fuel for the automotive age. In 1936 he constructed an even larger processing plant. The new facility was an elaborate industrial age marvel carved out of the thickly wooded wilderness. It had steam-powered scoops and long, sloping conveyor belts, flywheels and pulleys, big steel drums and tall smokestacks. The raw bitumen was separated into oil froth and sandy residue using a hot water process based on Clark's method, and a rudimentary refinery on-site transformed the heavy oil into petroleum distillate and asphalt. The whole apparatus was powered by two fifty-horsepower boilers fed constantly by spruce logs culled from the surrounding forest.

The endless task of felling and preparing the wood for the boilers required gangs of workers, and so there was a big bunkhouse to house the seventy men Fitzsimmons hired and brought out to run his Bitumount plant in the spring of 1937. Fitzsimmons registered the site to receive mail and had a radio transmitter installed there. It was a work camp on its way to becoming a boomtown, he was sure of it.

The Bitumount plant was an ominous start for the fledgling industry. While Fitzsimmons travelled across the country begging investors to back his new business, the Bitumount crew struggled mightily with the stubborn, sticky, scratchy oil sands sludge throughout the summer. Fitzsimmons's separation process was far from perfect, so the bitumen pumped from the separator to the refinery ran with abrasive sand that wore out the valves in the pumps. Valves, gears and belts gummed up constantly with gooey bitumen. The refinery's distillation tower clogged with sand. At the end of the working day, the crew's clothes would be so caked in viscous oil sands residue that they could barely bend their joints to walk, a crew of oil-black tin men filing back to the bunkhouse each evening for chow.

Fitzsimmons's fundraising efforts, meanwhile, failed to attract a single investor. No one working at Bitumount that summer earned a dime. Men with enough money to buy their way onto passing steamboats abandoned the site in a steady stream, but the rest were stuck. Tom Morimoto, the son of the first Japanese-Canadian to settle in Fort McMurray, had been hired by Fitzsimmons to operate Bitumount's radio, and he recalled the scene in his 2007 memoir. "Quite a few of us," he wrote, "had to wait for the river to freeze in December to make their journey on foot." When the freeze-up finally happened, the remaining crew attempted to hitch a sleigh to the horses on-site to drag their baggage, but the heavy animals kept breaking through the crust of ice on the river. And so Morimoto and his colleagues finished the journey on foot, heavy packs bending their backs, trudging through the snow on the frozen river for two exhausting days all the way to Fort McMurray. Dozens of men fleeing their work site over the ice like refugees—this was the inauspicious end to the oil sands industry's troubled first chapter.

OIL CENTURY

While bitumen refused to pay out, luckier strikes around the globe gave rise to a new chapter in the world's economic history: the age of oil, which rapidly transformed the entire world to fit its scale, needs and biases. The age had launched with the rise of the world's first great industrial behemoth and prototype of the modern multinational corporation, John D. Rockefeller's Standard Oil, which emerged from the nineteenth-century oil boom in the hills of western Pennsylvania to achieve a level of wealth and power without precedent.

The century born of Standard Oil and its brethren was an age of accelerating speed and escalating scale, rapid change and technological novelty that expanded as quickly as crude oil could be refined into gasoline and a cracked petroleum molecule could be stretched into giddy new polymer shapes and textures. The gusher—that sudden eruption of impossible quantities of oil from beneath the earth's surface—personified the instant fortunes to be made as modern business first grew to global size. The term originated with the first such triumphant explosion at Spindletop, Texas, in 1901. The many gushers that followed—in Oklahoma and California, in the deserts of Iran and Saudi Arabia, in the Amazon rainforest and the Indonesian jungle—fed an emergent age of gas-fuelled machines and boundless energy demand. The internal combustion engine launched a revolution in mobility and reshaped the cities of the industrial West in its image. The First World War was fought significantly, if not centrally, over vast oil deposits in the Middle East, and the Second World War was the first war at oil's full size and speed, a battle of tank engines and airplanes, fed by aviation fuel and continent-wide supply chains. And at war's end, the oil age roared on toward its zenith with the rise of North American suburbia.

This was a new consumer age of plastic fantastic engineering and abundant technological gadgetry, a time of expansive growth, bigger houses on broader lawns, braggadocious fins on ever larger cars. And all of it was thanks above all to bountiful supplies of cheap energy, oil and its by-products above all. The second half of the twentieth century was an age of hydrocarbon-powered High Modernity. And it was this grand narrative arc—this world-historical force—that finally gave rise, in time, to a thriving oil patch in northern Alberta.

The story of oil is the foundation story of the twentieth century, its primary motive force. Oil's abundance and power ignited dreams of limitless growth and impossible wealth. The whole modern world took on some of the delirious logic of the boomtown and the gusher, driven by the certainty that there would always be more. Every time oil approached a potential end, a plateau where surely there could be no vast reservoirs remaining to be tapped and no places left in the earth to be pocked with the deep boreholes of exploratory wells, the dream found its way somehow to a renewal.

As the Second World War ended, worries began to emerge about an end to oil's overheated fever dream. Resource scarcity had haunted the war on many fronts, but none was more troublesome than the constant challenge of securing steady supplies of oil. The German war machine had rapidly improved techniques for converting coal to oil after it failed in its catastrophic bid to seize the Soviet Union's oil supplies in Baku. The Japanese sneak attack on Pearl Harbor in 1941 was to some extent a preemptive strike to prevent losing control of its vital Indonesian oil fields. The extraordinary industrial machine of the United States turned time and again to novel ways to find and use oil in the war years. Nylon, for instance, derived from a by-product of oil refining and was originally perfected as a lightweight material for parachutes and army tents; the explosion in the petrochemical and plastics industries after the war was a direct result of wartime scarcity.

That same necessity spurred the Canadian government to take over Sidney Ells's Abasand processing plant in 1943, investigating ways to feed bitumen's hydrocarbon power into the war effort. The plant burned to the ground in June 1945, mere weeks after Canada's army and its allies had completed the project of liberating Europe from Nazi tyranny. But the war had demonstrated both the awesome power and the troubling fragility of a world fuelled by oil, and in the postwar era, global economies were driven as never before by the search for new sources of oil and innovative uses for it.

Across western Canada in those years, the High Modern church of technocratic progress and engineering prowess held sway—that secular faith in the limitless ability of new technology, large-scale industry and careful government planning to invent a wondrously prosperous future. Dams were built along the Nelson River in northern Manitoba, astride the roaring Peace and Columbia Rivers in British Columbia—great concrete slabs that rose from the valleys like mountain faces and vast manmade lakes manufactured by the pure limitless will of applied science and human industry, each blazing with enough electricity-generating might to power the greatest metropolis. Where the land was too flat to dam swift rivers, mighty shovels dug coal from beneath the prairie soil and uranium from the shores of Lake Athabasca to spin turbines in yet more power plants. Vast deposits of oil and natural gas were discovered above the Arctic Circle in the Beaufort Sea and the Mackenzie Delta, continent-wide pipeline networks built and a string of sci-fi radar stations laid across the islands of Canada's Far North to guard it all. Cars grew wide and gaudy in celebration of the achievement, and residential streets grew wider still and curved in lazy arcs across the prairie, the neighbourhoods erected with unprecedented speed on the rims of cities heated by natural gas furnaces and lit by high-pressure sodium, the sprawling young cityscapes punctuated by exclamatory neon.

Oil, which had seemed in such tight supply during the war, became wildly plentiful in these first postwar decades. Its bounty soon ushered in a golden age of motoring and aviation and space exploration. Geologists prodded the earth everywhere that ancient fossils had pooled in abundance a hundred million years back, uncovering deposits of staggering scope one after another. The greatest of them all was Ghawar, the mammoth oil reservoir discovered in 1948 beneath the Saudi desert that forever moved the oil industry's centre of gravity from America to the Middle East, though few fully understood the scale or permanence of the shift at the time. Fewer still now worried about scarcity—which, in the gleaming prosperity of postwar North America, seemed as relevant as a victory garden or a ration on tin. But those who remembered the lessons of the war most deeply knew there could never be too much of the stuff, that every oil well eventually had to tumble over the top of the production curve and down the dark slope of depletion.

By the early 1950s, just as the High Modern bacchanal was reaching maximum zeal, the vast unexploited bitumen deposits of the McMurray Formation landed on the radar of one of those fretful oilmen: J. Howard Pew of the Philadelphia-based Sun Oil Company. Pew's family had been refining oil almost since it was first discovered in Pennsylvania in the 1860s, and the Pew fortune expanded when the family company became a key player in the Spindletop boom. During the Second World War, Sun Oil produced aviation fuel and contributed petrochemicals for the manufacture of synthetic rubber after the war effort exhausted natural supplies. Pew was sixty-three years old at the war's end, rumoured to be the world's seventh richest man, a titan of the industry who had run Sun Oil since his father had died when Howard was thirty. Howard was a legendarily stern and domineering figure, a staunch Christian who wrote serious scholarly papers on dour Calvinism and loathed government interference in the marketplace with a messianic, anti-Communist fervour nearly as fierce as his faith. His company was a temple to free-market thrift; Sun's employees received no sick leave under his watch.

The commodity strains of the war convinced Pew that an era of oil scarcity would soon be at hand. He was also wary of relying on distant, untrustworthy countries such as Venezuela and the Persian Gulf states for America's vital energy supplies. In 1944 a Sun Oil executive met with Lloyd Champion, who had taken over Fitzsimmons's International Bitumen Company, and Sun Oil also consulted the Geological Survey of Canada to learn more about the oil sands deposits around the same time. After Imperial Oil struck conventional crude at Leduc in central Alberta in 1947, Sun Oil established a modest field office in Calgary. This would prove pivotal to the oil sands industry.

Postwar Alberta's self-image transformed overnight in the wake of the Leduc strike. The Depression years had been brutal on the province's predominantly agricultural economy, but now it was an energy business player, an emerging economic powerhouse. For the first time since before the First World War, Alberta was booming instead of barely getting by.

The province's premier at the time, Ernest Manning, was a deeply religious man himself and a cautious conservative. But the oil-driven boom of the late 1940s convinced his government to renew its interest in the risky oil sands. The province's reconvened Alberta Research Council invested in a new experimental plant at Bitumount and sent Karl Clark there to resume work on hot water separation. In 1949 Clark had refined his process to produce a steady stream of high-quality heavy crude oil suitable for refining as fuel, and he declared bitumen finally ready for the marketplace. The Alberta government sent a petroleum engineer named Sidney Blair to the site to gather information for a major report on the economic viability of oil sands production. His *Report on the Alberta Bituminous Sands*, published in late 1950, estimated that crude oil could be made from the bitumen of the McMurray Formation at around three dollars a barrel, cheap enough to be commercially viable.

The Blair report brought an unprecedented sense of purpose to the oil sands project, and the provincial government organized a major conference in Edmonton the following September to announce its bitumen breakthrough to the energy-hungry world. More than a hundred delegates from governments and oil companies across North America attended. Standard and Gulf, Shell and Imperial, Sinclair and Union and, of course, Pew's Sun Oil—all came to hear presentations on "Geology of the Bituminous Sand Deposits of the McMurray Area, Alberta" and "Proposed Methods of Mining Alberta Oil Sands." The proceedings were relentlessly technical and dry as toast—even in his closing remarks, Sidney Blair offered no rallying cry or note of triumph, fussing instead over such details as the removal of sulphur from coker distillate nearly to his very last word.

But still, here was the whole oil industry gathered in Alberta, talking about bitumen! It had been thirty long and fruitless years since Clark first reckoned he had the maddening bitumen puzzle sorted, but surely this was a true pivot point, not another false start. At the end of the conference, more than half the delegates loaded into planes and flew to Bitumount for guided tours presented proudly by Clark himself. It had to be only a matter of time, some technical details and, sure, quite a bit of money before the Alberta oil sands made their mark on the global energy map.

In truth, it nearly didn't happen. No private company had been more interested in the progress made in the boreal forest than Pew's Sun Oil. But before the conference, Sun's Alberta office manager, George Dunlap, advised the company against investing in oil sands development, arguing that it wasn't yet cost-effective and might never be. In a serious breach of protocol at highly hierarchical Sun, Ned Gilbert, a young field geologist who had been up to Fort McMurray to gather core samples of bitumen and inspect Karl Clark's work, wrote a dissenting letter to Dunlap just two months before the big meeting in Edmonton and sent copies to the senior executives back in Philadelphia. "I have long felt that our company should take a permit to explore for oil from the Tar Sands of Alberta," Gilbert wrote. He marvelled at both the size of the deposit and the rock-bottom cost of the leases—one patch of land after another, each containing two hundred million barrels of recoverable oil, at an offering price per acre available "no other place in the world." Gilbert's bosses were persuaded. After the conference, Sun sent Gilbert to start buying up leases.

Pew's peers were convinced his company had lost its collective mind. He was wasting good money on "moose pasture." Around the Palliser Hotel in downtown Calgary, where many oilmen lived and kept offices in the early days of Alberta's oil business, there was one lease in particular that came to be known as "Gilbert's Folly." (It would eventually become Suncor's Firebag River in situ operation, producing 200,000 barrels per day.) But Sun and its dour president were undeterred. Before long, Pew himself became a frequent visitor to Alberta, conducting business more often than not from a cabin at Jasper Park Lodge during the summer months. Premier Ernest Manning met with Pew there on several occasions to talk through the development of the oil sands. The two men quickly formed a

strong bond through their shared Christian faith, and Pew remained un-
wavering in his commitment to building a major commercial production
facility north of Fort McMurray.

Sun became the lead partner in a consortium that called itself Great
Canadian Oil Sands (GCOS), investing half a million dollars in the project in the 1950s. Blueprints for the facility design were drawn up by 1958,
and the Alberta government approved the project application in 1962.
With oil prices still around $3 per barrel and the projected costs of the oil
sands plant mounting, Sun's board of directors remained unsure whether
to commit fully to financing construction. In 1964 Pew had Dunlap and
Gilbert—both still on the job for Sun Oil in Alberta—prepare a final report on the project and delivered it to the board himself. "Gentlemen,"
Pew told the Sun board, "if you don't do this project, I will do it myself."
The board backed Pew's plan, and the oil sands joined the global oil industry for the first time.

Sun Oil's GCOS operation began digging bitumen from the earth at
commercial scale in 1967, marking the birth of an entirely new kind of oil
business—oil mining, essentially. The ceremony at the project's launch
on September 30 that year was a study in High Modern theatre. Out at the
mine site, which was not yet fully operational, the company erected a great
billowing white tent free of scaffold or frame. It was held aloft by air pressure alone, with mechanical pumps blowing wind steady and true into the
space until it was a cavernous temporary ballroom. Everyone up in Fort
McMurray called it "the bubble." It looked like it had been borrowed from
some futuristic pavilion at Montreal's Expo 67, the centennial Canadian
birthday celebration of High Modern progress that had captivated Canadians throughout the summer.

Inside the bubble, bunting hung from the sloping roof behind a long
dais draped in white. Behind the lectern, a broad banner was adorned with
the young company's logo—the letters GCOS forming the spokes inside
a sharp-toothed bucket wheel, the massive machine that chewed bitumen
from the earth out in the mine like a hungry dog gnawing at a gristled
bone. Above the logo, a semicircular arch of text read "Man Develops His

World." It was an incontrovertible statement of fact in this otherworldly prefab temple to the genius of engineering. This was the purpose of civilization, modernity's very apex.

Man Develops His World!

The whole scene looked like a production still from *Citizen Kane*. Serious men in dark suits and thick-rimmed glasses sat in a row at the long head table, and the seats arranged before them were filled with what seemed like the whole population of this remote outpost of High Modern triumph known as Fort McMurray. J. Howard Pew, now eighty-five years old and as stern and sharp-eyed as ever, was among the dignitaries. He made a short speech extolling this "great forward step in the development of the oil industry."

But the day belonged more than anyone to Ernest Manning. An evangelical preacher turned politician, Manning had been in charge of Alberta for so long the province seemed inseparable from his persona, and especially from his voice: thin and loud and reedy, a Bible-thumper's scolding wail that had been ubiquitous on Canadian radio during the 1930s on the Prophetic Bible Institute's *Back to the Bible Hour*. Manning had been an acolyte in those days of an English engineer's utopian economic theory known as "social credit," which argued for the perfectibility of society through the application of the precise machine logic of engineering to money and consumption and the social order they created. The theory never held much water in practice, but the Social Credit Party triumphed in Alberta politics nonetheless, first coming to power under William "Bible Bill" Aberhart (the Prophetic Bible Institute's founder) in 1935 and then, after Aberhart's death, under his disciple Manning.

On that crisp, sunny day in September 1967, Ernest Manning had been Alberta's premier for twenty-four years. Across a quarter century, he'd shaped the province around his core philosophy, a mix of staunch Christian social conservatism and sober market capitalism. Earlier that year, Alberta voters had handed Manning's Socreds their seventh electoral victory—another landslide, with just six of the legislature's sixty-three seats captured by opposition parties. As Manning stood at the lectern behind a line of gleaming silver microphones, his voice *was* Alberta, as far as most Albertans and much of the country were concerned.

"This is a historic day for the province of Alberta," Manning said. "It is fitting that we gathered here today should dedicate this plant not merely to the production of oil but to the continual progress and enrichment of mankind."

Man Develops His World!

All the decades of lab research with sample buckets of sticky bitumen, the failed commercial experiments and government-backed pilot projects had finally yielded a gusher in the bug-ridden backwoods of northern Alberta. The GCOS site was a far cry from the simple wood scaffolds and pumpjacks of previous oil strikes. It was overrun with great steel bucket-wheel rigs feeding a maze of conveyors and holding tanks and rock crushers, towering cokers and miles of labyrinthine pipe, all of it engaged in the elaborate process of turning the reluctant bitumen-rich sand into crude oil. Bitumen never gushed, of course. It oozed like heavy molasses in summer, gumming up these big new conveyor belts and crushers just as it had out at Bitumount in the 1930s. And it turned to jagged rock in northern Alberta's mean winter, sometimes grinding away an enormous bucket wheel's steel teeth in a single afternoon.

For so many years, bitumen had seemed a lost cause, and some executives at Pew's own company still thought it was a boondoggle. The plant the dignitaries were inaugurating that day would soon be riddled with technical problems. Power outages occurred daily, sometimes more than once on a bad day. The on-site offices at the GCOS plant had no insulation that first winter, and so secretaries were obliged to chip the frost off their desks with ice scrapers from their cars before starting the day's work. Fort McMurray was still more fur-trading outpost than functioning town, a frigid wasteland with dogsleds in the snowy streets in winter that turned to what one pioneering GCOS worker called a "sea of mud" in spring. Another reported that his wife burst into tears on first sight of the desolate town. Moose pasture would be an upgrade from this desolate backwater. In the industry, the joke went that GCOS really stood for "Gone Crazy Over Sand."

Still, the day had finally come. GCOS was up and running, making oil from ancient gummy sand most days. It was on the road—surely, *finally*—to steady, profitable production in the most important resource industry there was. What a time for the oil business, the nation, the whole grand project of Western civilization, riding smooth and fast toward its third straight decade of unprecedented growth and wealth, propelled by a roaring motor built of technological invention and engineering genius. Hydroelectric dams, nuclear plants, great coal-fired furnaces and, above all, oil and more oil—endlessly adaptable, limitlessly applicable oil, condensed into tidy hydrocarbon molecules of energy-dense light crude or strung out into miraculous polymer chains to be reformed as motor vehicle dashboards or children's toys, paints or fertilizers or Vaseline petroleum jelly.

What was High Modernity, after all, if not a great global church for the worship of large-scale energy production? How else did humankind come to possess something of the power of the divine if not by engines and turbines and rockets? And what fuel source was more vital to the High Modern church's holiest rites than the stuff now being dug out of the earth north of Fort McMurray? Progress was another word for energy—it was energy applied—and energy at its highest refinement meant oil, and oil meant power. To sit astride an oil deposit was to ride in High Modernity's cockpit, pointed straight at a brighter future on a golden horizon well within reach.

This was the narrative arc that connected the ceremony in the bubble to nearly a hundred years of progress and propelled the oil sands project across countless technological chasms and over daunting economic hurdles in the decades to come. The project stood at the very centre of modern civilization, even if it seemed as if it was located at the edge of the known universe. To seize control of such energy resources was to know the truest kind of freedom. Oil was the ultimate commodity, an absolute good.

Man Develops His World!

THREE

STANDARD OPERATING PROCEDURE

PAY DIRT

In the conventional oil business, the core problem of developing the resource has always been a question of exploration and discovery. The challenge resided in locating the oil. Scouting inhospitable terrain, producing and scanning seismic data, drilling exploratory wells, reconsidering and then drilling deeper and trying again somewhere else on the map—all of it to locate reservoirs worth tapping, pumping and piping. The twentieth-century history of the oil industry is rich with stories of tenacity and luck, a persistent field engineer's stubborn insistence on drilling just once more that yields a discovery of fortune-making scale. Imperial Oil spent years drilling 133 dry wells in the Canadian prairie before the Leduc No. 1 strike in February 1947 finally launched large-scale oil production to Alberta. "The prize," as Daniel Yergin called it in his definitive history of the business, was invariably a hidden treasure, the gusher always unexpected.

In the oil sands, unique among the world's major oil plays, there has never been any question of finding the oil. The whole mammoth apparatus of the twenty-first-century oil sands mine, all the workers on buses and in trucks and pouring in from the thousand-bed work camps and tidy new suburbs—this whole enterprise is dedicated not to locating oil but to separating the bitumen from the sand, clay and water it has been fused with for millions of years. Nearly a century of experimentation, lab research and investment, from Count von Hammerstein to Karl Clark, had all been aimed at the maddeningly complex goal of extracting bitumen from oil sands ore at commercial scale for a profit-making price.

"I felt I was going back in history and being an explorer and seeing a potential that was unbelievable." This is Clem Bowman, a chemical engineer who spent his career studying how to unlock all that bitumen, describing his first research trip to Fort McMurray in the early 1960s. "I can still remember standing on the floor of the valley just north of Fort McMurray and looking up and seeing this oil sands deposit where it was exposed. And picking up clumps of this sand, of the oil sands, and seeing the little grains of quartz sand embedded in this. And I thought, *This is a miracle material.*"

The miracle would wait a generation after Bowman first marvelled at bitumen's potential. But finally there came the years of $100-per-barrel oil, triggering a boom that lasted more than a decade and making oil sands production seem like a permanent fixture on the boreal forest landscape and the balance sheets of the Canadian economy. At the far end of it, in 2014, a crane operator named Dave McGregor, who working in construction on a new oil sands mine, told the *Edmonton Journal*, "It's the only place in Canada where you can look and see fifty years ahead of you."

Bitumen's secret was unlocked, and so the nation and the world descended on the Patch to find a role in its labour-intensive extraction. And there was no shortage of roles. McGregor came from Vancouver Island to operate mammoth cranes. He joined engineers from Pakistan and heavy equipment mechanics from small-town Nova Scotia and pipefitters from

Newfoundland and haul truck drivers from the Philippines and mill-wrights from the First Nations community of Fort Chipewyan and city planners from suburban Toronto, all of them filling the seats on those white luxury coaches alongside workers with certification in a dozen other trades from every province and seemingly half the world's nations. All of them off to the Patch and out to site, making Clem Bowman's miracle vision manifest.

Most days at Suncor's base site, perhaps 6,000 people march off to liberate another three hundred thousand or so barrels of bitumen from the black earth. The term is theirs, used frequently by executives and technicians in the industry: in the name of freedom and opportunity, progress and profit, they *liberate* oil from sand. And in doing so, they renew their belief in the essential truth of the blunt assertion on the banner that hung over the GCOS launch: *Man Develops His World*.

The basic apparatus of a modern oil sands site is deceptively simple, different from the old plant at Bitumount in scale more than in concept. In the huge open pits, industrial shovels gouge oil sands ore from the ground and drop it into the waiting beds of enormous dump trucks. The trucks haul the ore to a nearby hopper, where it moves by a series of conveyors and pipes to the main plant. The bitumen is separated from the sand, clay and water along the way. At the main plant, this heavy oil is either upgraded—chemically transformed into a synthetic copy of conventional oil—or else combined with petrochemicals called diluents that reduce its viscosity so it can be shipped by pipeline to an upgrader and refiner hundreds or thousands of miles away.

In its broad strokes, there's little to an oil sands mine today that wouldn't be familiar to Karl Clark. His hot water separation process remains at the core of every oil sands mining enterprise. The ore being mined is composed of about 10 percent bitumen on average. Around 5 percent of the ore is water. The rest is a mix of sand—mostly silica, some quartz—and a handful of clays rich in minerals with obscure names such as kaolinite, smectite and montmorillonite that are sometimes described collectively as "fines," a reference to their particle size. Bitumen, a heavy oil, does not rise as quickly to the surface in water at room temperature as lighter oils do. Clark's hot water process involves adding heated water to the oil sands ore and agitating it, at which point the aerated bitumen separates from about half of the fines and sand and rises to the surface as a "froth." Collect the froth, discard the rest, and there's your steady flow of boreal pay dirt.

At Suncor base and the seven other mine sites north of Fort Mc-Murray, Clark's process has been built out to the scale of the global energy economy. The shovel units are seven storeys tall, each wielding a steel bucket the size of a two-car garage that carves a hundred tons of oil sands ore from the ground with each scoop. A steady stream of gargantuan dump trucks—most commonly the Caterpillar 797B, until recently the largest dump truck ever made—make their way to the shovels, backing in to collect four huge scoops of ore. When the scoop lifts with its claw full of ore and the shovel unit swivels above its enormous tracks to deliver its load, the effect is like watching a small apartment building spin on its axis to drop a suburban lawn's worth of dirt into an Olympic-sized swimming pool on wheels. Fully loaded, the trucks crawl back along the open pit's road to a huge hopper-crusher apparatus several storeys tall. The crusher is a moveable unit, placed as near the active mine site as possible because the most expensive way to move bitumen around is to haul it as ore, laden with the excess weight of sand and clay, in the dump box of a diesel-burning truck the size of a two-storey Fort McMurray starter home.

The ore exits the hopper in a steady flow, dropping down through a set of steel grinders coated in exotic alloys like tungsten carbide to guard against wear. The grinders turn the slabs of the stuff—which gum together in warm weather and freeze into great stony sheets in the long frigid winter—into roughly uniform chunks no larger than beach balls. The crushed ore then moves by conveyor to a nearby way station (either a simple stockpile or a steel surge bin), and from there through screens or over enormous rotating drums, depending on the mine site, to be mixed with water heated to somewhere between 70 and 90 degrees Celsius and forms a slurry at a temperature of around 50 degrees. The ore spends just a few minutes in the drums, and then the slurry is pumped into pipes to be transferred to the main plant.

There are usually three parallel pipelines at least one kilometre long installed for this transfer process: two active pipes and a spare. This stage— hydrotransport, in the industry's argot—is not just a transportation method but also a vital first stage in the separation process. Hydrotransport adds ten minutes or more to the ore's "residence time," its interval as an aerated slurry. The turbulence along the way breaks down larger chunks of ore into smaller and smaller particles until individual sand grains remain, casting loose the microscopic oil drops to amalgamate into tiny pools of oil large enough to float. These pools attach themselves to air bubbles in the slurry, creating aerated bitumen that floats readily. The bitumen thus arrives at the main plant already "liberated from the sand grain," in the words of one trade magazine's procedural guide.

At the main plant, the hydrotransport pipes deposit their slurry into a "primary separation cell," an enormous, cone-shaped vessel that looks like a municipal water tower with a funnel attached to its base. Inside the cone, more hot water is added. The sand sinks to the bottom of the vessel, and the heated, aerated bitumen rises to the surface as a froth, which overflows into collection troughs. A layer of "middlings"—a clay-rich slurry with 1 percent to 4 percent bitumen still trapped inside it— remains sandwiched between the layers of froth and sand. The middlings are removed for further processing to capture the remaining oil. The froth, meanwhile, is now nearly 60 percent bitumen. It is injected with a much lighter hydrocarbon—naphtha or paraffin—to lower the viscosity, help in the removal of the remaining water, and settle out the last of the clays. At this point, perhaps three or four hours after the ore was scraped from the pit, the product has begun to roughly resemble the resource that flows readily from the reservoir at a conventional oil drilling site.

This is all tidy enough in theory, and it confirms what Clark knew by 1949, which was that the oil sands could be persuaded to yield marketable crude at industrial scale. The devil is in the details, though, and the oil sands project has been haunted by a thousand mean demons every step of the way. Nothing about turning bitumen-rich ore into profitable flows of crude oil has proven to be straightforward, and not a single step was without glitches and bugs and plain old snafus of such frequency and stubborn, knotty intransigence as to give heartburn and high blood pressure to several generations of the best engineers oil money could persuade to make their careers in the remote northeast of Alberta, mucking around with oily sludge. Just the teeth mounted on the grinder drums in an oil sands crushing machine—pyramids of hard steel coated in wear-resistant tungsten carbide—can occupy handfuls of engineers for years, experimenting with tooth shapes and coating mixes to try to get them to last longer as they gnaw away at abrasive chunks of bitumen all day.

There is nothing consistent about the ore. It changes from gum to stone with the weather in a climate of subarctic extremes. The composition of ore varies infinitely across the oil sands formation: a scoop from the ground in one spot in the mine can pull much more bitumen per ton than a scoop somewhere else. The mine must be mapped carefully to produce a balanced mix of lower-grade ore (overly laden with clay) and higher-grade ore (much coarser with sand) to keep the whole operation steady. There is a crucial range of density for the slurry as it enters the hydrotransport phase (1,500 to 1,600 kilograms per cubic metre, for the record), and a necessary portion of froth that must be bitumen (more than 50 percent but never more than 65 percent) to keep the main plant humming. Hydrotransport itself was born of necessity, discovered and developed by earlier generations of oil sands mines that required too much water and too much heat to produce a barrel of crude, driving up costs. The original GCOS plant's separator equipment would get so gummed up with sticky bitumen that it would take a crew eight hours at a stretch to clean it. The ore's abrasiveness haunted the length of the production line, eating away at pipe and vessel walls. (A saying passed around by old hands at Syncrude had it that the slurry pipe walls lost a pickup truck's worth of steel every day.) The first oil sands tailings ponds were designed to the specifications of a contemporary copper mine, and it was anticipated that the fine tailings in the pond—the yogurty goo of fines left over after the separation process—would settle out within three years and could then be remediated and removed. But oil sands fines turned out to be singularly stubborn clay, stymying site engineers and convincing chemists in the early days that they might not separate even if they were left to sit for a thousand years.

"The oil sands have hit a wall again and again and again," Clem Bowman said, "and each time, a visionary has led the industry over the wall."

From the very day the VIPs gathered beneath the GCOS banner to inaugurate the first commercial oil sands mine, the entire project presented the High Modern technocratic order with a particularly enticing and maddening conundrum. Here is a fossil fuel deposit of staggering size, but it comes in the form of a substance singularly unwilling to yield its bounty.

"The oil sands, it's a wonder of the world," said George Skulsky, who spent a quarter century overseeing extraction at the site. "It's really an oil field on the surface of the ground."

In response, engineers—those secular priests of this technological church—have met the challenge as only engineers can, with a practical wizardry of inventive genius and jaw-dropping scale. There's perhaps no better example of the thorny problem and its aggressively engineered solution than the most visible symbol of the oil sands enterprise: the Caterpillar 797 mining truck.

THE HIGH MODERN HAUL TRUCK ZENITH

When GCOS began mining bitumen in northern Alberta in 1967, it did not employ trucks and shovels as its primary open-pit tools. Instead, relying on the best practices of the conventional mining industry, it imported the largest bucket-wheel excavators it could find. The bucket wheel, developed in Germany's Ruhr Valley industrial heartland for the coal mining industry, was an enormous tractor with a long arm of iron scaffold, at the end of which was an enormous steel wheel. The wheel had big buckets around its perimeter, twenty-four in all, with hard steel digging teeth on each of them, like a weaponized Ferris wheel. Bucket wheels would chug slowly along the floor of an oil sands mine, the wheel spinning away, teeth chewing up ore to fill the buckets, which carried the pay dirt up and around to a conveyor belt built into the machine's arm.

The bucket-wheel excavator, though, had never met a substance quite like oil sands ore, and it had never operated in a climate as harsh as the subarctic boreal forest. The teeth on the bucket wheel, which weighed forty kilograms each, would sometimes wear away to nothing in less than a single twelve-hour shift. In the early days of bucket-wheel excavators at GCOS, the teeth would often snap off entirely in the coldest depths of boreal winter, and you could hear them rattling around in the separation drums "like a million church bells," as George Skulsky put it.

At the GCOS site, there was eventually a staff of four hundred charged solely with handling wear and tear on the machines. By the early 1990s, the bucket wheel had become the icon of an industry—an industry stuck in embryo seemingly forever and understood to be teetering on the brink of total failure.

Big dump trucks and shovels had been part of oil sands operations since the beginning, used to dig up and truck away the thick layer of bitumen-free sand, clay and shale covering the oil sands seam, known in the industry as "overburden." But then Suncor—the publicly traded company that evolved out of the GCOS project—brought in a new CEO, Rick George. Instead of hiring another oil business veteran to rethink Suncor's mining operations, he brought in an executive who actually had a background in conventional mining, an engineer named Dee Parkinson-Marcoux. Among Parkinson-Marcoux's key changes to site operations was the introduction of large trucks and shovels to replace the beaten-up, ground-down old bucket wheels. The truck-and-shovel approach to mining oil sands ore improved speed and efficiency so significantly it was credited with reducing the production cost of a barrel of bitumen by $5 or $6 all by itself. The other oil sands operator, Syncrude, made a similar switch soon after, and when the oil sands boomed around the turn of the millennium, trucks and shovels had emerged as the industry standard.

There was no shortage of huge dump trucks on the market when the oil sands companies went looking. The Caterpillar 777, for example, was a towering behemoth in yellow steel and black rubber, with a dump box capable of hauling a hundred tons of ore at a time. Many such trucks were purchased and set to just that task. But it was soon determined that none of these vehicles was truly *enormous*, none built quite all the way up to the oil sands industry's wild scale. And so, beginning in 1994, Syncrude engineers entered into a partnership with Caterpillar, the world's largest manufacturer of mining trucks, to develop a genuine giant for the Patch.

Caterpillar Inc. was born as the Holt Manufacturing Company, and it first started producing steam-powered farm equipment in Peoria, Illinois, in 1909. Steam tractors powered by gasoline engines had been in use for more than a decade when Benjamin Holt introduced his great innovation to the machine—a continuous track made of wooden planks that wrapped around the tractor's wheels, keeping them from getting bogged down in the mud of a farm field. A Holt company employee observed that the track-equipped machine resembled a caterpillar, and the nickname soon attached itself to the tractor itself and eventually to the whole company. Holt developed his innovation in California farm country, but the company became a major manufacturer only after it was rechristened the Holt Caterpillar Company in Peoria in 1910. Holt sold tractors to the British and French governments at the start of the First World War, and the design soon inspired the invention of the tank.

Back in Peoria after the war, the company was renamed Caterpillar and introduced its first full product line in 1925—a range of tractors that varied in hauling capacity from two tons to ten tons. The company prospered in the explosive economic climate of midcentury America, opening one new factory after another in Peoria, expanding to other cities across the Midwest and becoming a worldwide leader in heavy equipment manufacturing. The company's biggest tractors are still made in Peoria, but its largest truck assembly plant is in nearby Decatur. This is the factory where the Cat 797 heavy haul truck was born.

The scale of Building D at the Caterpillar facility in Decatur is nearly

as staggering as the enormity of an oil sands mine. The building is a series of interlocking rectangular warehouse structures, two to three storeys
high, alternating brown brick and grey siding, that stretch away from the
main entrance virtually to the horizon. An enormous Cat 785 truck stands
sentry over the main entrance, mounted there like a national monument
behind an informational plaque. The truck's iconic yellow exterior—a distinct shade patented by Caterpillar in 1979—works at least as well as a
nameplate as the company name bolted to the side of Building D. The
Cat 785 was the first outsized mining truck manufactured in Decatur,
starting in 1984. In the years since, Building D has turned out more than
ten thousand mining trucks. The one on display is nearly as tall as the
building behind it. But just the tires on a Cat 797 would reach about halfway to the highest ceiling in Building D all by themselves, which is why
they can't be fully assembled here in Decatur.

The Cat 797 is a child's sandbox fantasy come to life at Godzilla scale.
More than that, it is an industrial symphony, a carefully orchestrated feat
of industrial design, advanced engineering and material science, aided by
highly skilled assembly, global supply-chain management and digital-age
monitoring and control. The truck was built to the specifications of the
largest mine sites the world has known, and, in northern Alberta, it forms
the motorized front line of the global energy industry. It is the triumph of
the whole industrial age made manifest, an avatar of modern engineering's
limitless might filled up with diesel fuel and sent rumbling down a mine
road to haul raw energy from the earth at four hundred tons per load.

The sheer size of an oil sands haul truck is jaw-dropping. For this
reason, a replica Cat 797 is the centrepiece of the Visitors Center at Caterpillar's headquarters in Peoria, where a 62-seat auditorium has been built
inside its dump box to screen movies about the company's history. The Cat
797 stands 25 feet tall to the top of that dump box, and it's about 30 feet
wide and 50 feet long—the dimensions of a 1,500-square-foot, two-storey
home. The cab where the driver sits is more than 20 feet off the ground,
a self-contained operating station with eight on-board computers in addition to the steering wheel. The truck's six tires are 14 feet tall and together

contain enough rubber to tread five hundred cars. Its 24-cylinder engine, the largest truck engine ever made, is more powerful than the motor in an M-1 Abrams tank. The Cat 797 weighs more than a Boeing 747 passenger jet. Every detail and data point about the truck is superlative.

The manufacturing process is a related study in the expanding scope of advanced materials engineering, manufacturing skill and continent-wide logistics. Nine separate castings are made at a foundry in Louisiana, the molten steel poured into enormous moulds from a remote-controlled ladle the size of a hotel hot tub. The nine pieces get shipped to Caterpillar's heavy equipment assembly plant in Decatur, where robot welders spend twenty hours per vehicle fusing the frame together.

At this stage, the construction of a Cat 797 has at least as much in common with crafting a custom piece of furniture as it does with the work carried out on a conventional automotive assembly line. There are individual welds that can take four hours. Robotic arms perform the less delicate welds in a twenty-hour process. The product is a duplicate of every other Cat 797, but the work is specific and highly skilled. For example, a welder working on the truck's drop tubes—the enormous steel supports that raise and lower the truck's bed a hundred times a day to dump oil sands ore on-site—uses a unique carbon steel wire and a welding process that looks like hand stitching. While it is being welded, the spot where two tubes meet resembles a zipper—a series of crisscrossing lengths of wire, which is the diameter of a pencil and engineered to cool very quickly. This is so that the welders can work up the weld without the whole thing turning into a dripping mess of liquid metal. They execute a series of slow, precise, back-and-forth manoevres with their torches, the flame melting the wire like a needle pulling thread across the seam, stitching together the two pieces of steel.

"When I first got over here," a welder explained on the National Geographic Channel program *Ultimate Factories*, "this is the job I wanted to do, because this is so neat."

The finished frame is sixty-one thousand pounds of steel measuring thirty-seven feet front to back. The engine is built from separate mammoth castings in Indiana, the giant tires hand-assembled at a Michelin factory in South Carolina from 130 huge sheets of rubber each, in a process that resembles a sort of industrial-scale mix of weaving and pottery. The cab and its digital monitors and controls and soundproofed walls are put together at a plant in Joliet, Illinois. All of it gets shipped to Caterpillar's Decatur plant, where the engine is mounted on the frame.

The fully assembled Cat 797 is far too large to be driven on any highway, so the constituent pieces of the haul truck are loaded onto thirteen flatbed trucks and driven three thousand kilometres to a warehouse in Fort McMurray. The warehouse is owned by Finning International, a Vancouver-based company that is the world's largest Caterpillar heavy equipment dealer, due in large part to its steady sales of Cat 797s and huge bulldozers and tractors to oil sands companies. The dump box is shipped to the same Finning warehouse in five pieces—five more enormous slabs of precision-cast steel—and then seven-person technical teams, working around the clock, spend seven days assembling a single Cat 797 from all the parts. The whole process usually takes about eighty days from first casting to final assembly, and the price tag is $5 million or more per truck.

The first full order of Cat 797s—eight in all—arrived at Syncrude's Aurora mine in 2002. When the boom hit its full swing a few years later, the truck became the icon of the whole industry—the default photo for breathless stories about the explosive growth and mounting profits of the oil sands business, the triumphant image of High Modern engineering at its maximum skill and size.

In short order, a whole cottage industry arose in northern Alberta to service the trucks, a range of mechanics and refurbishers and parts suppliers in addition to the folks at fast-growing Finning. An Edmonton company called Titan Supply, for example, developed a special "towing sling" just for the Cat 797s. The packed dirt of an oil sands mine's road has a tendency to grow soft and mucky in spring, and the dramatic shifts in weight as a Cat 797 dumps its load can cause the huge tires to sink ten feet or more into the mud. Drivers were using thick steel-wire ropes as towing cables, but the ropes weighed more than three hundred pounds and had a habit of kinking and springing back savagely when they snapped. The steel in the ropes also tended to develop sharp burrs, and it gummed up easily with bitumen. It was all a costly, dangerous mess. So Titan built a new cable out of synthetic fibres, space-age bullet-stopping stuff like Kevlar and aramid. The new tow rope was just as strong, but flexible and light—only fifty pounds or so. Even the smallest of the Cat 797 drivers could get their stuck truck hitched to another vehicle on their own.

In this and countless other ways, the Cat 797 became part of the local culture and a symbol of the industry. In the business, they're referred to generically as haul trucks, acknowledging the presence of Liebherr T 282s and Cat 793s, but the huge Cat 797s are the real icons. A hundred of them had been shipped to oil sands mines by 2007. In 2015, Syncrude's fleet numbered more than a hundred all by itself, representing a $39 million investment in truck tires alone. At a more recently developed site—Shell's Muskeg River mine, say, which first began digging bitumen in 2002— the first phase of operation was driven by twenty-five heavy haul trucks carrying the excavations of five shovels. In 2002 Keyano College in Fort McMurray added a heavy haul truck simulator to its heavy equipment operator course. In the summer of 2006, when the Alberta government was invited by the Smithsonian Institution in Washington, DC, to assemble a public display of "the culture of Alberta" on the National Mall, the centrepiece was a Caterpillar 777 haul truck, standing in for the true colossus of the oil sands.

The haul truck was the booming Patch in shorthand. You couldn't readily show visitors or TV cameras the byzantine chemical processes taking place inside a separation vessel or a hydrocracker, but anyone who laid eyes on a steady stream of house-sized trucks chugging up and down a mine road understood immediately the scale of the operation, its deceptive simplicity and perhaps even something of the complex engineering it had taken to make the world's third largest oil reserve finally pay out. As the media from across the country and then the world descended on booming Fort McMurray, the Cat 797 inevitably became a recurring motif.

When company officials showed journalists around, they liked to point out how it was already part of the industry's lore that women made better haul truck drivers than men did. They were more careful, more focused. A Suncor promotional video series about its workforce, released in 2012, featured a haul truck driver named Sonja Peteriet, posed in front of a Cat 797 in her blue, reflective-striped coveralls and hard hat. "They're the biggest truck in the world," she said, "so that's pretty cool in itself."

Several media features on the diverse face of Fort McMurray's workforce have focused on a diminutive Filipina woman named Mucharata Minog David, a self-described "tough princess" who arrived in Fort McMurray as part of the Canadian government's Temporary Foreign Worker (TFW) program. She trained as a haul truck driver and landed a permanent job on a Suncor site. An *Edmonton Journal* feature in 2005, meanwhile, profiled Tracey Gladue, a Metis woman raised in Fort McMurray who left a career in law enforcement to drive Cat 797s for Suncor. Prince Philip, Duke of Edinburgh, visited Fort McMurray that year, and his itinerary included a stop at the Suncor mine, during which Gladue gave him a tour of her truck. "I like working on my own," she told the *Journal*. "I pick up a load, dump it off and go pick up another one. I feel in control and like I'm accomplishing something."

All told, the Patch's daily workforce numbers 28,000 on the sites themselves, as well as 25,000 contractors engaged in routine upkeep and the labour-intensive "turnaround" maintenance that occurs when production facilities shut down for major refurbishment. There are also nearly 10,000 construction workers employed in the industry's continuing growth. And this is just the front line of an industry-wide force that the Canadian Association of Petroleum Producers estimates at 150,000 nationwide, all employed due to direct investment in the project of liberating bitumen from the oil sands.

Down in the mines, the workhorses remain haul trucks and shovels. They only stop long enough for one operator to take over from another, and then the machines all go right back to work. The haul trucks run up and down the winding dirt roads in and out of the pit, one after the other, evenly spaced, a colossal clockwork. The truck arrives at the shovel, backs in. The shovel has already begun to gouge away another 100 tons of dirt before the truck has moved fully into place. A single scoop takes less than half a minute, then another and another, and in barely a minute and a half, 400 tons of ore sits in the Cat 797's dump box. The operator can keep an eye on the load on a monitor in her cab. The haul truck pulls away from under the shovel, and another rolls up to take its place. The operator pilots the vehicle up the road out of the pit to the waiting hopper, backs in, dumps the load, heads back into the pit.

If there are no mechanical problems, if the great tires don't choose that shift to finally wear out (as they tend to do on around the three-hundredth straight day of nonstop work), if the truck stays free of mud and snow—if all goes well, the average 797 will make four trips to the shovel and back per hour, roughly thirty to fifty total trips per shift by each driver. On average, each 400-ton load will produce 172 barrels of oil. In the giddy days of $120-per-barrel oil in 2008, a driver might have hauled a million dollars' worth of oil in a single twelve-hour shift. In 2015, with oil stuck in the doldrums of $50 or less, the total was between $250,000 and $450,000. Not every job in the mine—or in the industry—can be enumerated quite so tidily, and all of them are ultimately required to turn those 100-ton scoops of ore into barrels of crude sold on the open market, but this, in any case, is what a day's work is worth on an oil sands mine.

BURIED TREASURE

The haul truck hides a secret. The size of the Cat 797, the bright yellow paint and the roaring twenty-four-cylinder engine, its great symbolic weight on the landscape, the lunar vastness of the open-pit mines—all this obscures the basic fact that since 2012, the majority of the Patch's 2.4 million barrels of oil per day is not extracted from surface mines. Any given day in 2015, a slim majority of 1.3 million barrels came instead from in situ operations.

The development of technology to extract deeply buried bitumen deposits was made necessary by the geology of Alberta's oil sands. The Mc-Murray Formation approaches and even breaches the forest floor on the banks of the Athabasca and its tributaries in and around Fort McMurray. This is why you can take a stroll down a path out back of the Fort Mc-Murray suburb of Abasand Heights to the site of the plant that burned down at the end of the Second World War and pull away pieces of bitumen from an exposed seam along the way. The oil sands mines north of the city all dig into the same slab of bitumen just below the boreal forest's muskeg floor. Mining is cost-effective to a depth of eighty metres. But the overwhelming majority of the proven reserves in the Patch are deeper down, south and west of the city, where the McMurray Formation is buried much deeper below the earth's surface.

For many decades, this was the greater riddle, the more precious and abundant prize hidden deeper underground, locked away even tighter in a sandy sludge that would not flow to the surface. There was a half-serious proposal back in the 1950s, notorious in the business, to detonate a nuclear bomb in the middle of this deeper deposit, liquefying it and—so it was hoped—creating something like a conventional oil reservoir that might yield to standard wells and pumpjacks. The idea was never pursued seriously. Instead, starting in the depths of price-shocked OPEC scarcity in the early 1970s, university labs and oil company research-and-development (R&D) departments in Alberta began to investigate other means of turning oil sands into crude. Premier Peter Lougheed established the Alberta Oil Sands Technology and Research Authority (AOSTRA) in 1974 with a $100 million research budget—nearly half a billion dollars in today's money and a huge sum at the time, one of the largest dedicated public R&D investments ever made in Canada—to develop new technologies for extracting in situ bitumen.

Lougheed was the political architect of modern Alberta and its first true postwar premier in terms of his world view. He had come to power in 1971 as leader of a young, dynamic new political party—the Progressive Conservatives, with Lougheed's emphasis sharply on the progressive side—that felt like a popular movement with modernization as its goal. His repeated showdowns with the federal government over control of Alberta's oil and gas business, including the oil sands, earned him the nickname "the Blue-Eyed Sheik" and a national reputation for skilled bare-knuckle politics.

Lougheed was a forceful but cautious champion of Alberta's fossil fuel resources. He pushed for slow, orderly development in the oil sands and established a sovereign wealth fund, the Alberta Heritage Savings Trust Fund, to collect 30 percent of all fossil fuel revenues and save their mounting value for future generations of Albertans. The establishment of AOSTRA garnered fewer headlines than Lougheed's showdowns with federal politicians, but it would prove pivotal to the industry a quarter century later.

AOSTRA was a quintessential High Modern progressive's initiative— a Crown corporation charged with the goal of unlocking a valuable but underdeveloped natural resource. It began modestly, headed by a highly regarded research engineer at Imperial Oil named Clem Bowman, who Lougheed recruited personally for the job. As he settled into the role, Bowman recalled the obscure research work of Dr. Roger Butler, a fellow chemical engineer in the research department at Imperial. Butler had an idea he'd been talking up since the early 1960s, a handful of differential equations and diagrams sketched freehand on gridded engineering paper that purported to show how a pair of wells drilled horizontally through an oil sands deposit could coax the oil out of the sludge.

The mid-1970s represented an anxious, ambitious gold rush sort of time in the oil business. OPEC, the Organization of Petroleum Exporting Countries, had launched an oil embargo in response to American support for Israel, cutting production and hiking prices. The embargo demonstrated overnight the fragility of global supplies and their susceptibility to unstable Middle Eastern politics, while demand continued to mount unabated. The industry responded with a frantic hunt for new oil plays, from the northern slope of Alaska to the bottom of the North Sea and the

Gulf of Mexico. AOSTRA emerged in the midst of this frenzy, looking for a key to unlock the billions of barrels everyone knew waited deep under the muskeg in the McMurray Formation.

One day a couple of years after its launch, Bowman and his team heard from Jack Haston, an engineer at the Calgary office of an oil-field engineering firm called Williams Brothers. The company had been investigating technology exchange opportunities with the Soviet Union. One of the possibilities was a unique mining operation in northern Russia, where heat was being used to extract oil. And so it came to pass that in November 1976, with the Soviet Union gearing up for lavish celebrations commemorating the sixtieth anniversary of the Communist revolution, a delegation of eight oilmen from conservative Alberta went to Moscow.

Bowman sent his AOSTRA deputy, Maurice Carrigy. Officials from Petro-Canada, Husky Oil, Cities Service Company and Atlantic Richfield Company joined him. Haston figured the group needed at least one guy who knew how mines worked, so he recruited an engineer named Gerry Stephenson, who had coal mining experience in the Alberta Rocky Mountain town of Canmore.

After a few days of meetings with officials in Moscow, the AOSTRA delegation boarded a small plane for the flight to Ukhta, the industrial hub of the Yarega oil field, 1,300 kilometres to the northeast. Looking out the airplane window, Haston marvelled at how familiar the view was. Farmland and deciduous forest at first, giving way to boreal forest and muskeg as they neared Ukhta. It was almost a precise mirror image of the landscape on the ride from Edmonton to Fort McMurray.

The oil production facility at Yarega was a classic industrial age mine. The Soviet hosts led the Albertans into a cage elevator that took them down several hundred feet into a mine shaft. Tunnels led away from the shaft through the sandstone at mild downward angles, reinforced at intervals by wooden trusses.

When they reached their destination, they stepped out into a broad mining tunnel—a "stope," to use the miners' lingo—with troughs running down either side. "Jesus, look at that!" Gerry Stephenson said to the

others in a shocked whisper. He was the only one with intimate knowledge
of conventional mines, but all of them knew immediately they were surveying a singular and dangerous industrial scene. Somewhere high above
them in the sandstone, a well was pumping steam into the rock formation.
All along either side of the stope, a series of spigots that looked like lawn
sprinkler heads dripped crude oil, which gathered in the troughs below
and flowed in the open down to a central pooling area. Haston thought
giddily that it was a good thing nobody was wearing steel-toed boots—
there was surely highly flammable crude oil vapour all around them in the
stope, and it would take only a single spark from a steel toe scraping rock
to ignite it. But what do you know, the crazy apparatus worked. "Gravity
drainage" was, technically speaking, a viable way to mine oil from stone.

When they returned to the surface, the Albertans filled their lungs
with fresh northern air and gratefully accepted shots of vodka from their
Soviet hosts.

The vodka would flow freely throughout the tour, and on the last
night in Ukhta, Haston and his colleagues joined the Soviet mining officials for a banquet at the city's grandest hotel. At dinner, the officials
proposed a toast to the sixtieth anniversary of Vladimir Lenin's return
to Moscow and the October 1917 Revolution he inspired. Their glasses
raised high, the Alberta oilmen drank to the glories of Communism.
Much later that night, in the square near the hotel, Haston staggered
gleefully around the base of the city's great fountain with Stephenson,
the two of them singing every Canadian kid's best-known French children's song, "Alouette." Haston was originally from Toronto and Stephenson from England, and they sang in poor schoolboy French about
plucking a pretty bird's feathers. They didn't know it yet, but they'd just
seen the prototype of the industrial process that would turn in situ bitumen into a viable multibillion-dollar commodity.

Back in Canada, Stephenson dutifully prepared a report and filed it
with AOSTRA. "It said, basically, the system works, it's very primitive, but
we should study for application in the oil sands, where we have similar
problems," he recalled in an interview years later.

THE PATCH

70

The report sat with Bowman and his team at AOSTRA as oil continued its dizzying rise in price through the final years of the decade and royalties flowed into Lougheed's Heritage Fund at a clip of $2,000 per minute. By 1982, Stephenson had convinced AOSTRA to back a full field test of a concept combining Yarega's mining processes with Roger Butler's technical equations, which came to be known as steam-assisted gravity drainage (SAGD). In the mid-1980s, with the global oil industry now reeling from a supply glut and collapsing prices, AOSTRA's pilot project team went from office tower to emptying office tower in downtown Calgary, looking for industry partners. The AOSTRA team was convinced they had cracked the ancient oil sands puzzle, that horizontal wells and steam injection would open up hundreds of billions of barrels of oil to commercial production. But in the gloom of the Patch in the mid-1980s, not one company was willing to sink money into a risky new technology. Breaking with his mandate, AOSTRA's acting director, Maurice Carrigy, decided the organization would back the SAGD field test on its own. A colleague would recount it years later as "the gutsiest call in our industry."

With AOSTRA's full support, the team began work on what came to be known as the Underground Test Facility (UTF). On the banks of the Athabasca River just south of the GCOS site, they brought in a drilling rig built to dig missile silos and excavated a mine shaft of their own. (As with the Yarega site, the UTF's rough-hewn design would often spook visitors; one provincial politician remembered a trip down the shaft into the mine in a rattling elevator "that looked like it had come out of an old horror movie.") Horizontal wells were drilled from the shaft, tests conducted and the concept proven: by injecting the uppermost of the paired wells with steam, in situ bitumen would turn to liquid and drip into the lower well. In time, a handful of companies were persuaded to make small investments of $1 million or so to keep it running and conduct tests of their own.

AOSTRA's field test overlapped with rapid advances in horizontal drilling in the conventional oil industry. By 1996, SAGD was ready for its first commercial test. Encana Corporation, a major Canadian natural gas company, built the first pilot well at Foster Creek, 200 kilometres southeast of Fort McMurray. The first full commercial production facility came online at the same site in 2001, and SAGD rode the same wild boom as the rest of the Patch in the years to come, as oil prices skyrocketed north of $100. The technology was widely adopted by industry veterans like Suncor, ConocoPhillips and Statoil, as well as a host of "junior" oil sands players, mostly smaller companies out of Calgary hoping to use the new technology and its less onerous start-up costs (or similarly scaled operations using other in situ innovations) to fully unlock the tens of billions of barrels of bitumen far beneath the forest floor.

Drilling for in situ reserves using SAGD and similar processes has been greeted as a technological marvel, broadly understood as the engine of the industry's brightest future. This isn't just because 80 percent of Alberta's oil sands deposits are buried too deeply for surface mining but also because SAGD arrived on the scene with such an enticing high-tech sheen. It was laboratory-driven and innovative. Its physical impact on the landscape was relatively gentle—no oil-slicked duck-trapping tailings ponds or gaping-moonscape open-pit mines. It was a twenty-first-century replacement, finally, for the brute force of shovels and dump trucks.

"It's a dramatic shift in the extraction of oil sands," a Cenovus Energy executive told the *Calgary Herald* in 2010. "We're really a tech company that produces oil and gas." Cenovus, the company spun off from Encana to develop its in situ assets, had come to think of itself as a bridge between the industrial and digital ages, an analogue to the fleet-footed, research-driven enterprises that vaulted telecommunications into the internet age. "Welcome to a different kind of oil sands," read the tagline on a Cenovus ad campaign launched in 2011.

And so as the thousands trudge to the mine sites north of Fort McMurray day in and day out in 2015, a smaller workforce heads out for morning shifts on drilling rigs and in control rooms at dozens of tidy little SAGD plants scattered across the quiet forest south of the city. MEG Energy, possibly the most successful of the oil sands juniors—at the very least, one of the few juniors not watching the cratering price of oil like it was a dire electrocardiogram reading of its own fiscal health—produces eighty thousand barrels each day at its modest facility not far from a pretty little body of water called Christina Lake.

Many of MEG Energy's employees wake up in a resort-like lodge called Pirate's Cove, overlooking the lake. The scene is tranquil enough that MEG's work camp shares the lakeshore with a resort lodge noted for its fishing. (MEG employees have been known to land a northern pike or two between shifts, casting their rods from the lodge's emergency evacuation boats.) In white work trucks and shuttles, they depart for an orderly site out in the woods northeast of the lakeshore. The scale of a SAGD site is still unmistakably industrial, but there's none of the High Modern massiveness of an oil sands mine site. The cluster of buildings that forms the core of the facility—a tank farm, a few low warehouse buildings, water recycling ponds, several cogeneration plants—wouldn't be out of place in a suburban industrial park.

The oldest SAGD plants, and still among the largest producers, are operated by Cenovus. The company traces its roots to a Crown corporation, the Alberta Energy Company, established in the 1970s to develop new oil and gas projects. After AOSTRA demonstrated the potential of SAGD in the early 1990s, Alberta Energy (which became Encana after a 2002 merger) set up the first commercial test plant, expanded it to commercial scale in 2001, and built a second plant near Christina Lake that began producing oil in 2002. The Christina Lake plant produced 18,000 barrels of oil per day that year. As the industry boomed in the years that followed, both plants grew, and Encana spun its SAGD operations off into a company—Cenovus—dedicated exclusively to in situ production. Christina Lake expanded to 76,000 barrels per day in 2013 and was pumping 150,000 barrels by 2015.

The heart of a SAGD production facility is essentially a large power plant run on natural gas—specifically a cogeneration plant, which takes in water and burns natural gas to produce steam and electricity. A large portion of the electricity is superfluous to the plant's requirements and flows onto the provincial power grid, a sort of by-product generated alongside the plant's vital steam production. At Cenovus's Christina Lake plant, twelve gas boilers—"steam generators," as the technicians call them—stand in a neat row like sentries, their hundred-foot-tall white chimneys mounted on boxy bases. Water arrives pressurized and preheated to 195°C and is converted to steam at 300 degrees. The steam is piped from the plant to a range of well pads scattered through the surrounding forest. From above, the well pads resemble broad dirt parking lots, with an insectlike arrangement of shed structures and protruding pipe at their centre. The sheds form a backbone from which well pipes extend in pairs like spidery legs. Cenovus, always keen to appeal to Canadian patriotism, describes its average well pad as "about the size of ten hockey rinks."

At a typical Christina Lake well pad, each pair of wells has been drilled 600 metres straight down. There, at the depth of the oil sands deposit, the wells turn 90 degrees and travel horizontally two kilometres through mud and rock to their target. Ideally, the well pairs are perfectly parallel and the steam injector is as near as possible to five metres above the collection well. The superheated steam from the plant flows from the injection well to saturate the deposit, the bitumen melts and flows, and a steady stream of water and oil seeps into the lower well, from which it is pumped to the surface. In a separation tank back at the plant, the water is removed, and almost all of it—98 percent or more at Cenovus's plants—is recycled back through the steam generators to melt more bitumen.

In theory, the process is an elegant closed loop, but like all else in the Patch, it is dogged by complications and costly inefficiencies. At a control room back at the base plant, half a dozen or more technicians monitor pressure and temperature throughout the process. Minor changes in the quality of the deposit or the steam temperature can eat away at production volume and profitability. Governing it all is a single merciless statistic: the steam-to-oil ratio, or SOR. This is a simple metric indicating how much steam is being used per unit of oil produced. It is tracked and tweaked in the in situ business more zealously than the price of oil.

Harbir Chhina, executive vice president for oil sands development at Cenovus, has been obsessing over SOR his whole professional life. When Chhina was a young research engineer at AOSTRA in the 1980s, just

graduated from the University of Calgary, the SOR at an experimental
SAGD operation was as high as 10 to 1. When he moved to the Alberta
Energy Company to oversee the first commercial tests of the technology, it
had declined to 4 to 1. A tighter SOR soon became the primary measure
of economic viability. Cenovus's first full commercial production plants
came online around 2.3 to 1. This is still at the efficient, profitable end of
the industry spectrum—Cenovus's combined Christina Lake and Foster
Creek production averages an SOR of 2.1 to 1, while new in situ technologies and operations working less robust deposits often fall in the range of
4:1 to 6:1. At Cenovus's highest-performing Christina Lake well pads, the
SOR has dropped as low as 1.8 to 1.

"It is the most important metric in our business," Chhina says. "It
controls not only the economics, it controls your footprints, it controls
your emissions, your water usage. It has an impact on everything in your
business, the steam-oil ratio does. Because we're basically building water
recycling plants."

Water is heated, injected, removed, stored in ponds, treated, recycled,
reinjected. And the technicians pore over SOR data all the while. An uptick in the ratio means more steam being generated, which means more
natural gas used, which means rising per-barrel costs and shrinking profit
margins and increasing greenhouse gas emissions. The oil—the ostensible
pay dirt—can seem almost incidental at a SAGD plant. But off it goes nevertheless, separated from the water that liberated it from the oil sands ore
and injected with lighter diluents to make it easier to transport.

Finally it flows! The heavy crude, liberated after countless millennia
through the genius of engineers, flows by the hundreds of thousands of barrels. It washes down feeder pipelines, through interconnections and down
trunk pipelines and dedicated connector lines—1.3 million barrels per
day of in situ bitumen joining 1.1 million from the great mines in a more
or less steady southward flow. All of it is bound by one route or another to
upgraders and tank farms, oil terminals built at wellheads and railheads to
intersect with continent-wide pipe and rail networks. Eventually it all finds

its way to open ports and open markets, joining a dizzyingly scaled deluge of 91 million barrels worldwide daily.

A barrel of oil is 159 litres of hydrocarbon energy, and 91 million barrels is a volume beyond the limit of anyone's reckoning, really. Fourteen billion litres a day, 10 million every minute. Four Olympic-sized swimming pools every sixty seconds, if you prefer more tangible metrics. Enough oil for every car and bus and lifted pickup truck on earth, enough for all the diesel engines and diesel generators cranking away at work sites or remote villages beyond the reach of power grids. Enough for every backyard barbecue's propane tank, every butane-filled Zippo lighter, every jar of Vaseline, every tube of lipstick. Every length of PVC pipe and every key on every keyboard in the whole digital world. Suncor likes to brag that it supplies the hydrocarbons that give the shine to gummy bears, so all of that, too. Bite into a gummy bear on the ride home from the grocery store and wonder whether some handful of those hydrocarbon molecules started out as Lower Cretaceous oil sands sludge turned to liquid far beneath the boreal forest floor in northern Alberta.

MIDSTREAM

Long before it burns in the engine of a Ford F-150 or shellacs a gummy bear, the 2.4-million-barrel daily ration of bitumen exits the boreal forest scene, heading southwest and entering the phase known in the industry as midstream. Upstream refers to mines and SAGD wellheads, exploration and production. Refining, delivery, marketing and petrochemical manufacture lie downstream. Midstream is the point in between, the point at which resource becomes commodity.

For Alberta bitumen, midstream is a place a few hundred kilometres south or southwest of its origin. Not quite half of the day's oil sands production is upgraded on-site, transformed from raw bitumen into synthetic crude oil at processing facilities located at oil sands base plants near the mines. There are four on-site upgraders in the Patch, one each at Suncor's base site, Syncrude's Mildred Lake, CNRL's Horizon and CNOOC/ Nexen's Long Lake in situ operation. The other half of the flow is dilbit, bitumen mixed by its producers with those lighter hydrocarbons called diluents to lower its viscosity so that it can flow down a pipeline. Either way, the destination is one of a handful of oil way stations, waiting clusters of storage tanks, oil terminals, railheads and pipeline termini on the outskirts of Edmonton, or else a transport hub such as the small prairie town of Hardisty, 550 kilometres south of Fort McMurray, on the Canadian National rail line.

The land northeast of Edmonton is broad, flat and fertile, fed amply by the North Saskatchewan River and the prairie sun. The northeastern part of the city has long been a heavy industrial area, and its suburban industrial parks spill out toward Fort Saskatchewan, a satellite city 25 kilometres farther northeast. Beyond Fort Saskatchewan, there are fields of wheat and canola, some of them dotted with pumpjacks liberating conventional crude oil from the ancient seafloor of the Western Canadian Sedimentary Basin. Just past the city limits, between the river and the rail line, is a strip of densely industrialized land that has been turning hydrocarbons into consumer products since the first Alberta oil strikes in the 1940s.

The whole region, from the northeast suburbs of Edmonton out past Fort Saskatchewan, has recently been branded "Alberta's Industrial Heartland" by local business boosters. Locals also refer to it colloquially as Upgrader Alley, testimony not so much to the presence of Shell's long-serving Scotford upgrader in the area but to a decade-old dream of greatly expanding its upgrading and refining capacity that has not been fully realized yet. As the breakneck pace of the booming oil sands swept up Edmonton and Fort Saskatchewan in its dizzying flow, most midstream and downstream companies decided it made more economic sense to reconfigure existing refineries in Illinois and Texas so that they could receive dilbit rather than produce refined petrochemical products in distant, landlocked central Alberta. In 2015 there was still only one operating upgrader in Upgrader Alley—Shell's Scotford upgrader and refinery, then being outfitted with Alberta's first on-site carbon capture and storage (CCS) operation to bury one million tons of carbon dioxide under the prairie soil each year. A second upgrader and refinery project began construction in 2013, but it was still under construction and over budget, a sinkhole for provincial money in addition to the private capital invested in it. The majority of Alberta's bitumen upgrading continued to occur at six facilities in the Fort McMurray area, and more and more in situ oil went into pipes as dilbit, without upgrading.

The self-proclaimed Industrial Heartland of Alberta remains a busy industrial scene nonetheless. The stretch of prairie on the outskirts of Fort Saskatchewan is covered over with mazes of steel towers and snaking pipes, a signature on the landscape similar to the oil sands plants farther north, flanked here by train tracks and lines of waiting tanker cars stretching to the horizon. In addition to Shell's enormous facility, there are storage terminals and oil-by-rail terminals and petrochemical plants. Dow Chemical Company makes ethylene and polyethylene here from the oil's by-products, and a company called MEGlobal produces monoethylene glycol and diethylene glycol, the raw material for ubiquitous plastics such as polyester and polyethylene terephthalate (PET). On the edge of the nearby village of Bruderheim, Cenovus has a new terminal capable of loading tanker cars with a hundred thousand barrels of its dilbit each day. MEG Energy stores up to nine hundred thousand barrels of oil a day in a new tank farm in the area. From the outskirts of Fort Saskatchewan southwest to the Strathcona Industrial Park on the southern fringe of Edmonton, more than forty industrial facilities, mostly hydrocarbon related, operate in the heartland, representing more than $30 billion in investments to date. More than four hundred thousand barrels of oil are processed at three refineries here each day. There's enough storage for more than twenty-three million barrels of oil, and terminals ready to load most of that oil into pipelines and onto rail cars. Another twenty-six million barrels of storage capacity awaits at the pipeline hub of Hardisty.

There are, in all, eight upgraders and four refineries across Alberta, seventeen tank farms at six terminal sites and fourteen oil-by-rail terminals. There are also pipeline mouths and railroad sidings by the dozens, and pipe and track that connect to transport networks spanning the continent. All of it assembled to do what the pioneering prospectors of the oil sands— though they knew they had a bonanza under their feet—could not manage, which is to deliver bitumen in such quantity and quality as to make it an essential piece of the global energy industry.

FOUR

MIDDAY

HIGH MODERN NOON

At lunch time any given day in 2015, Fort McMurray is a tranquil little city. Odd-hour shifts and twenty-four-hour-a-day operations mean there's always some bustle, but by noon the streets are no longer filled with Diversified buses and white trucks heading to and from site. There's less sense of single-minded purpose. Thousands are out at the mines, and only a tiny portion of the city's workforce commutes into the city centre for standard office work. Traffic moves smoothly even on Franklin Avenue, the main downtown thoroughfare.

Franklin Avenue achieved some notoriety during the most manic years of the Patch's boom. Starting around 2005, the world's attention turned to the oil sands region and its fast-growing hub, and journalists descended from across Canada and around the world to file breathless reports on this new Klondike in Alberta's north. With scant access to the mine sites, reporters were left to soak up some local boomtown colour along Franklin Avenue, lingering in particular on a couple of square blocks at the north end of town. There they found the Boomtown Casino, just around the corner from an old hotel complex housing the Oil Can Tavern, Teasers Strip Club and the notorious Diggers Variety Club, where young men coming off lucrative shifts on Thursday payday nights would wait for their name to be called over the club's public address system to cash their cheques at the bar like lottery winners.

A 2005 *Calgary Herald* feature described the corner of Franklin Avenue and Main Street, in the shadow of the government building that serves as Fort McMurray's city hall, as an open-air "drug den" and prostitution stroll. Fights and police interventions, the *Herald* reported, were pretty much a nightly occurrence. Easy money and hard partying, cocaine and methamphetamine, prostitutes in the 7-Eleven parking lot at Franklin and Main and escort services filling ten pages of the local phone book— this was the portrait of Fort McMurray's social life the wider world saw in the boom years. A 2012 feature that ran in British *GQ*, loathed with particular intensity by locals, read like a twenty-first-century reboot of a dime novel about the lawless Wild West. The *GQ* writer toured seemingly every licensed establishment on Franklin Avenue to arrive at the conclusion that Fort McMurray was a place "synonymous with crime, an explosion in prostitution and the tough, young, bored single men with too much money and too little to do who are fuelling the chaos." The story also hinted ominously at "Somali gangs and Hell's Angels" running drug and prostitution rings in town.

Virtually every media outlet in Canada ran similar if more restrained stories on "Fort McMoney" during the boom years. Few gave any indication of how concentrated their salacious scenes were, how you could circumnavigate the entire bacchanal on foot—from the casino parking lot, past Diggers and the midrise apartment blocks where drug busts often went down, back around to the intersection of Franklin and Main—in less than half an hour. And British *GQ* certainly didn't return for a follow-up report when the Diggers complex closed for good just months after its

story ran, razed to the ground before the year was out in the first stages of
a downtown redevelopment project.

The reality of Fort McMurray is much more complex and far less chaotic than those magazine scenes. The city's 2015 census counted 82,724
people living in the "urban service area" of Fort McMurray (an unwieldy
way of differentiating the city itself from the vast hinterland of work camps
and small, predominantly First Nations communities that together make
up the Regional Municipality of Wood Buffalo). Less than 15 percent of
that total resides in the Lower Townsite area, the original downtown on the
Clearwater River floodplain anchored by Franklin Avenue. A substantial
majority of the city's residents—more than fifty-six thousand of them—live
in three suburban developments on the other side of the Athabasca River
from the Lower Townsite, neighbourhoods named Thickwood Heights,
Timberlea and Parsons Creek, built mostly in the last twenty years in response to the rapid growth of the oil sands workforce.

Crossing the Athabasca from downtown over the bridge from the
Lower Townsite, the first exit on Highway 63 leads to Thickwood Boulevard, a wide, split-laned suburban thoroughfare. It cuts through the older
subdivisions of Thickwood, circles north, and becomes Confederation
Way as it arrives in Timberlea. There it bisects the length of the newer
suburb and returns to the highway one exit farther north. This broad suburban semicircle, lined with strip malls, supermarkets, big-box stores, fast-
food joints, hockey arenas, churches and midrise office buildings, is in
many ways the city's true main street.

Fort McMurray is predominantly a tidy, suburbanized company
town. A local blogger named Andrew Farris described it in a sardonic
"Get Rich Quick at the Oil Sands" guide, published online not long after the infamous GQ story, as "more Cypress Creek than Dawson City."
Dawson City, of course, was the brash, bawdy boomtown born overnight
to service the Klondike gold rush in the 1890s, while Cypress Creek is
the place name of a hypermodern, spotlessly clean, relentlessly upper-
middle-class company town in a particular episode of *The Simpsons* TV
show. To drive the length of the Thickwood Boulevard–Confederation

Way loop is to see much of Cypress Creek and practically none of Dawson City.

Here, along the looping suburban boulevard and up curvilinear secondary avenues and down winding crescents and cul-de-sacs, is a bountiful suburban idyll. In half the neighbourhoods along the Thickwood-Confederation loop, the scene in 2015 looks almost eerily new, like the last sheets of vinyl siding were tacked up this morning and the final stretch of pavement dried yesterday. Rows of houses back onto newly turned earth, piles of rock and stacks of assorted building materials. New streets stretch past suburban driveways into nothing. In Parsons Creek, the newest of the city's suburban developments, there is a kind of central square formed by a broad swath of barren dirt boxed in by new roads and surrounded by half-finished avenues. A row of sandwich boards and billboards advertising show homes greets you on your way into Parsons Creek.

Here are the usual assortment of customized late-model F-150s and Silverados, white work trucks, RVs parked in driveways, backyards littered with ATVs and snowmobiles and speedboats. Here are standard starter homes with the requisite nuclear families. Here as well are starter homes bought as investments by new arrivals from Newfoundland and Ontario and West Africa and Colombia — young engineers renting out bedrooms to colleagues and listing their basement suites on Airbnb to make mortgage payments in a market that was among the most inflated in the country for much of the past decade. (The average price of a home in Fort McMurray was $740,000 in 2012.) Here in older split-levels are long-established families with teenage kids living side by side with shift workers crammed six to ten per unit, as in the boarding houses of another era. And here, in places, are For Sale signs in front of houses that provide evidence not of departing families but of growing real estate fortunes. There was fast money to be made in recent years flipping houses in Fort McMurray's overheated, perpetually undersupplied housing market; in the city's South Asian community, immigrants from the Indian state of Gujarat have a reputation for savvy real estate plays.

Here are immaculately landscaped lawns and parks, brand-new schools and recreation facilities. Here are the YMCA and the Suncor Energy Centre for the Performing Arts and the Multicultural Association of Wood Buffalo. Here are lavishly equipped big-box gyms, where men doing solo twenty-and-tens, their families back in Quebec or Prince Edward Island, spend their very little downtime working out, counting reps in lieu of counting the days till they head home again. Here are strip malls with long-established bars featuring karaoke nights and down-home fiddle bands tucked between Lebanese-run donair places and dental offices. Here's a sign advertising "Tar Sand Betties Roller Derby" in front of a hockey arena. Here, on the very western edge of Timberlea, is the Syncrude Athletic Park, as new and lavish a collection of sports fields as you'll find in any small city in the country. Beer-league softball teams fill a half-dozen baseball fields with friendly chatter, alongside four soccer pitches where cheers ring out in at least that many languages, alongside Fort McMurray's first-ever cricket pitch, put in after the rest of the park had been built at the behest of the city's first-ever cricket club.

Here, on MacDonald Island, which lies across the river just north of downtown and just south of the highway exit leading to Thickwood, is maybe the most elaborate multipurpose recreational centre a company town has ever built, finished in 2009 at a cost of $127 million. Here, surrounding a wide parking lot, is upper-middle-class suburban leisure at its High Modern apex and in many of its most popular forms. Here is the Miskanaw Golf Club, its clubhouse staring across the parking lot at Shell Place, a brand-new outdoor stadium and concert venue. In between the stadium and golf course is the enormous Suncor Community Leisure Centre. Its marquee facility is the Syncrude Aquatic Centre, an expansive, tropical-themed retreat from the merciless boreal winter, climate-controlled and artificially humid and equipped with several pools and multiple waterslides. There is also the CNOOC Nexen Field House (for basketball and other court sports), the CNRL Arena (for hockey and figure skating), the Total Fitness Centre (named for the French oil company, not the comprehensiveness of its workout gear) and the Oilsands Curling Club. The city's public library, with its Total Aboriginal Cultural Corner and Syncrude Corner, is on the second floor.

MacDonald Island is a sober middle-class pleasure dome. It is the suburban antithesis of a raunchy boomtown tavern. It is what you build from fast-flowing oil riches if your intent is to defy nagging boomtown stereotypes. It speaks to permanence and optimism, to raising families and living well. In the three years after MacDonald Island opened, Fort McMurray had one of the highest birthrates in Canada: 37.4 per 1,000 population, far above the national average of 11 per 1,000. In July 2012 alone, there were 147 births in the hospital at the other end of downtown from MacDonald Island. This is no city of single young men—certainly not exclusively, not anymore.

Suburban Fort McMurray barely needs the city that spawned it. Suburbia is the fossil fuel era's signature urban form and most widely dispersed aspirational lifestyle. And in Fort McMurray, where it has been built with oil-worker pay to house oil-worker families and their oil-powered trucks and toys, it has achieved some kind of maximum expression. This is self-contained, self-perpetuating suburbia—suburbia if not quite perfected then certainly better crafted and refined than the norm.

Here, along one quiet Timberlea lane in a neighbourhood of streets named for boreal forest wildflowers and trees, is the home of Kiran Malik-Khan, who greets guests in her comfortable living room with its overstuffed couches and framed passages from the Koran on the walls and revels in explaining how people like her have come to find a home in a place like this.

"Everybody you will speak to will tell you it's a land of opportunity, because it is," Malik-Khan says. "But when you start giving back, and you start making it home, it's also the place where you want to be."

Malik-Khan was born in Pakistan, passed her teenage years in suburban New Jersey and married a Pakistani-American engineer. She first came to Canada in 2000, when her husband landed a job in suburban Vancouver. The work vanished within months of their arrival. They had just had their first child, and the shock of unemployment was troubling.

Her husband found another job, a short-term contract with Syncrude in Edmonton. He called one day to say he'd taken a permanent position in Fort McMurray. Malik-Khan had never heard the name before; she asked him to spell it for her.

She returned home to Pakistan to visit family and landed back in Fort McMurray just after New Year's Day 2001.

Coming into the city from Edmonton or the airport south of town, there is a moment when Highway 63 crests a hill and descends into the Clearwater Valley. It's an experience that sticks with many new arrivals. Years later, they readily recall details, emotions, the raw beauty of the valley or the eerie sense of fragility in the vast, frozen landscape. For Malik-Khan, just off a plane from Karachi, there was nothing in her previous experience even in wintertime New Jersey to prepare her for Fort McMurray in January.

"I still remember coming down the hill and just looking at Fort McMurray, and not understanding—you know, when I get out of this car, I'll be hit by minus-forty. My husband had told me that it's very, very cold. But hearing about it and experiencing it are two very different things."

The shock of it passed. Soon they were settled into an apartment building with a handful of other Pakistani families, caring for babies together and sharing potluck dinners after nightfall during Ramadan. Malik-Khan started on an English degree by correspondence and found work as a freelance reporter for *Fort McMurray Today*, the local newspaper. Her beat was the rapidly diversifying community. Before long, she was filing ten stories a month—on Fort McMurray's modest downtown mosque, on the work of the Filipino-Canadian Association, on the food traditions of new arrivals from central Africa and Southeast Asia.

By day, Malik-Khan worked as a director of stakeholder relations at the United Way of Fort McMurray. She and her husband had a second boy after the one that came with them in frigid January 2001, and both were growing up within a tight-knit but wildly diverse Muslim community. In the evenings and on weekends, Malik-Khan still freelanced, taking pictures at the annual general meeting of the Multicultural Association for

Your McMurray magazine and helping to publish a local literary journal titled *NorthWord*. She gave a talk called "Who's Afraid of the Hijab?" at a Fort McMurray TEDx conference in February 2015. And she volunteered in a variety of roles at the city's only mosque, the Markaz-ul-Islam. She was as fully ensconced in her community as a character in a 1950s family sitcom.

The Markaz-ul-Islam is housed in a converted bungalow just off Franklin Avenue. Its prayer hall can fit 250 people at most. For Friday midday prayers during Ramadan in 2015, more than 2,500 Muslims would be looking for a place to pray together. Most went to a rotating roster of school gyms and community centres. This was a stopgap solution, and work had begun on a more durable one. On the western edge of the city's suburbs, in a wide field right around the spot where Thickwood Boulevard becomes Confederation Way, there was a newly built road heading into the empty distance and a low gate to one side, like the sort that tells you the name of a suburban subdivision. It read simply, "Abraham." The Markaz-ul-Islam's members had been fundraising and planning since 2005, and in May 2015 they turned earth on an enormous new prayer hall and multipurpose community centre in the field behind the sign, a place they had decided to call Abraham's Land.

The first phase of the project is the new mosque itself, a $50-million complex housing a prayer hall for more than 2,500, an Islamic school, a recreation centre and a pool. The long-term plan, though, is much more ambitious: a place of faith perhaps without parallel anywhere else. It is a very Fort McMurray sort of plan, and it might one day produce a singularly Fort McMurray institution. Sacred space has been in short supply in the city throughout the boom years, and one of those surprising things about Fort McMurray is its social fluidity. The concentrated population of workers in the same industry, so many of them on the other side of the country or the planet from their traditional communities, have developed a sort of frontier knack for collaboration. The Markaz-ul-Islam's directors and congregants had been working side by side with leaders and practitioners of the city's many other faiths for years, and so as their vision for the new mosque expanded, they saw an opportunity to meet an even broader need. There are substantial plans already to build Catholic and Protestant churches on the same site, and there have been discussions about adding a Hindu temple to the mix. In Fort McMurray, the barriers just seem more readily overcome.

"I see that to be a huge plus here, that people feel at home the moment they come," said Waj Arain, who is in charge of public relations for the mosque.

Arain himself arrived from Toronto at the peak of the boom in 2007, his story typical of the oil sands business. He was a young man with a newly minted engineering degree, actively recruited by an oil company. The job interview was strange, quite unlike the others he'd had as a neophyte engineer. The recruiters wanted to know about his credentials, of course, but they spent nearly as much time talking about Fort McMurray, what a great community it was, its amenities. As part of the hiring process, Arain was brought out to the city on an orientation visit. He learned where the mosque was and about all the opportunities there and elsewhere to volunteer. The Muslim community itself was like nothing in Toronto or anywhere else, a seamless mix of Sunni and Shia, a veritable United Nations of cultural traditions.

"It's a melting pot," Arain said. "You'll see all cultures, all ethnicities. So that to me is a great thing."

The city's social calendar any given day in 2015 supported his point. Fort McMurray hosted celebrations of the Independence Days of both Botswana and the Democratic Republic of the Congo. The Filipino-Canadian Association's dance troupe had rehearsals almost every weekend, and the Gujarati Cultural Society hosted a celebration of Diwali, the Hindu festival of lights, at a local hotel. If there was a nation on earth that matriculated B.Eng. students or obliged ambitious immigrants to look worldwide for opportunities, some small knot of them now met in Fort McMurray. The same is true of most Canadian cities, of course. Nearly half a century of federally enshrined multiculturalism and liberal immigration policy has obliged urban Canada to conduct one of the planet's most rapid and dramatic experiments in social transformation, reconfiguring them in a generation or two into some of the most brazenly multicultural metropolises the world has ever seen. Fort McMurray has hosted the same urban experiment in microcosm and in fast-forward, condensing half a century mostly into a single decade and conducting it amid a total population of less than a hundred thousand.

This is not a work camp, and it is not a lawless gold rush town. This is the crazy-quilted social fabric that led a family-oriented, community-minded woman like Kiran Malik-Khan to embrace the place.

"If you don't see it, you can start it in Fort McMurray," she said. She has little patience for the boomtown myth. "If all you're going to focus on is angry men, prostitutes and drugs—then all three exist in every community in the world. Name one city that doesn't have all three."

And so here, on a bright Friday in late June 2015, in the middle of Ramadan, was a midday scene that might not have an equal anywhere else in the world where Muslims gather to pray. Just off Confederation Way in Timberlea is a new school in blond and grey stone called McTavish Junior High. The school's main entrance faces Parsons Creek Drive, a quiet suburban avenue that curves gently past the adjacent athletic fields and a Catholic high school farther along.

Around one o'clock, cars, trucks and an inordinate number of taxis began to fill either side of the street. Soon a crowd of people flowed down the sidewalk toward the school entrance, waving hello to one another and calling *Assalaam alaikum!* The Markaz-ul-Islam had booked McTavish Junior High's big gymnasium for its midday prayer, and the faithful arrived in twos and threes, in extended families of eight and twelve. Cab drivers and shift workers back from the site arrived solo, some still in their steel-toed boots and blue coveralls, the reflective stripes gleaming in the summer sun. They came wearing hijabs, *taqiyahs*, embroidered *salwar kameez* and immaculate white dishdashas. One woman wore a baseball cap over her hijab, another had hers tucked into the hood of a Montreal Canadiens sweatshirt. There were groups of women in heavy black cloth and groups of men in crisp, flowing white. Small talk came in a dozen languages and a dozen more accents. There was no differentiation between Sunni or Shia, Pakistani or Indian, Nigerian or Sudanese, Jordanian or Syrian or Iranian. They walked down Parsons Creek Drive and turned into the school parking lot and spared a glance for the two men selling mangoes by the crate near the door. Then they all disappeared inside to pray together.

The Friday prayer procession during Ramadan 2015 in Fort McMurray was a time-lapse photo of the last quarter century of Canadian immigration, a crowd more than two thousand strong, far larger than any that had ever filled the Boomtown Casino on a luckless Friday night. There might not be another mosque in the world outside Mecca, makeshift as this one was, that had welcomed a single congregation this diverse in nationality and belief. If Fort McMurray hosted a scene in 2015 that distinguished it most starkly from any other resource boomtown, this might have been it.

When Ramadan falls in June, it presents a unique challenge to Muslims in Fort McMurray. Subarctic daylight is at its peak, and the interval between darkness and dawn—the only time when devout Muslims may eat during the holy month—is just a few hours long. Kiran Malik-Khan knows her dishwasher's cleaning cycle takes three hours and fourteen minutes, and in late June she would often sleep for less time than the dishwasher took to clean last night's *iftar* dishes. But there she was, a radiant smile beaming out from under her hijab among the crowd outside McTavish Junior High, walking with her husband and two boys into the school.

Inside, the men and women filed into separate gyms. The whole congregation faced east and kneeled and touched their foreheads to their prayer mats. They faced Mecca and prayed, as Muslims do wherever they are. The ritual was over in barely half an hour, and the crowd dissipated even faster than it had gathered. If you hadn't happened to pass by that afternoon between one and two o'clock, all you would have seen was the same kind of quiet avenue you could see anywhere else in the suburbanized world.

THE GREAT INDOORS

The Patch's midday ritual in Calgary, seven hundred kilometres south of Fort McMurray, is undertaken with some small measure of the same urgency as a rush to midday Ramadan prayer, though none of the piety. It is the opposite of fasting. Nearly every building in downtown Calgary's high-rise core is stitched together by a series of elevated walkways at second-storey level, climate-controlled concourses that cross the streets below at mid-block, and many of the second storeys of those towers have been developed as food courts. This is where the corporate workforce that manages much of the oil sands industry gathers in its greatest number for lunch on a typical weekday.

The raised walkway network is called the Plus 15, referring to its elevation in feet above the streets below. It links buildings largely or entirely leased by the major oil companies to those filled by smaller companies that occupy only a floor or two, offices housing teams of lawyers and bankers, financiers and consultants, energy industry analysts and oil-field service companies. The Plus 15 network stretches from the corner of Eighth Street and Eighth Avenue in the southwest corner of the city's central business district to First Street and Fourth Avenue in the northeast—48 square blocks of gleaming postwar steel and glass, somewhere in the vicinity of 125 buildings in total, all of it tied together by those 60 or so walkways, forming a rambling ersatz shopping mall on its collective second floor. There are dry cleaners, banks, travel agents, massage therapy and dental clinics, jewellers, drug stores, printers of business cards and sellers of business suits. Buskers often set up in certain busy Plus 15s. Craft merchants sometimes put out tables along the concourses, and panhandlers ask for change in the doorways.

There is more to the business of downtown Calgary than the oil sands. There is the conventional oil and gas industry, of course, and there are substantial workforces engaged in high technology, agribusiness, education, media and the arts. The Plus 15 network counts among its number the logoed towers of telecom companies, insurance brokers, the Calgary

Public Library, the Calgary Board of Education, the offices of the National Energy Board and the federal government's main Calgary office. The Canadian Pacific Railway, still one of the city's largest employers, fills a floor of an office building on the southern edge of the high-rise core beside the CPR tracks. But this is above all the Patch's corporate headquarters, the home of Suncor and Syncrude and the birthplace of Cenovus and CNRL and MEG Energy. It is home as well to Enbridge and TransCanada Pipe-Lines, and the Canadian offices of CNOOC, Statoil, Shell and Total. And at lunchtime, punctually, a few minutes after noon, the corporate workforce flows out of the high-rises into food courts, upscale eateries and cafeteria-style restaurants scattered throughout the Plus 15s.

The centre of the whole network is a knot of buildings on the block of Fifth Avenue between Third and Second Streets. The southwest corner of this block is occupied by a generic midrise office tower called Calgary Place. At Plus 15 level inside the building, there is an entrance to the Metropolitan Conference Centre, a conference space of 1970s vintage where politicians often come to affirm their support for Alberta's oil and gas industry. Heading east, Calgary Place connects to the Stock Exchange Tower. From glass windows there, you can look south across Fifth Avenue at the Calgary Petroleum Club, a two-storey structure with a modernist facade of black stone and pink marble. The private club traces its origins to a hospitality suite at the nearby Palliser Hotel, the enormous old CPR hotel that was home to American oilmen during the first Alberta oil boom of the late 1940s. The Petroleum Club's interior is modest by the standards of twenty-first-century wealth, more like a reasonably well-appointed small-town country club than a palatial deal-making space for Big Oil.

The next Plus 15 heading east provides a view of an outsized bronze statue of Outlaw, the most formidable riding bull in the history of the Calgary Stampede rodeo, installed on the plaza below. In seventy-one rodeo appearances, Outlaw shook off seventy cowboys before they reached the eight-second mark of an official ride. The bull died in 2004, a month after the bell around its neck substituted for the closing bell on the New York Stock Exchange live by satellite TV. When the statue was unveiled six years later, just as the Alberta energy business was rallying from its post-2008 doldrums, a spokesperson for the financial sector organization that commissioned it said Outlaw stood for "the entrepreneurialism, grit and determination symbolic of the capital markets."

Past Outlaw's memorial plaza, the Plus 15 network connects to Fifth Avenue Place, a pair of high-rise glass towers with a newly renovated second-storey retail concourse. The complex used to be called Esso Plaza—Esso as in S.O., for Standard Oil—and its offices remain enmeshed in the vast web of former Standard companies. Its primary tenant is still Imperial Oil, Canada's oldest and long its largest oil company, which operates Esso gas stations in Canada. Imperial is majority-owned by ExxonMobil, a merged conglomerate of two former Standard Oil descendants and the largest private oil company on earth.

Such an ostentatious concentration of wealth and power is relatively new to the city. At the end of the Second World War, Calgary was little more than an outsized ranching town, one of a string of rail hubs along the transcontinental CP line. It was slightly larger than Regina, Saskatchewan, but nowhere near as big as Winnipeg. When Ned Gilbert, who would persuade Sun Oil to make its first investment in the oil sands, arrived after graduating from the University of Wisconsin in the late 1940s, it felt to him about as substantial as the college town of Madison he'd just left. But the city soon grew up and out, expanding in loping strides with the fortunes being made producing fuel used to heat suburban homes and move vehicles in and out of suburban garages. And so the hub of Calgary's business district is, rather fittingly, an artificially lit, climate-controlled homage to suburban retail commerce.

There is an obvious practicality to the Plus 15 network. Winters are long and sometimes harsh here where the prairie meets the Rockies, the streets and sidewalks filling with snow that turns to slush and back again when a warming winter chinook wind blows through. But the Plus 15 represents as well a rejection of place, a suburbanite's thermostat-controlled denial of the realities of the local climate. Fifteen feet above the sidewalk, weather has been rendered irrelevant. The landscape is a picture framed by an office tower's window. The heart of the city, the main street where you bump into an old friend or pick up your dry cleaning, is an indoor concourse lined with retail outlets, set to a soundtrack of office-tower HVAC white noise. All of it gets locked up at night, and much of it is a desolate ghost town on the weekends. From suburban garage to heated underground parking lot, from meeting to lunch to a quick haircut, the white-collar oil sands employee's working day can transpire entirely, effortlessly indoors. In Calgary director Gary Burns's 2000 film *Waydowntown*, shot documentary-style in the Plus 15 concourses, a group of office workers in buildings connected by elevated walkways wager to see who can go the longest without setting foot outside. There is no indication, from the setting alone, in which city the movie transpires.

Just after twelve o'clock on any given day in 2015, the food court at Fifth Avenue Place starts to hum with the burbling echo of multiple quiet conversations and shoes scuffling on institutional tile—that distinctive sound of shopping mall bustle. Fifth Avenue Place has something of a town square feel. The common seating areas have skylights, stylish drop ceilings of slotted wood and clusters of padded chairs. Office workers stream in through the Plus 15 halls in four directions to form neat lines at Subway and Wendy's and Ginger Beef Express, a chain specializing in an ersatz Chinese dish invented decades ago by a Chinese restaurateur to please Caucasian Calgary palates. There are knots of young men in the tattered jeans and spackle-flecked sneakers of the construction trades, evidence of a city still growing to catch up with the last boom, as well as groups of older men in dark business suits and ties. The bulk of the workforce, though, dresses in a sort of eclectic way that gestures at classic business attire while rarely fully achieving it—a look that could perhaps be called "engineer formal." Men wear pressed shirts, plain or checked and open at the neck, tucked into jeans or chinos or pleated dress pants. Those wearing jackets are tieless often as not. Women are dressed in slightly-less-than-formal business pantsuits and skirt suits or casual dresses over leggings. Security badges dangle from every other neck or belt. The gathering throngs carry their food to the tables on plastic trays and trade gossip or scroll away on their smartphones. Billion-dollar business deals have been finalized more than once over the years by CEOs slurping from polypropylene straws at food court tables.

The corporate headquarters of the oil sands, like its satellites in the boreal forest, defaults to the informal, the middle class and the suburban. The parking garages below the office towers hold far more luxury SUVs than the average Fort McMurray parking lot—the BMW X5 and the Mercedes GLE taking the place of the Ford F-150 in the social hierarchy—but nearly everyone drives home at the end of the workday to a house, however large, that resembles a split-level suburban ranch house more than a mansion befitting a Rockefeller or Pew.

The lunch hour wraps up, and the crowd disperses in the same erratic rhythm with which it gathered, and by midafternoon, the Plus 15 concourses are quiet and the food courts begin to close up. Many Calgary offices shift their business hours to overlap with Eastern time in Toronto, which is two hours ahead, so the city's downtown core starts to fill before eight in the morning and empties out in significant measure before four o'clock. You could wander through Plus 15s at four o'clock on a Friday afternoon and think Calgary was a sleepy backwater or a half-empty miniature empire in decline.

For much of the city's history, Calgary has felt marginal to the Canadian economy, a distant overgrown farm town on the far end of a wide prairie, most of a continent away from Toronto and Montreal. No one there thought much about New York or London or Beijing, and, needless to say, no one in New York or London or Beijing thought much about Calgary. But in recent years, Calgary has begun to see itself as central for the first time. The workers return down Plus 15 hallways to ride express elevators to high-rise offices connected to supply chains that stretch down thousands of miles of pipe and rail and highway and shipping lane to heavy equipment manufacturers in Illinois, oil refineries in East Texas, head offices in Houston and the Hague, Oslo and Paris, Beijing and Tokyo. Statoil, Norway's partly state-owned oil company, has offices in a building just across the street from Fifth Avenue Place. The Bank of China has a branch two blocks west. The United Kingdom and Mexico maintain consulates nearby.

During the boom years, Calgary emerged as Canada's number two city for corporate head offices, a bigger business hub than Montreal or Vancouver, second only to Toronto and gaining fast. The flow of companies and capital may have slowed by 2015, but the sense of importance and centrality remained. Calgary was a city in full, and despite the modest shopping mall trappings, the Plus 15 network linked together a major global business network. Canada has always been a resource-driven economy, and now it was an emerging energy superpower. At least that's what the politicians liked to say in their luncheon addresses at the Metropolitan Centre. Canada was now a player on the world's biggest economic stage, a leading oil producer. And this was its hub, its brain trust, its seat of power. The whole nation now looked to Calgary to gauge the pace of its growth and check the engine of its economy.

"My government will support vigorous and beneficial environmental standards while ensuring the continued responsible expansion of the oil sands." This was how Jim Prentice, a former federal environment minister, addressed the crowd at the Metropolitan Centre in May 2014, summing up his responsibility to the city's booming industry.

Prentice was in downtown Calgary that day to launch his campaign for the leadership of the Progressive Conservative Association of Alberta (PCAA or PCs), the province's reigning political dynasty. For more than forty years, winning the party's leadership was the only real contest en route to the premier's office. The PCs, backed heavily by Calgary's oil execs and financiers, came to power in 1971 under Peter Lougheed, ousting the Social Credit government that Ernest Manning had left to a hapless henchman, Harry Strom, when he retired in 1968. Lougheed and his PC successors had been seriously challenged in only one provincial election since.

Prentice, a Calgarian, delivered his Metropolitan Centre speech as a formality. He knew the crowd, and they knew him, and everyone knew the PC government would look after the energy sector and do whatever it took to keep the Patch booming, the office towers bustling and the expense accounts happily covering the steak dinners around the corner at Caesar's and Buchanan's. In September 2014 the PC membership elected Prentice as its party leader—and the sixteenth premier of Alberta—in a landslide. A new lord of the long boom, thus anointed.

And what a boom it had been. Starting around 2002, the fast-rising price of oil and rapid expansion of Alberta's oil and gas production—conventional crude and natural gas as well as bitumen—turned the province into Canada's perennial economic powerhouse. Midway through the boom's first wave, in 2006, a Statistics Canada study reported that Alberta was in the midst of "the strongest period of economic growth ever recorded by any Canadian province." Annual provincial gross domestic product (GDP) and population growth both cleared 10 percent.

When the oil sands industry's champions first pitched the federal and provincial governments on more favourable tax and royalty regimes in the mid-1990s, they promised $25 billion in capital expenditure on oil sands projects within twenty-five years. They hit that mark inside of five years and kept on charging. More than $200 billion was invested in the oil sands from 1999 to 2013. In 2014, the peak year for investment, $34 billion more in capital poured into the Patch. Alberta collected $5.2 billion in royalties from oil sands production the same year. The province's name became synonymous with economic success, and as the corporate capital and financial epicentre, Calgary was the urban face of the boom. After so many years of trial and error, the promise of the Patch had been fulfilled beyond anyone's dreams.

Calgary didn't explode at quite the same rate, proportionally speaking, as Fort McMurray did, but the much larger city added new residents at a rate of forty thousand a year throughout the boom—a Fort McMurray's worth every two years—and became a twenty-first-century metropolis in full. Its downtown grew thick with construction cranes and glittered with new office towers. New suburban communities sprung from the prairie earth on the city's periphery with the speed of sweetgrass in summer. In 2006 alone, Calgary issued building permits for commercial and residential development projects worth $4.7 billion—more than double the volume of investment it had seen in 2002 and a full $1 billion more than the figure for Toronto, which is more than twice Calgary's size. There were five times as many million-dollar homes in the city in 2007 as there were at the start of 2005. The local homebuilding industry had to ration concrete for pouring foundations. Wages skyrocketed, and businesses from retail to oil-field services still couldn't keep fully staffed. Year-end bonuses equal in size to the annual salaries of the employees receiving them were not unknown.

Along the way, Calgary found a swagger and cosmopolitan sophistication never seen before. The prime minister was a Calgarian for most of those years, and so were the CEOs of many of Canada's most successful companies. The formerly sleepy prairie town and poor cultural cousin to the older eastern cities became known for edgy theatre and high-end dining. There was one downtown restaurant that rimmed its martini glasses in gold dust, just to say it could. A Ferrari dealer opened up down the road from a Honda lot in the northeastern suburbs, and Tiffany & Co. and Burberry became tenants at Calgary's biggest mall. In the mountain resort towns west of the city—Canmore, Invermere, Radium Hot Springs, Golden—holiday condo complexes went up one after another, and their sale prices rose dizzily along with the skyrocketing price of oil. The lakefronts and vineyards of British Columbia's Okanagan Valley became a retirement hub for wealthy Calgarians who cashed out of the Patch.

The city had ridden the ups and downs of global oil prices before. But this boom was longer, more colossal, and it was fed by enough young newcomers who hadn't seen the last major collapse (in the 1980s) to fuel illusions of a party that went on forever. The phrase *energy superpower* dripped like free-flowing golden honey from the tongues of provincial politicians and industry executives and their steadfast champion in the prime minister's office in Ottawa. Calgary ran the country—maybe next, the whole world! Perhaps the oil sands would produce eight million barrels a day by 2035. How soon would the city double in size? Was there a better place on earth to make a fortune?

Man Develops His World! Now without qualifications, delays, setbacks and frustrations. Faster than ever!

FIVE

GROWING PAINS

THE SWING PRODUCER'S REVENGE

The oil game is a tough business, capricious and merciless. For every gusher, there is a dry well, and vertiginous upward price spikes are premonitions of gut-wrenching freefall. And so, the dizzy decadent heights of the boom years notwithstanding, it remained well understood in at least some Calgary executive suites that the city's economic fortunes still rose and fell with the price of oil. And the price of oil was a fickle thing, far beyond local control, now and forever. Like any market commodity, oil's price fluctuated constantly, sometimes wildly, owing to factors so poorly understood that the annals of energy business journalism are littered with a far greater number of ridiculously inaccurate price predictions than accurate forecasts. Middle Eastern wars and Gulf coast hurricanes send oil prices reeling. So does the sudden arrival in the marketplace of fracked shale oil by the millions of barrels, or OPEC's snap decision to change its general disposition toward supply and demand.

Though much of the world talks about "the price of oil" as a single metric, there are more than a hundred different crude oil prices in the global marketplace—a bewildering technocratic array of place names and regional blends. There are more factors than anyone can readily track and predict governing the price of each kind of crude, but the basic governing principles are density, sulphur content and distance to market. "Light sweet" oils—less dense, less complex hydrocarbons that are lower in sulphur and can be readily and cheaply converted into high-quality gasoline—fetch higher prices; so does oil produced near major ports.

Alberta's oil flows down continent-wide pipelines and over long train tracks to gush into a global marketplace where the ambitious hubris of the province's energy superpower boast has been affirmed by mounting revenues. But that's where it has also confronted cold economic realities.

The Patch's oil is at the troublesome end of the spectrum by all three key metrics. Alberta bitumen is a heavy hydrocarbon mixture freighted with sour sulphur and pulled from the ground in a place surrounded by thousands of miles of land on all sides. About 60 percent of oil sands bitumen is shipped and sold without refining as dilbit, which becomes part of several different blends, including Western Canadian Select (WCS), Access Western Blend and Christina Lake Dilbit. It is usually priced in the market using the WCS benchmark, a blend of low-grade heavy oils sold at prices below West Texas Intermediate (WTI), which is itself often sold at a discount to the Brent Blend benchmark price usually quoted as "the price of oil." Owing to its distance from ports, WCS also fetches a lower price than blends of comparable quality such as Mexico's Maya. WTI is discounted because it is drawn from landlocked sources and costs more to bring to market. WCS is further discounted because it still needs substantial refining before it can enter the marketplace. And even the 40 percent of Alberta's bitumen that is upgraded and refined into synthetic crude is often sold at a discount below WTI because it exported almost exclusively into the United States. The huge American boom in oil extracted from hydraulically fractured shale has created a continental supply glut in recent years, obliging Alberta producers to sell at a discount in order to ensure the pipeline access they need to get their product to US refineries and ports. This persistent oversupply crisis—which the Alberta government started calling the "bitumen bubble" in 2013—became just the most recent factor driving the industry's push to build new pipelines, particularly ones that go directly to Canadian ports and open up access to overseas markets. (The supply glut had a similar impact on all other North American oil production, as well.) And all of this is before taking into account the larger factors bearing down on the global prices that set the benchmarks.

There has never been anything like precision control over oil prices, but the roller-coaster ride has been smoothed out somewhat over the years by the actions of a role player known in the business as the swing producer. The job of the swing producer in the global oil marketplace is to cut oil production when prices sink too low and step it up when prices inflate too high. For the first half of the twentieth century, the "Seven Sisters"—the world's seven largest oil companies, comprising three former Standard Oil subsidiaries, plus Texaco, Gulf, Royal Dutch Shell and British Petroleum—dominated the industry, and the United States was far and away the world's largest oil supplier. For byzantine bureaucratic reasons dating back to the great Spindletop oil strike of 1901, the Texas Railroad Commission served as the first market-stabilizing swing producer, setting well-by-well production quotas for the often-reluctant Seven Sisters to meet. The quotas cushioned against price shocks by creating spare capacity that could be brought online quickly to respond to supply shortfalls or demand spikes. With the great Middle Eastern oil discoveries of the postwar era, prices dropped and global oil demand surged, while the United States fast approached peak production. America's spare capacity vanished, and the Texas Railroad Commission abdicated its position as swing producer, eliminating its quotas entirely in 1972. The job had already begun by then to shift to OPEC, with Saudi Arabia's state-owned oil giant Saudi Aramco the first among equals in the cartel. The price

shocks of the 1970s and 1980s, driven by politically motivated OPEC production quotas and boycotts, cemented the cartel's supremacy.

And so it held until mid-2014, when Saudi Arabia, which for years had
maintained around two million barrels per day of spare capacity to keep
prices from falling, decided to abandon its swing producer role. Supplies
were surging worldwide at the time, driven by oil prices that were hovering
above $80 per barrel for the fourth straight year. This drove massive new
investments in Alberta's oil sands, but it also fuelled a raucous fracking
boom in the United States, which boosted American oil production from
5.5 million barrels to more than 9 million in just five years. The global
economy entered a sluggish phase in 2014, however, owing in large measure to slower economic growth in China, and an oil supply glut began
to emerge around the middle of that year. OPEC, as swing producer, was
expected to cut production until the glut abated and prices stabilized. But
the Saudis refused, and the rest of the cartel followed suit. Oil prices plummeted below $50 and stayed there. Weeks became months, and the slump
stretched into 2015 and became a worldwide oil bust.

As the world waited on the Saudis, oil industry analysts speculated
widely on their strategic goals. These ranged from near-term geopoliti-
cal aims—punishing the economies of Iran and Russia, for example, for
supporting Saudi enemies in the Middle East—to long-term environmental concerns like the erosion of global oil demand as nations around
the world aimed to reduce their dependency on fossil fuels to combat
climate change. The swing producer role is predicated on a demand
curve sloping ever upward, but global oil demand was already expanding slower than anticipated. And if it stopped? If it shrunk? This would
negate the swing role. The oil game would become a pure zero-sum
competition for market share. Whether that was happening yet, the Saudis wanted to redefine their status in the game now, for all the reasons
anxious analysts thought up.

This, in any case, was Paul Spedding's read on the Saudi strategy.
Spedding spent a decade as cohead of HSBC Bank's global Oil and Gas
Research Division, retiring the year before the price shock took hold.

Spedding was one of the first analysts at a major bank to report on the risk to the industry posed by climate change, back in 2008. He specializes in wider angles and long views.

"Saudi Arabia just said, 'We're losing market share,'" Spedding said. "The way things are going, the way the investment is going into tight oil and was beginning to go into new oil sands projects, they said, 'Well, this is not sustainable for us. We will have to keep cutting, and ultimately we'll get to the stage where we won't be covering our budgets.'"

By budgets, Spedding meant not Saudi Aramco's operating budget but the Saudi government's budgets, the vast trough of oil wealth out of which it covers the cost of running the country. The Saudis, he explained, have the luxury and the anxiety of being pure harvesters in the oil business. They know what their reserves are, and they can extract those reserves at a range of rates. They know how many barrels they need to sell and how much they need to earn per barrel to cover the national budget. They also know how long they can operate in the red, starving out competitors, before the toll on the government's coffers becomes too onerous. And they know that once they run out of oil, or the world no longer wants enough of it, they are well and truly sunk. And so whether it was Russian encroachment in the Middle East or fracked shale's intervention in the oil futures markets, all of it ran counter to their interests.

The Saudis understood that if they kept producing at their current rate in 2014 and 2015, the price of oil would fall. And falling prices would make their enemies bleed—particularly the high-cost unconventional oil plays that were attracting tens of billions of dollars per year in new capital investment but were profitable only if prices stayed high. Oil plays like Alberta's oil sands, which was a known target, if not a specific or primary one.

"I don't think they cared where the cuts come from, they just wanted capital expenditure to cut back," Spedding said. "If they did think about it beyond that, I think they'd be definitely concerned about the wave of very-long-term oil sands projects. Because an oil sands project takes market share that they can never get back. Once an oil sands project is there, it stays. And that's the worst possible outcome for them. Whereas at least with shale oil, if a shale play takes market share from Saudi Arabia, if Saudi Arabia stops the capital expenditure going into that shale play, Saudi Arabia gets that market share back. With oil sands, they never get it back."

Wherever the outcome ranked on Saudi Arabia's priority list, the impact on the Patch was exactly as Spedding suggested. New investments shrunk—after the record $34-billion year in 2014, capital expenditures in the oil sands dropped to $23 billion in 2015 and plummeted further in 2016. Eighteen projects in the planning or construction phase were cancelled. One oil company after another announced layoffs and cutbacks. The unemployment rate in Alberta, long the envy of the nation, skyrocketed.

And in May 2015, one year almost to the day after Jim Prentice declared his candidacy for the leadership of the Progressive Conservative dynasty, he stepped up to the podium at the Metropolitan Centre, the throne room of downtown Calgary's Plus 15 network, and delivered the most shockingly unexpected concession speech in the province's history, addressing a sparse crowd of loyalists stunned into eerie silence. After forty-four years in power, the PCs had lost the election and the government. Adding insult to injury, they'd lost to the left-leaning New Democratic Party, which had never held more than 20 percent of the seats in the legislature. Prentice resigned the party's leadership on the spot, even as votes were still being counted.

The bust of 2015 had a dark aura at its edges, a hint of a deeper doom than most people working in the Patch had ever seen. It was portentous and cataclysmic enough to send the longest-standing dynasty in North American politics packing. Later in 2015, the federal Conservative government and its proudly Calgarian prime minister fell to a rejuvenated Liberal Party led by Justin Trudeau, the son of the prime minister who had launched the National Energy Program in the early 1980s, an initiative still virulently loathed in the Patch as an attempt to seize control of Alberta's hydrocarbon wealth from its provincial minders. The new provincial and federal governments promised to safeguard the Patch's health—as every politician hoping to win votes in Alberta must—but they also spoke of the need for real action on climate change and an accelerated transition to a low-carbon economy. From the vantage point of downtown Calgary, the shifting fortunes of 2015 could feel not just big but tectonic, a realignment of the energy world now underway. Could it be that the emergent energy superpower was the lord of an outmoded manor with crumbling foundations?

DOLDRUMS

If you were a Calgary office worker, the twisted, unpredictable logical knots governing oil price fluctuations were easy to push out of your mind when the stuff was selling at $80 or $100 or even $120 per barrel. The baseline, everyone understood, was that there was no commodity more vital than oil, none more essential to the purring daily hum of the global economy. Prices rose and fell in the short term, companies grew and contracted. There were cycles. There were even busts. Every office had old hands who'd lived through the dark days of the 1980s in Calgary, when OPEC drove the oil price into the floor and it felt like half the city emptied overnight as geologists and engineers packed their belongings into U-Haul trucks and fled back east.

The necessity of oil, though, was incontestable. If you pulled it from the ground, there was a buyer for it. Catastrophic spills made the industry many enemies, and environmentalists liked to fret about dead ducks and mounting greenhouse gas emissions—and that was fine, that was their prerogative. The industry would give a little thought to that. That stuff was on the agenda, it came up at board meetings. Companies had sustainability reports now alongside their financials, and everyone put trees and reclaimed wetlands on the covers of their annual reports. But as long as billions of people around the world had a car in the garage (or aspired to both car and garage ownership), as long as airplanes roared through the sky and container ships churned across the oceans, as long as farmers needed to plow vast fields and protect their crops against pests, as long as people tapped out messages on keyboards and smartphones and wrapped

themselves in Gore-Tex against the chill wind and sided their homes in vinyl against the elements and cooked dinner on non-stick pans and popped
little sealed detergent packets into the dishwasher to clean up afterward
and brushed their teeth with nylon bristles before settling in on soft mat-
tresses stuffed with polyurethane and memory foam to dream of another
day in the good fossil-fuelled life—as long as life as just about everyone
knew it carried on, in other words—as long as all that held, the folks shuffling back to their desks after lunch understood theirs to be a useful and
durable place in the world.

An employee of the SAGD pioneer Cenovus heads back to work after
lunch at Fifth Avenue Place by following the Plus 15 through the Trans-
Canada Tower—as in TransCanada PipeLines, the company behind the
Keystone XL pipeline—and then a nondescript parkade. The route then
veers south to the Suncor Energy Centre on the other side of Fifth Avenue.
There is another food court here, filling a sort of indoor plaza connecting the two towers of the Suncor complex. It was originally christened
the Petro-Canada Centre when it opened in 1984, for its primary tenant,
Petro-Canada, the locally reviled state-owned oil company and beachhead
of Pierre Trudeau's National Energy Program. The taller of the towers,
fifty-three storeys high, was Calgary's tallest building for more than a quarter century, and the buildings' rust-coloured exterior earned the complex
the nickname "Red Square." It was a symbol imposed on Calgary from
distant Ottawa, standing arrogantly for all that had gone wrong during the
crippling mid-1980s bust. The Saudi decision to glut the global oil market
and push prices below $10 per barrel may have been the prime driver of
that bust, but for Calgarians working in the energy business, it was that
imperious Pierre Trudeau and those eastern-bastard Liberals with all their
federal meddling who were the real villains.

As the Cenovus employee passes through the former Red Square, joining a flow of fellow workers who chose Thai or burritos from its food court
for lunch that day, does she wonder at the changing fates of the industry, notwithstanding the continued necessity of the resource? That 1980s
bust had once felt almost permanent, eternal. Calgary limped through the

middle of the decade drought-stricken, office towers half empty, new sub-urban houses gone vacant and surrounded by broad lawns of dead grass. Suncor nearly pulled the plug entirely on its oil sands operations in the early 1990s. When the industry finally found its footing again a few years later, oil sands CEOs talked about needing twenty-five years or more to build out their projects to full scale. Instead, it all changed in a single de-lirious decade of escalating oil prices, with billions in capital investment pouring into the city and new residents landing in Calgary by the tens of thousands each year to cash in on the mother of all booms.

The Cenovus employee walks from the Suncor Centre to the Bow Building via the newest and most elegant Plus 15 of them all. Floor-to-ceiling glass offers postcard views of the Calgary Tower to the south and the century-old stone Centre Street Bridge over the Bow River to the north. Permanence reigns as far as the eye can see. By the time ground broke on the Bow Building in the summer of 2007, Calgary's economy was roaring with such ferocious might it made international headlines. The oil industry—and especially the growth of the oil sands—was the nation's top priority, both on Parliament Hill and on Bay Street. And even in the face of the 2008 financial crisis, the boom didn't really end so much as shrug momentarily before regathering itself and racing on. It went on so long that it was easy, as a Cenovus employee—moving into the tallest Canadian skyscraper west of Toronto in 2012, gaping at the glamorous architectural touches, the soaring lobby and multistorey atria every dozen or so floors and the geodesic triangles and squares of glass in British architect Norman Foster's signature curtain walls—it became easy, didn't it, to think this boom might never end?

Perhaps every boom is expected to last forever. Every boom con-tains within it some skewed logic in which the impossible growth and rapidly amassed wealth undergo a transition from fantastically fluid to some simulacrum of a solid state. The careening boom logic becomes the norm. Luck becomes a strain of genius, and opportunism starts to re-semble a chess master's grand strategy. The boom was built of stuff as solid and true as glass and steel, crafted from the technological brilliance and entrepreneurial daring of a generation of the smartest engineers the nation has ever known, its credibility renewed daily at a rate of 2.4 million barrels. With such lofty heights near enough in the Patch's collective memory, even the deepest troughs can seem like mere hiccups on a journey headed ever upward.

A Cenovus employee entering the building through the Plus 15 concourse any given day in 2015 has likely shed such illusions. She takes the escalator down to the main floor to swipe her security badge and wait with her coworkers between banks of elevators, surely fretting over how long the trough will last this time. Oil languishing below $50 a barrel, new projects cancelled, layoffs slashing through the fifty-eight floors of the Bow and every other tower in town seemingly by the week. Would the Bow, like Red Square before it, become a lasting symbol of a certain strain of fossil-fuelled hubris?

MOVING THE NEEDLE

The thinking in the executive suites at Cenovus entertains no such lasting doubts. From the vantage point of Harbir Chhina's expansive office on the Bow Building's twenty-sixth floor, with its panoramic southwest view of the downtown core and the snow-capped Rockies on the horizon, the future is as bright as sunshine on mountain snow. Here the talk is of an industry just getting started, an industry that even in its infancy shook the whole nation—if not the world.

Chhina's office is decorated with a career petroleum engineer's random assortment of oil business bric-a-brac. There are plaques, oil-themed desk trinkets, grip-and-grin photos commemorating company milestones. He is proudest of the large, framed photo hung near his office door, showing Chhina beaming as he stands with the chief of the Heart Lake First Nation—an Indigenous community near Cenovus's SAGD operations—after they had cosigned a long-term benefit agreement. Chhina was born in a Punjabi village called Malikpur, and he moved to Canada with his family at ten years old, came of age in British Columbia, and likely didn't think his B.Eng. would lead to a career smiling broadly in a ceremonial photo with the chief of a First Nation. It's a marker, perhaps, of how far his career has taken him, how surprising its rewards have been.

Chhina's working life has been momentous in many ways that a petroleum engineer would never expect. In particular, he was instrumental in creating an entire new kind of oil extraction. A whole subindustry—in situ oil sands production—now exists where there was none before. It is the reason Cenovus exists as a company, and it is to some degree the reason that the tallest skyscraper in western Canada stands on the eastern edge of downtown Calgary. Aside from the small cluster of research scientists who developed and patented SAGD technology, there might be no engineer anywhere who has spent his career as deeply engaged as Chhina has been in turning SAGD into a viable commercial process and unlocking the vast in situ bitumen deposits buried under Alberta's boreal forest.

In the early 1980s, when Chhina first started working in the industry, many of his colleagues believed in situ oil sands resources would never be profitable. AOSTRA, where he started his career, had been charged with developing the technology to make the business work. But when the research team took its SAGD prototype to every boardroom in town looking for partners, not one was willing to invest money in it. Calgary's economy was a shambles at the time, the hated Red Square towers rising on the skyline to taunt a wounded industry. The oil sands looked like a great stumbling white elephant, and what little money was being invested in the oil and gas business in Alberta in those years was not going to be bet on a wild long shot that was surely decades from even a slim chance at payback.

As Chhina tells the tale, he rises from his chair and strides over to a steel valve displayed on the wall near his desk. The valve had once been mounted on a wellhead at Foster Creek, the very SAGD test well that proved the technology. Chhina takes the valve in his hands, remembers turning it in 1997 at a well pad at the end of a lonely dirt road deep in the woods. He had by then spent fifteen years working on SAGD, and that Foster Creek wellhead was the ignition switch on his twenty-sixth pilot project. He turned the wheel, and he opened the valve, and oil began to flow. And just like that, Chhina and his colleagues changed the whole industry, the whole country.

"I call this a twenty-billion-dollar wellhead for us," he says. "I call it a hundred and fifty, two-hundred-billion-dollar success story for our industry. Because of this one success, this first well at Foster Creek, our company went on to invest twenty billion dollars in SAGD."

He takes his hands off the valve and comes back to the table.

"That's how much we've invested. And I think as an industry, we have at least one-fifty, if not two hundred billion dollars invested. So this technology has made a big move in the employment, in creating jobs in this province and across Canada. And I believe it's moved the GDP of this country."

How many engineers can say a thing like that with a straight face? Who else could plausibly boast they moved the needle on the whole damn nation's GDP? But then, wasn't this exactly what engineering was for? Wasn't it what made engineers the quiet masters of the High Modern, its primary architects, the practical wizards of progress itself? To build an industry, to tap a source of power and wealth never before harnessed. To put people to work, to create jobs and build office towers and mount the valve that opened the first spigot on the wall next to your desk and look at it every day and know—and *know*—there was a distinct sliver of the nation's prosperity with your name on it.

Man develops his world.

By the late 1980s, Chhina was convinced that SAGD was a legitimate enterprise. So he took a job with the company that would spawn Cenovus and spent the next twenty years making it work. In the oil business, when a well earns back its development costs and begins to pump pure profit, it's said to be "paid out." In 2010 the first commercial SAGD plant at Foster Creek paid out. Chhina figures that by 2011, it was generating $1 million in royalties for the province every single day. Funding for schools and hospitals and good roads, not to mention the income taxes flowing from thousands of jobs in the gleaming office tower from which he now surveys the city. A million bucks a day, because someone—some *engineer*—had been willing to gamble on an idea a generation back. And even with the cratered oil price and the anxiety coursing through the Plus 15 network like a high-frequency radio wave in 2015, he believes his business is still in its infancy.

"So where are we now on the technology side is, I compare it to a baseball game," Chhina says. "I believe we just finished the first inning. We've got eight more innings to play. And so we have a long road ahead in terms of applying new technologies in the oil sands. To make them even more economical. And it turns out that economics and environmental benefits go together."

What Chhina means is that the two great challenges for the oil sands—and especially for in situ operations—are cost and greenhouse gas (GHG) emissions per barrel. And cutting costs for a SAGD operation means primarily reducing the amount of energy used to produce a barrel of oil, employing less steam and thus improving the almighty steam to oil ratio, which in turn means reducing the amount of natural gas used and shrinking the GHGs. Solve one problem, and you fix the other one too.

Still, it's an entwined challenge that verges on existential for the oil sands. While Chhina and his colleagues were off solving the in situ riddle and making SAGD pay out, the basic structure of the energy economy altered in its fundamentals. Meeting endlessly rising demand by any means necessary was no longer the central organizing principle of the oil business. Demand and supply were locked in a volatile seesaw match across a long plateau at somewhere between 90 million and 100 million barrels per day, and global demand's upward march to a long-forecasted daily rate of 120 million barrels or more, once thought to be as little as a decade away, might well never materialize. In 2015, with oil prices lingering below $50 per barrel and long-term forecasts—unreliable as they might be—predicting $100 barrels were far away on the horizon (perhaps even receding to a place that might never again be reached), Chhina's SAGD barrels were at the outer margin of profitability. His toughest opponent now was all that "light tight oil" being cracked from shale deposits in North Dakota and West Texas and Pennsylvania, which was coming to market faster and cheaper. The ability of guys like Chhina to move the needle on the nation's GDP was dissipating by the day, or so it seemed. It was a faint memory already in the doldrums of 2015, like the afternoon sun falling behind gathering storm clouds on the Calgary horizon.

What's more, Chhina's barrels were among the world's most carbon intensive. Owing to the natural gas needed to make the steam that got the bitumen flowing, oil from SAGD wells emitted more GHGs per barrel than all but the dirtiest heavy oils out of California. And carbon intensity—the contribution of each barrel of oil to the mounting calamity of climate change—was not a tangential or future-tense concern anymore for the oil industry. It was no longer sufficient to point at the 80 percent of a barrel's emissions that came from burning it as fuel—the puffs of exhaust blowing out the tailpipe of every car on earth, for example—and insist the climate problem would have to be solved there alone. If bitumen was to stay in the game for another eight innings, it would have to find some way to reach markets much more efficiently and with far less carbon dioxide emitted in its production.

There was never any time to rest on your laurels in the Patch. From the gooey bitumen gumming up the gears at that first Bitumount plant to the sand grinding away tons of steel each month at GCOS to the oversized emissions footprint needed to get to 1.8-to-1 SOR, some gnawing problem was always chewing away at the industry's stability.

From the heights of the Bow Building, Chhina surveys the city his oil helped build and indulges only the slightest skepticism at the scope of the problem. Sure, he concedes, the oil sands business was designed to operate in a marketplace where benchmark WTI oil was being sold for at least $80 per barrel, maybe as low as $70. And since the conventional wisdom now had it that the world would be a $55-per-barrel WTI world for the foreseeable future, these were trying times for the oil sands business. But just twenty years ago, conventional wisdom argued that Cenovus's in situ barrels were never going to make it to market at a profit. And the conventional wisdom a decade or so before that had it that bitumen might never turn a profit at all. And so Chhina, like the executives in spacious offices on the upper floors of buildings all over downtown Calgary, insists that his company and his industry are ready once again to prove the conventional wisdom wrong.

"We have started a challenge," he says, "starting last year in our organization, to what I call forty-forty-forty-forty. And that means that in order for us to compete with light tight oil, we need to shave off 40 percent on our capital, 40 percent on operating cost, 40 percent on G&A and 40 percent improvement in netback." Chhina's list consists of three kinds of cost—the cost of the production facility, the everyday cost of producing a barrel of oil and the cost of "general and administrative" tasks—followed by a calculation of those costs against revenue.

The cost reductions, though daunting, are the stuff of keen-eyed red-blooded engineers and managers in any business. Reduce inputs, improve efficiencies, use fewer people and less stuff to do more. A 40 percent cut might sound like quite a lot, but it's well within the everyday ambitions of the profession. Chhina rattles off the progress to date: already nearing a 40 percent reduction in capital costs, operating costs down 20 percent, G&A down 30 percent. But netback?

"We have not really moved the needle on the netback," he says.

Cenovus has not moved the needle on netback because the netback issue is by far the trickiest. The term *netback* is specific to the oil business, industry jargon for the profitability of a barrel of oil. Add up your costs per barrel—production costs, the cost of transporting a barrel by rail or pipe, storage costs, upgrading and refining costs, marketing costs, royalties and fees taken by governments or other resource owners along the way—and subtract that total from the barrel's selling price. The remainder is a company's netback, its profit per barrel, a handy shorthand for how profitable the whole enterprise is.

From the point of view of the roadside gas pump, a barrel of oil is a barrel of oil. But the tangled way it goes from deep beneath the ground to the gas tank of an F-150 makes for substantial variances in the netback. There is a whole hidden universe of elaborate formulas and byzantine financial rites that determines the netback for a given stream of oil production—benchmark prices and long-term contracts derived from those benchmarks that were signed months if not years ago, future prices and differentials, all of it combining to explain why the netback rate for this barrel from Saudi Aramco's Ghawar field is so much greater than for that barrel from Cenovus's Christina Lake operation. The price of oil is a spectrum that expands and contracts to its own strange rhythms within the larger drumbeat of the benchmarks.

Overall, every barrel of Saudi light sweet crude is higher in quality, more cost-efficient to extract, and cheaper and easier to bring to port, refine and deliver to customers, so it sends at least $20 more sloshing back up the supply chain to its producers than does Cenovus's SAGD-produced heavy crude. And unlike readily altered variables—the cost and efficiency of a new gas plant at Christina Lake, say, or the number of middle managers currently sitting at desks and drawing Cenovus paycheques in the Bow Building—there are factors in that nasty netback equation that are far beyond the control of Harbir Chhina or any other executive (or company) toiling away in the glass towers of downtown Calgary.

The great hindrance to improving netback, as far as Chhina sees it, is a factor that haunts the Patch like a spectral cloud, impossible to dissipate and almost as hard to grasp. It's the missing link, the last piece of critical infrastructure not fully accounted for across a decade-long boom—the totemic condition long known as "market access" and these days sometimes referred to more precisely as "access to tidewater." Alberta's oil is landlocked. For decades, the trickle of bitumen flowing out of the province's north didn't amount to enough for this to matter all that much. There was a vast network of pipes moving crude oil all over North America: to Vancouver on the Pacific coast, to Chicago on the Great Lakes and to Houston and Port Arthur, Texas, on the US Gulf coast. A well-established pipeline network also moved oil from central Alberta via Illinois to Sarnia, Ontario, the chemical-plant hub near Detroit where Canada's oil industry was born in the 1850s. When the first Suncor and Syncrude operations started producing oil in the 1960s and 1970s, they flowed easily into this existing pipeline capacity. As the Patch boomed along with the rest of the global oil business in the first years of the millennium, midstream companies expanded rapidly, building parallel pipelines alongside existing ones ("twinning" them) and launching new pipeline projects from scratch, the same as they had for decades. They submitted applications and checked off regulatory requirements and laid pipe by the thousands and thousands of kilometres across the continent and back again, with no more fuss than electricity companies stringing up high-voltage wires.

Around 2008 or so, the sheer scale of the Patch's expansion triggered a new wave of pipeline development. Oil sands producers were tired of absorbing the discount against WTI, so they came to covet tidewater of their very own. The term evokes brackish shores and open oceans, but to Chhina and his colleagues, what it specifically meant was a direct route to Asia. To China and India, with their roaring economies and their unquenchable thirst for energy. A marketplace where WCS and other heavy crudes would no longer be such poor cousins. Applications went in for wider pipes covering greater distances. Not just TransCanada's Keystone pipe to Cushing, Oklahoma (where WTI prices are set), already under construction, but also a newer, bigger model: Keystone XL. A twin for Kinder Morgan's existing Trans Mountain pipeline system from Edmonton to Vancouver. A whole new route, an arrow-straight shot from northern Alberta to the tiny port of Kitimat in northern British Columbia, which its developer, Enbridge, christened Northern Gateway. A conversion of a continent-wide natural gas pipe—Energy East—to carry bitumen to refineries in Quebec and New Brunswick. Build at least one, perhaps build them all. Do it yesterday. Harbir Chhina and his movers of the national GDP needle need market access. Man develops his world!

"When it goes to Asian markets, we find that the value of our oil improves by ten to fifteen dollars a barrel," Chhina explains. "Which has a big impact on not just our economics, it has a big impact on Alberta and Canada in terms of our project gets paid out faster, the royalties start collecting faster. And so that money gets spread for social benefits, whether it's education or health care and stuff. So that fifteen dollars is a big thing, if we can get that. Which is why pipelines are so important."

The importance of tidewater access was self-evident to everyone in the Patch a decade ago. But Chhina still yearns for market access because the necessity is no longer self-evident beyond the industry's office towers and well pads. And he and his industry colleagues find that making the case for that access grows harder by the day. Oil, that most precious and vital of commodities, has become one of the most controversial, the most fraught and fought over, the most contentious and politically volatile. And of all the 90-odd million barrels of oil in all the world's daily supply, none is more highly contested—none to date has had its necessity as thoroughly audited—as the 2.4 million barrels extracted daily from the Patch.

THE PIPELINE PROXY WAR

As oil sands operators hunted hungrily for market access in the years after 2008, Alberta's remote bitumen mines found themselves thrust to the very centre of a global debate about whether oil was such a wonderful thing after all, whether it had anything to do with progress as it was being redefined in the age of climate change. When Chhina speaks of netbacks and market access, he is skirting the edge of an international political argument about the place of Canada's bitumen in the future of the global energy economy. The pipe he covets is serving as the unlikely proxy for at least his whole industry, if not the entire fossil fuel age and every sin of omission or emission it ever committed, going all the way back to those first wells near Sarnia.

Even as recently as the first wave of the Patch's boom, pipeline projects had been straightforward business transactions. In 2008, for example, Enbridge launched plans to build the Alberta Clipper, a $2-billion, 1,600-kilometre, 36-inch pipeline to carry the rapidly expanding flows of oil sands products from Hardisty to Superior, Wisconsin, a long-serving Great Lakes port of call for Canadian oil. The Alberta Clipper proposal moved through National Energy Board hearings in Canada with little friction and was approved in February 2008. Construction began soon after, the new pipe laid diagonally from Hardisty across southern Saskatchewan and Manitoba. There were sporadic protests against the project by First Nations along the route, primarily demanding larger shares of the pipeline's revenues and more jobs in its construction. A few lesser known environmental groups in Minnesota attempted to block the pipeline's progress in court citing regional environmental concerns—worries over spills, damage to flora and fauna along the route, that sort of thing. Enbridge made concessions sufficient to end the protests, and the construction carried on without incident. An Enbridge spokesperson told a reporter from the *Regina Leader-Post* in Saskatchewan that the pipeline was "the biggest project nobody knows about." The newspaper dubbed it an "invisible megaproject."

South of the border, the US State Department consented to the Alberta Clipper in August 2009. A State Department press release announcing the approval argued that the pipeline "will advance a number of strategic interests of the United States" by increasing oil imports from "a stable and reliable ally," as well as sending "a positive economic signal, in a difficult economic period." Workers in Superior sealed the final welds on the pipe in March 2010, and oil began to flow down the pipe from Hardisty at the rate of 450,000 barrels per day soon after that. But the pipeline must already have seemed to some in the business like an artifact from another time, a product of an era when the necessity of oil and its central role in the onward march of progress were virtually unassailable.

Enbridge and its competitors had several other pipelines of similar or greater length and volume in the works by the time the new pipeline began transporting oil. By then, however, the entire political context of oil pipeline megaprojects had begun to change so radically that it would soon be no hyperbole to suggest the Alberta Clipper might be one of the last major pipelines to be laid under the Canada-US border for at least another generation.

In March 2015 a cross section of the Patch's senior executives and engineers convened in the grand ballroom of the Shaw Conference Centre overlooking the North Saskatchewan River in downtown Edmonton for the World Heavy Oil Congress. The first morning's opening keynote panel was entitled "Maximizing Market Access for Albertan Heavy Oil Products," and among the panellists was Norman Rinne, an executive at Kinder Morgan. His company had spent the previous fall in a legal battle with the city of Burnaby, a suburb of Vancouver, which had filed an injunction to try to stop preliminary planning work on Burnaby Mountain for Kinder Morgan's proposed twinning of its Trans Mountain pipeline. For weeks in November 2014, the courtroom drama was accompanied by a round-the-clock protest camp on Burnaby Mountain itself. Hundreds of protestors were arrested, including the grand chief of the Union of British Columbia Indian Chiefs.

Pipelines, Rinne explained to his colleagues in Edmonton, had become "the nexus of the debate about energy." And the impact on what the industry had taken to calling its "social licence"—that crucial but amorphous consensus of public opinion, political will and economic utility by which a democratic populace gave sanction to large infrastructure projects in the twenty-first century—had been substantial. By way of example, Rinne talked about the Anchor Loop, an expansion to the Trans Mountain pipeline that Kinder Morgan had completed in 2008. Anchor Loop was a 158-kilometre twinning of the existing pipeline, which involved excavating and laying pipe through two treasured swaths of Rocky Mountain wilderness—Jasper National Park and Mount Robson Provincial Park. Kinder Morgan had submitted its application to the NEB in 2004. There were, Rinne said, exactly four "interveners." Just four people, mostly federal employees from relevant departments, asked to give testimony to the NEB panel considering the application. It was summarily approved and built without fanfare or rancour and now helped deliver thousands of barrels of bitumen from Edmonton to the port of Vancouver each day.

When Kinder Morgan submitted its application to twin the rest of the Trans Mountain pipeline in 2013, the NEB received more than four hundred intervener requests, as well as written submissions containing more than twenty thousand questions about the pipeline, its route, its viability and safety and necessity. The municipal government of Burnaby lobbied actively against it in addition to taking Kinder Morgan to court.

The conflict made international headlines and played a decisive role in the 2013 provincial election in British Columbia.

By the time of the 2015 World Heavy Oil Congress, midstream companies like Kinder Morgan, Enbridge and TransCanada PipeLines had grown used to the calamity that accompanied their pipeline applications. TransCanada's Keystone XL project had ignited the battle, drawing ferocious protest from ranchers and Indigenous people in Nebraska. This in turn had attracted opposition from regional and then national and global environmental groups, which had long searched in vain for a catalyst to intensify and expand climate change activism. Keystone XL turned oil sands pipelines into an international political issue and a proxy of the first resort for the much broader debate about climate and energy policy. In the process, the pipeline—eventually *any* pipeline intended to move bitumen to tidewater—became the symbol of the entire fight. It was the line in the sand, the first full and direct conflict between progress in the age of fossil fuel—defined by expanding energy use and industrial megaprojects—and progress in the age of climate change, which sought to balance economic growth and industrial development with sound environmental stewardship and reductions in greenhouse gas emissions.

The protest message soon reached the office towers of Calgary, and it was even addressed in the industry's distinctive way. The Patch's executives were not ignorant of their industry's environmental footprint. They had been grappling with pipeline spills and toxic tailings for decades, and for the most part they conceded that their emissions had to shrink. But let's be fair, they replied. The protesters—some of them, anyway—claimed that a barrel of bitumen emitted three times as much carbon dioxide as a conventional barrel. But if you looked at "wells to wheels" emissions—all the CO_2 emitted in the life cycle of a barrel of oil, not just the emissions during production, because didn't the whole life cycle of the fuel matter the most in the end?—if you looked at it that way, the result was nowhere near triple. The US State Department, for example, went with 17 percent more emissions per barrel than a barrel of Saudi or North Sea crude. Was that a problem? Fine, then it's a problem. Let's do something about it. Let's look

at the emissions intensity of the barrel of bitumen, which is down 31per-
cent since 1990. Could you say that about coal?

This is a parallel that former Suncor CEO Rick George likes to make
explicit. In his 2013 book *Sun Rise*, a memoir of his life in the Patch,
George asserted that the entire carbon footprint of the oil sands was
smaller than that of just the fleet of coal-fired power plants in the state of
Wisconsin. This is no longer accurate—oil sands emissions have grown
significantly since George wrote his book—but they remain smaller than
the coal emissions of Missouri and seven other states. Why are the Patch's
68 megatons of carbon dioxide per year carrying the blame for the whole
world's climate change mess? Why do those emissions make an archvil-
lain, when the 76 megatons emitted by coal plants in Missouri or the 151
megatons generated by coal in Texas do not? What makes the oil sands
business singularly culpable in a global energy system that derives more
than 85 percent of all its power from GHG-spewing fossil fuels?

This is how it looks from those Calgary office towers, how they talk
about it over lunch at those food court tables in the Plus 15, should the
topic arise. And this is what they'd like you all to understand: they responded to demand. That's all they've done. They met *your* demand.
Every single glass tower in Calgary, every comfortable suburban McMan-
sion at the end of every cul-de-sac, every truck bound north on Highway
63 laden with oil sands plant modules, every white Diversified bus and
buggy-whipping work truck, every drilling rig and separation cell and hydrocracker stack—all of it is there only because all of us burn ninety million barrels of oil every day. *All of us.* The protestors drive to the protests,
don't they? Except those Hollywood celebrities who fly in on private jets,
of course. What do you think those use for fuel? What material goes into
those keys on your keyboard that you're clacking away on to tell everyone
who reads your blog about that evil "carbon bomb"? How did the tofu in
your vegan lunch get to the grocery store, and what went into the fertilizer
and pesticide that allowed it to grow in such cheap and plentiful abundance? This is what perplexes the workers of the Patch.

But even if they wouldn't all admit it, there was a streak of denial running through this line of argument, a tendency toward motivated reasoning and cherry-picked data. They liked to look at wells to wheels emissions for the footprint of a barrel of bitumen, for example, but they considered only the emissions *intensity* per barrel and not the entire cumulative emissions of the whole Patch when they talked about the trend in upstream GHGs. If the protesters sometimes played fast and loose with their numbers, the oil sands business often did the same with their own.

In recent years, many in the Patch have come almost all the way around. They pretty much get it. In addition to being residents of a city and citizens of a country as broadly concerned about environmental stewardship and avoiding climate catastrophe as any other, they as an industry are aware how high a priority this needs to be. Sure, there are some old dinosaurs from the early wildcat days who still think the UN cooked up this climate crisis in Geneva to punish them for their wealth and genius, some who insist that there's still enough doubt about the causes and impacts of climate change to recommend caution in shutting down lucrative mining operations and slaying golden geese. But mostly they get it. Some, like Harbir Chhina, even believe they have begun to address it.

"Look at the whole value chain," Chhina says. Don't just talk about the 20 percent of a barrel's emissions produced extracting it from an in situ deposit. Talk wells to wheels. Set a goal of zero. That's the real target: emissions-free oil. "We think it's important to solve the whole problem," he says, "not just worry about your own backyard."

To that end, Chhina throws rhetorical pitches very much like a guy on the mound in the first inning. He talks about next-generation technologies—not just elaborate, expensive bolt-on gear that might sequester carbon dioxide from a SAGD plant deep beneath the ground but also the sci-fi stuff. Technologies that will take a CO_2 stream, whether from a SAGD plant's boiler or a car's exhaust pipe, and convert it back into a synthetic fuel, closing the emissions loop for good. Or perhaps turning carbon dioxide into a useful material, a replacement for laminated wood tables or steel auto bodies. Research of this sort is already underway in elite university labs.

"This is our moon shot," Chhina says. "How to get to zero emissions." He betrays no doubt. He's the confident engineer again, standing at the wellhead, valve in his hand, knowing that when he turns it, the oil will flow. And it will be good.

Calgary is a city that has begun to nurture pretenses of world-class cosmopolitanism, but at its core, it remains a city of boosters and true believers. During the 1988 Winter Olympics, greeters in big white cowboy hats, vests and bolo ties could be seen all over town, welcoming visitors with a friendly cartoon cowboy's *Howdy!* And that seemed so thoroughly Calgarian that you'll still find senior citizens in that exact same uniform saying howdy to arrivals at Calgary International Airport. The city's social life revolves around Canada's biggest, rowdiest, booziest rodeo, and everyone from bank tellers to corporate lawyers to your family dentist dons stiff cowboy boots and hayseed plaid shirts for the occasion. They put hay bales and plywood stage-set corral fences all over town—you see that stuff up and down every corridor in the Plus 15. Calgary has always been a city that saw itself as a maverick chasing a long-shot dream, and in the face of doubt and a distant business and political elite far to the east that still thinks there's nothing much happening there, Calgarians default to optimistic yahooing boosterism. The city's official slogan is "Onward!"

A zero-emissions barrel of oil from the so-called dirtiest industrial project on earth? That might sound far-fetched. But so was the first Great Canadian Oil Sands plant, and so was Chhina's test well at Foster Creek. And so the city and the business and the chattering lunch mates in the Plus 15s all remain ready—for another miracle, another boom, another wild ride. Onward!

SIX

SHIFT CHANGES

HARVESTERS

When Harbir Chhina and his colleagues in downtown Calgary moved the national needle on GDP, the economic reverberations radiated out far well beyond the Patch. They rattled down pipelines to distant ports, to the Gulf of Mexico and the Pacific coast and the port of South Portland, Maine. They roared down highways to distant suppliers, makers of luxury coaches in Quebec and giant yellow trucks and tractors in Illinois and manufacturers of oil sands production plant "modules" in South Korea, China and the Philippines. They blipped down fibre-optic cables and back again at the speed of light, to pension funds in Ontario and British Columbia, and to hedge fund managers and investment bankers in New York and London.

A project of such wild scale and a boom of such gee-whiz magnitude sends out shock waves of money and hype that circle the globe, and those waves create a kind of magnetic pull in return. As it boomed and boomed again for a decade or more, the Patch pulled things to it with little discretion, like a feudal lord or an agitated toddler. It sucked up materials, machines, money. And people.

The people came to the Patch from seemingly every nation, every creed, all walks of life. They filled Fort McMurray's mosques with engineers and technicians and taxi drivers. They filled Calgary's office towers with French executives and Norwegian engineers and Chinese bankers. And most of all, they came from the rest of Canada: from fading manufacturing burghs in southern Ontario and dying resource towns in the British Columbia interior. They came in such numbers from Canada's east coast that the joke in Fort McMurray was that it had become Newfoundland's second largest city.

For Atlantic Canada—the provinces of Newfoundland and Labrador, Nova Scotia, New Brunswick and Prince Edward Island—the Patch's epic boom arrived at a desperate time, in the wake of an economic and social upheaval of similar magnitude. The traditional resource industries of the region—fishing and seafood processing, pulp and paper, coal mining—had been fading for decades. And then the collapse of the Atlantic cod fishery, once the most abundant on earth, had descended in 1991 with the force and finality of a knockout punch. Provincial economies throughout the region reeled for years and spent more years after that struggling for stable footing and even a hint of recovery. Federal government bailout money and economic diversification schemes arrived in waves, but none filled the hole left by the cod fishery's absence. By 2001, fifty thousand Newfoundlanders had left the province for good. Populations also began to plummet in eastern Nova Scotia, where coal mine and pulp mill closures further amplified the catastrophe. The Cape Breton Regional Municipality, an urban district containing seven of Cape Breton Island's largest cities and towns, shrunk by 10 percent from 1996 to 2006. Guysborough County, a quiet rural stretch of mainland Nova Scotia coast just across the Canso Strait from Cape Breton, saw its population decline by a full quarter from 1996 to 2012.

At first, Atlantic Canada's decline and emigration was a scattershot phenomenon. But as investment in new oil sands projects rained down on the Patch after 1998, the great Atlantic Canadian exodus found a preferred destination, an ersatz Promised Land. Alberta's fossil fuel boom began to echo across Canada just as the permanence of Atlantic Canada's loss had fully sunk in. The wave of westward migrants grew in parallel with the rise in oil prices year after year throughout the first decade of the new millennium. From 2001 to 2006, at least 33,000 Atlantic Canadians moved to Alberta. By one estimate, an additional 5,500 Newfoundlanders were commuting back and forth to Fort McMurray by then as "fly-in, fly-out" workers on oil sands sites. From mid-2006 to mid-2007, as Alberta experienced the greatest period of economic growth of any province in Canada's history, the migrants came in ever greater droves. About 13,000 Atlantic Canadians relocated to Alberta in that twelve-month period alone, joining an influx from the rest of Canada that reached a pace of 100,000 per year. The premier of New Brunswick called it the greatest exodus his province had seen since the Great Depression. By 2006, unemployment across Atlantic Canada fell below 10 percent for the first time since 1976. An estimated 17 percent of Fort McMurray residents were Newfoundlanders, and nearly twice as many Newfoundlanders worked in Alberta as there were employed in the decimated fishery back home.

Year after year booming throughout the decade that followed, Atlantic Canadians poured into the Patch. The Newfoundlanders, with their unmistakable accents and tendency to colonize local clubs and pubs, became the most visible sign of the mass migration on the ground in Fort McMurray, but all of Atlantic Canada sent its young men and skilled tradespeople in droves. Welders and pipefitters left the shuttered shipyard at Marystown, Newfoundland, to work in Alberta. So many men went off to the Patch from New Waterford, Nova Scotia, that the fire department and high school sports teams wanted for volunteers. A columnist at the *Charlottetown Guardian*, Prince Edward Island's biggest newspaper, described Fort McMurray in 2014 as "the province's largest employer" without a word of qualification and just the barest hint of hyperbole. With median incomes soaring above $170,000 per year in Fort McMurray and plenty of overtime guaranteed—a place where you knew for certain you could "get your hours" in a skilled trade quicker than anywhere else, a fast track to full accreditation—there was nothing back home to compete with the promise of the Patch. "If we didn't have the oil sands—the McMurray factor, as we sometimes call it—we would be in economic chaos," the mayor of Cape Breton Regional Municipality told a Reuters news agency reporter one day in 2015.

The Cape Breton town of Port Hawkesbury is a microcosm of the story of collapse and exodus across Atlantic Canada. A town of 3,300 astride a substantial deepwater port, Port Hawkesbury grew up in the nineteenth century around a bustling shipbuilding industry. The port still moves millions of tons of gravel every year and serves as an oil transshipment point, but the lumber industry that once produced timber for the boats and gave the town its vigour in the twentieth century has entered a slow but likely terminal decline. In the boom years around 2009, representatives from oil sands companies would sometimes arrive at the Port Hawkesbury campus of the Nova Scotia Community College and hire up entire graduating classes of welders and pipefitters and electricians.

After the town's paper mill in Port Hawkesbury closed down in 2011, the town's long-serving mayor, Billy Joe MacLean, whose own son had settled in Fort McMurray, became a particularly vocal booster of the Patch's economic wonders. As MacLean watched skilled Cape Bretoners jet off to the Patch to earn their trade certifications and make top wages, returning to spend their money and build their homes in Port Hawkesbury, he reckoned that was a fair trade-off. "They're making quite a sacrifice for their families to go in that direction, but if they didn't have that direction to go to, they'd have nowhere to go," MacLean said. "If we didn't have the oil patch, the economies of eastern Canada would be in tatters."

The cultural tradition of economic exile ran deep in Atlantic Canada long before anyone had figured out how to turn bitumen into crude oil. The Atlantic provinces were among the first parts of Canada settled by Europeans, and the region had a thriving industrial sector for much of the

1800s, built on bustling trade with booming New England, which was just a short sail away. The newborn Canadian federal government's protectionist National Policy of 1879, however, brought the New England trade to an abrupt end and triggered an exodus of young skilled labourers and fortune seekers that would carry on largely uninterrupted for more than a century. It soon became commonplace for an Atlantic Canadian family to send a second son or third daughter to "the Boston states" to find work, a tradition that would continue well into the nineteen hundreds. Later generations of Atlantic Canadian migrants ventured into central Canada's industrial heartland, settling in Montreal and Toronto to work in the rapidly expanding postwar economy.

The most direct parallel with the migration to the Patch in the early years of the twenty-first century came at the beginning of the twentieth century. The Canadian prairie, which had just witnessed its first widespread settlement following the completion of the two national railroads, was emerging as one of the world's most bounteous breadbaskets. Prairie farmers of the time, most of whom had cleared their land on their own, were now desperate for labour. They convinced Canada's railroads to run special "harvest trains" in the late summer and early fall to supply the farmhands needed to bring in their crops. The trains were composed mainly of third-class "colonist cars"—simple coaches with wooden benches and space for as many as seventy-two passengers, plus a stove for heat and a water cooler. The trains ran from Sydney, Cape Breton's main city, to Calgary on the western rim of the prairie, picking up more cars and still more able-bodied young men clutching discounted tickets all along the route. At railheads west of Winnipeg, farmers and agents waited with job offers—often simply handmade, handheld signs reading "Men Needed" and the number of positions to be filled. At the end of the harvest season, the vast majority of the Atlantic Canadians returned home on the same special trains.

The first of the harvest trains ran in the 1890s, but the tradition exploded in the first decade of the twentieth century and continued to grow well into the 1920s. At the peak of the migration, as many as fifty trains made the trip in a single harvest season. The harvest trains took on many of the same socioeconomic trappings and mythological dimensions that would inspire the Maritime exodus to the Patch a century later. Here was the same promise of fast and easy money, with salaries for labourers on the prairie four times higher than the going rate in Atlantic Canada. In the early 1920s, labourers felling trees in the New Brunswick woods made $1 a day. The menial work on the prairie was at least as backbreaking—the most common job, stooking, involved long days stacking heavy sheaves of freshly cut wheat into piles to dry—but it paid $4 to $7 a day. Teachers' salaries were also three to four times more generous on average; one young woman from Antigonish, Nova Scotia, recalled leaving a position in her hometown that paid $90 per year in 1917 for a teaching job out west that paid $90 per *month*. "Everybody wanted to go west," a woman from Pictou County, Nova Scotia, recalled years later of her 1910 journey on a harvest train.

The thousands of descendants of harvest train riders who arrived in Fort McMurray at the dawn of the twenty-first century surely thought of themselves as pioneers of a similar sort, encountering a forbidding climate and unfamiliar culture. In short order, they would make it their own and reshape the culture back home in Atlantic Canada at the same time. It's difficult to say whether the Patch has become fundamentally Atlantic Canadian in some respects or whether Atlantic Canada has become a sort of distant colony of the Patch, but, in any case, the Patch never felt very far away from the towns and villages and quiet country roads of the Maritimes in 2015.

It was there in Nova Scotia towns like Stellarton and Truro, the tattered old industrial-era downtowns giving way to newer suburbs where expansive houses opened on driveways filled with big new pickup trucks and recreational vehicles, much like you'd find in Thickwood and Timberlea back in Fort McMurray. In the coastal village of Tatamagouche, on the Northumberland Strait, the newspaper runs a story on a former local junior hockey hero whose young son is now captain of the Tatamagouche Atom League hockey team; the story mentions in passing how the hometown hero splits his working time now between a lobster boat on the Northumberland Strait and an oil sands site north of Fort McMurray. It is a commonplace detail, an oil sands mine being no more exotic here than the Tatamagouche wharf.

New Glasgow is the industrial hub of Pictou County and home to the Sobeys grocery empire, and the pizza in town is known for its distinctive tangy sauce, an Anglophilic brown concoction with a flavour like nothing you can find on a pizza anywhere else. You know how it is when there's a taste like that, a craving that can't be satisfied any other way. On a street in downtown New Glasgow, there is an outlet of Acropole Pizza, a beloved local chain, and for $100 the UPS outlet in the strip mall just around the corner will ship two of those frozen Acropole brown sauce pizzas to homesick New Glasgow boys in Fort McMurray. It was doing a pretty brisk business back in 2013, though of course the pizza-by-mail trade had grown quieter in the $50-oil doldrums of 2015.

From the rugged east coast of Newfoundland to the rolling farmland of Prince Edward Island to the pulp towns of New Brunswick, these migration scenes repeat themselves. Young men (and more than a few women) gone west out of rare opportunity or grim necessity or some admixture of both. Populations in decline, old ways of fishing and shipbuilding and felling trees replaced by long-distance commutes and absentee husbands and a new Silverado Z71 in the garage. Walk into any Tim Hortons in any small town in Atlantic Canada, and you'll find no shortage of lament for the situation, but not much in the way of a plan to reduce its necessity or the will to change course in any substantial way.

GONE FISHING

Midafternoon one particular fine August day in 2015, Nick Martell of Georgetown, PEI, hopped in his Chevy pickup and headed down North Royalty Road toward town to run an errand or two and check on his fishing gear before he started his Fort McMurray commute. Martell was 36 and wiry in the way of a man who spent his working days either on a lobster boat or operating a 550-ton crane and spent his downtime lifting weights. He has two kids from a previous marriage—a daughter at university in New Brunswick, a teenage son in high school—and he lived in a comfortably appointed bungalow with his new girlfriend out in the royalty, which is what they call a rural township in PEI. The home's long driveway had plenty of room for the lobster boat in dry dock, a minivan, Martell's truck and the trailer he used to haul his speedboat to the wharf and back. He'd taken the speedboat out a couple times on this visit home, and that was one of his errands—he had to get that boat out of the water before he headed to Charlottetown to catch an evening flight to Toronto and from there to Fort McMurray. With the three hours of time difference he gained flying west, he'd land at Fort McMurray airport around eleven that evening and be up the next morning before five to head out to a twelve-hour shift at site. There were a lot of different routes from PEI to Fort McMurray, but this was his favourite, the one where you got a good last day with the family back in Georgetown and landed at night for a morning shift the next day. Right back into that otherworldly life of twelve-hour shifts and near-zero downtime—that locked-in, narrow-focus, workaholic Fort McMoney life, with the intervals between sleep and work defined by a bedroom in a friend's suburban house and the nearest gym in a city he barely knew, despite having worked there more than ten years.

Martell knew he was lucky for the work. He's a heavy crane operator, a specialized trade perpetually in high demand on an oil sands site. Even with the industry's economic woes, there was still plenty of work, more than the contracting firm Martell worked for could manage sometimes. There were routine repairs and annual maintenance shutdowns and new construction out at Suncor's Fort Hills site or an Enbridge tank farm near the SAGD operations, all of it needing monster loads of material and sometimes people lofted high into the sky on the end of the two-hundred-foot boom of the Grove GMK7550 crane Martell operated.

Martell drove through town to the fishing dock and found a parking spot. The wharf is postcard pretty. The small town hugs Georgetown Harbour, a sheltered inlet on the east coast of PEI that opens onto the lobster-rich waters of the Northumberland Strait. A thin strip of concrete pier stabs out into the water. Boxy lobster boats tethered to either side of it sway in the waves, their peaked upward-swooping bows jutting up like stiff upper lips in a midway caricature. Where the pier meets the shore, there's a cluster of wooden sheds, peak-roofed with walls of weather-beaten unpainted plank, the doors and window trim done in candy hues of green, yellow, red and blue. The scene looks timeless, unchangeable, an unbroken link to the first boats that arrived on Atlantic Canada's shores hunting for cod, for herring and halibut and bluefin tuna, for lobster and crab and the oysters that have made the names of some of PEI's cozy little bays famous the world over.

Martell strolled out across the dock like it was his front porch, waving hello and trading small talk with the couple of locals still fishing this time of year. The lobster season in this stretch of the Northumberland Strait runs through May and June, and during those months, the Georgetown wharf hums day and night with a commercial fishery's business. The rest of the year, though, there are only a few worthwhile catches—barely worth it, as far as Martell is concerned. A few boats go out to fish herring, and some boat captains catch silver-siders and other bait fish for their lobster traps, the catch flash-frozen and stored in big freezers in the quaint little wooden sheds. There's a little money to be had in sightseeing cruises and big-game fishing. But that's mainly for guys who have been at it for years, who own their boats and licences outright and pull enough lobster from the strait in season to turn a profit.

This was Martell's goal, his modest dream. But he was not there yet, not by a long shot. So once the small talk was done, he had to keep going up the dock to untether his speedboat and drag it to the launch, because he had to get it out of the water in time to report for the job that pays for it all.

Martell first went to Alberta when he was nineteen, fresh out of school, unskilled and hunting for work. The Patch was just starting to roar to life, and he easily found work in the conventional oil business. His first job was a classic roughneck gig, working on a surface casing rig, the apparatus that "completes" an oil well, driving perforated steel pipe and concrete deep into the newly drilled hole. There was a "picker truck" they used on the job, a flatbed truck with a small crane on it. Martell was the only rough-neck on-site with the license needed to drive it. Such is the haphazard way of career opportunities in the booming Patch.

Martell soon found work in Fort McMurray. Along the way, he got his journeyman ticket as a crane operator, gaining more experience day by twelve-hour day. He moved on to larger cranes and then to mobile cranes, towering devices built to oil sands scale, so large they have opera-tor cabs built into the crane assembly and sit on a sort of modified, built-in eighteen-wheeler that moves them from site to site. The Grove GMK7550, his current rig, is a freakish giant—a vehicle like a flattened, widened long-haul freight truck sitting on fourteen heavy tires packed close together like a Lego moon rover. The crane itself is a mammoth yellow tower mounted on the back of the truck, the telescoping end of it protruding over the top of the truck's cab like a fist when it is lowered for travel. The crane can lift loads up to 550 tons at a time and extend effortlessly 200 feet into the sky. Once, the year before, Martell had a job out at a Suncor site helping a crew working on the top of the "fire stack," the tallest chimney in an oil sands plant. The Grove crane has an attachment called a "megawing"— a pair of steel arms that protrude from the top of the crane's main boom, making it look like a cross. With the megawing extended, the crane can support another couple of hundred feet of boom. So there was Martell in his operating station on the back of the truck, his crane's arm stabbing 400 feet into the Alberta sky above him, a "man basket" at the end of it for workers to ride in, bringing that massive boom up and down smooth and safe so that these guys could work on the fire stack. Some days as a crane operator, Martell would spend wearying hours on end just waiting on a maintenance crew running behind schedule. But on days when he was swinging guys 400 feet up in the air with a few expert twists of the Grove crane's control stick—those were the days when he knew there was more to the job than just the money. There was fun and responsibility and power in the work. Every kid with a sandbox full of Tonka trucks dreamed of a shot at this kind of gig, let alone making more than $50 an hour at it.

Back on the dock in Georgetown, Martell winched his speedboat out of the water and onto the trailer. The view south from the pier is across the harbour to a larger dock with a large grey warehouse built on it. This is Seafood 2000 Ltd., the seafood processing plant where much of his catch goes in season. Martell worked on a lobster boat off PEI's north coast for a few years after high school, and from his early days in the Patch, he'd had plans to get back to PEI and own his own "fleet." This is the catch-all term used in Georgetown to describe everything you need to pull lobster out of the water: the boat and license, the gear and traps and a picturesque wooden shed on the dock for storing it all. Lobster fishers ready to retire with no heir to hand their fleet over to will sell off their license and some portion of the rest of their fleet to someone like Martell.

A lobster fleet is not a cheap business to launch. Martell worked nearly a decade before he had enough capital and credit to make it happen. His license cost him $220,000, a debt he's still repaying. It entitles him to fish all the lobster he wants in season from District 26A of the Northumberland Strait, though in practice each license has been attached to a smaller and more specific area of water as long as anyone remembers, and it was expected that Martell would keep fishing the same grounds as the fisherman he bought it from. Martell found a boat in a fishing village on the other end of the island and bought it for $30,000. It needed a new engine and new electronic equipment. There was fishing gear and all the rest of a fleet's accoutrements on top of that. The total investment ran more than $300,000. When he bought it all, Martell reckoned he could work a few successful seasons out in the Strait and spend the rest of the year making top dollar as a heavy crane operator, and before long—maybe five years or so—he'd clear his debts and own his fleet outright. Then he could cut back the work in Fort McMurray to just a few months of the off-season, maybe eventually be done with 550-ton cranes forever.

Martell launched his fleet in May 2013. Lobster prices in PEI cratered that season, falling lower than anyone had seen in decades, to barely $3 a pound at Seafood 2000. In theory, a lobster fisher could take his catch elsewhere, but the time demands of a short season and the logistics of transporting live lobster mean the plant and pound at Georgetown have a local monopoly. Martell and his fellow fleet owners knew there were better prices over in Nova Scotia and New Brunswick, so they blocked the entrance to the processing plant with a lobster boat and staged a protest. Prices crept up, but Martell still finished the season spending more to fish than he made with his catch, a net loss of $16,000 before he even factored in the debt payments. Prices rose the next year and the next, but not enough to speed up Martell's pursuit of his goal all that much.

Martell got the speedboat secured to the trailer and drove back out toward his place in the royalty. He took a side road this time, so he could swing by his buddy Josh's place. Josh was working on a new boathouse beside his suburban-style home. He had the posts in place and was cutting wood for the base of the big shed's frame. He came over as Martell pulled up, and they chatted a bit about the boathouse and about Fort McMurray. Josh had spent almost ten years working in the Patch, and then he came home and bought a lobster boat and hadn't looked back for several years. But with the ebb and flow of catch sizes and the persistent low prices, Josh was thinking he might head back out to Fort McMurray this fall. Martell thought he could probably get his company to bring Josh on as an apprentice. After all, they were perpetually short-staffed. Martell said he'd talk it over with the guys at his company and be back in touch when he got back from the twenty straight days of work in his twenty-and-ten. Then he said good-bye and drove home to start his transcontinental commute.

PATCH AIRWAYS

Like a lot of long-distance oil sands commuters, Martell travels with a simple carry-on. The most common version is an overstuffed backpack identical to the ones the Patch's workers carry to site every day, but Martell has a small gym duffle. He picked it up from home and said his farewells to his girlfriend and son and drove forty-five minutes to the Charlottetown airport. By dinnertime, he was en route to Toronto, and he would land in Fort McMurray before midnight.

When Martell's flight hit the tarmac at Pearson International Airport in Toronto, he joined a great mass of long-distance commuters spread across Canada, electricians and pipefitters and a dozen other trades who make up the oil sands industry's substantial itinerant workforce. Academics call them mobile workers, and the Fort McMurray municipal government refers to them as a "shadow population" in a whole separate section of its census dedicated to tracking them. Locals in Fort McMurray sometimes call them FIFOs, short for "fly-in, fly-out." It sometimes takes on a derogatory air—the mobile workers, like Maritimers on harvest trains a century before, are blamed for all manner of crime, rowdiness and general detriment to community spirit in some circles in town. The stereotypical FIFO is a young man, uneducated and barely skilled, a fast-buck thrill-seeker making too much money with no connection to Fort McMurray or any other community, possibly homesick and definitely contemptuous of the city where he earns his outsized pay.

In truth, the typical mobile worker is a lot like Martell. More than half of the Patch's mobile workers are thirty-five years old or older, 51 percent are married and more than 60 percent have a postsecondary education or a skilled trade certification. As recently as 2007, more than nine in ten were male, but by 2012 that share had declined to 83 percent and falling. The 2015 Fort McMurray census counted forty-three thousand people in its shadow population. This was slightly off the 2014 peak of fifty-one thousand but still far beyond the six thousand mobile workers first surveyed in 2000 as the boom revved its engines, and nearly double the mobile workforce of twenty-three thousand counted in 2010. The vast majority of them—thirty-eight thousand as of 2015—stay in the dozens of work camps scattered throughout the Patch. But perhaps two thousand live, as Martell does, in a buddy's spare bedroom in a Fort McMurray suburb or some other informal arrangement, while maintaining a permanent address elsewhere.

The mobile workers make up a third of the total population of greater Fort McMurray—the Regional Municipality of Wood Buffalo, as it's officially called—and any given day in 2015, thousands of them were in motion, airborne or in security lines or waiting at airport gates for connecting flights. They filled seats on planes from Charlottetown and Sydney and St. John's, Toronto and Montreal, Kamloops and Saskatoon. They filled whole airplanes that hopped relentlessly from Calgary and Edmonton to Fort McMurray and back a dozen times per day.

In addition to the regular commercial flights on Air Canada and West-Jet, there was an entire shadow airline industry serving the shadow population. In 2012, near the peak of the oil sands boom's second wave, more than 750,000 passengers per year flew in and out of the Patch on private aircraft. Suncor runs its own fleet (SunJet, by informal name), a trio of Bombardier Canadair Regional Jets and two other planes. Weekly SunJet schedules are routinely posted in the lobby of nearly every work camp in the region. For a time, it was somewhere around the tenth largest airline in Canada by passenger volume, flying twenty-five thousand passengers per month to and from oil sands jobs in 2012, and it was known in the industry for serving tasty banana bread on board. North Cariboo Air, a charter airline based in northern British Columbia, moved as many as nine thousand passengers a month at its peak; the company grew by a factor of eight in just the six wildest years of the boom.

Some of the private flights land alongside their commercial cousins at Fort McMurray International Airport, which in 2014 opened a new terminal five times larger than its predecessor. But they also bounce in and out of a half-dozen or more private aerodromes on or near oil sands sites—the Shell Albian Aerodrome and Suncor Firebag Aerodrome, Conklin (Leismer) Airport, aerodromes at CNRL's Horizon, Syncrude's Mildred Lake and Cenovus's Christina Lake sites. Some of these private airstrips are substantial enough to have full-time baggage handling and check-in staff. All together, they represented the largest single-industry air commuter network in North America, surely one of the largest in the world with a single destination in mind—a loosely affiliated Patch

Airways for one of the world's largest mobile workforces. The traffic was down in 2015 along with the price of oil—commercial passenger volumes into Fort McMurray Airport declined by 12 percent that year and charter passenger volumes by nearly 50 percent—but the mobile workers remained an omnipresent, though largely invisible, phenomenon on airplanes across the country.

The fly-in, fly-out tradition is certainly not unique to the oil sands. It's quite common in the fossil fuel and mining industries worldwide. There are mobile workers air commuting to North Sea offshore oil rigs, oil and natural gas production centres in remote Siberia, coal mines across the barren northwest quadrant of Australia. But there might be none with the single purpose and multiyear permanence of Patch Airways.

Fort McMurray's shadow population was born of the long, lunatic boom and the economic exigencies of the industry. By 2008, when the global financial crisis gave the Patch a moment to catch its breath, permanent accommodations were in critically short supply in Fort McMurray, and every logistics company in the business was racing to build and expand hotel-like work camps. The additional travel and logistical costs of a fly-in, fly-out worker can exceed $40,000 a year, but a highly skilled, ticketed tradesperson like Nick Martell could cost $25,000 in training alone—if you could even find such a person in a labour market that seemed to grow ever tighter. Better to retain the right people than hunt for new ones, even if it meant transporting them across an entire continent twice a month. By the time the second phase of the boom was in full swing around 2012, the shadow population was as crucial to an oil sands site's daily operations as the Cat 797 truck.

The impact of all that air travel and dislocation was significant—both in Fort McMurray and in the far-flung communities across the country that remained the real home for most of the mobile workers. The combination of absentee spouses and outsized salaries could be toxic to a marriage and family, even as it served as a source of new prosperity or welcome economic stability. It also fed a hyperconsumer culture with a desperate tinge to it. With guilt over being away flowing as easily as the money, many oil sands workers filled their short visits home with the outsized gear of a lavish vacation lifestyle—the biggest and best new RVs and camping trailers, off-road vehicles and snowmobiles, fishing boats and speedboats and Sea-Doos. Younger mobile workers went for the biggest and most tricked-out trucks as status symbols.

Back in Fort McMurray, permanent residents had taken to blaming the excesses of the industry's downtime on the shadow population—disproportionately, for sure, but not without evidence. The city's boomtown party scene was overhyped, but it was undeniably part of the local culture. Drug dealers and escort services did brisk business in a city where thousands of young men without families to fly home to poured into the streets at the end of gruelling work schedules bearing fat paycheques and a binge-friendly multiday holiday interval. A 2008 feature in the popular Canadian women's magazine *Chatelaine* probably made too much of a stereotype in which an anxious wife waited back home in the Maritimes for a husband soliciting prostitutes at the end of a long, lucrative workday, but it was grounded in at least some truth. Fort McMurray has its dark, wild side, and it is overfed by the transient culture of the mobile workers.

The more common reality for the shadow population, however, is a kind of institutionalized workaholism. The Patch offers exceedingly well-paid work, as much of it as a person can handle, at the cost of an anxious and sometimes alienating double life. The world of an oil sands work camp is almost monastically devoted to the daily grind of digging and processing bitumen. The culture of the camp and work place alike can be lonely and intimidating. In 2015 there were worries in abundance at either end of a mobile worker's commute: the price of oil and the next round of layoffs loomed over the Patch, while the strain on families left behind in fading towns waited at home. With a keen eye, you could see the stress of it scattered across the country. There's a look common to oil sands workers in transit. They stand in airport security lines and last calls at the gate in scuffed work boots and faded denim, their shoulders slumped under the weight of overstuffed backpacks and duffle bags. There is sometimes a weary middle-distance cast to the eyes, like the workday has already begun or stretched on too long. From Calgary International Airport to Pearson in Toronto, it's common to find middle-aged men sprawled across four seats at a departure gate, their heads mostly hidden by battered baseball caps or sweatshirt hoods, resting on those big backpacks, dead asleep. At Air Canada's Maple Leaf Lounges for frequent flyers, the mobile workers—many of whom qualified for the airline's highest frequent flyer status—have earned a reputation for much harder drinking than the usual business lounge denizen. There is a grass slope outside the main doors of the new Fort McMurray airport, and in the warm months of 2015, you could frequently find a handful of mobile workers there, seated or prone, some napping, others leaning on their stuffed bags like schoolkids, all of them waiting on some delay or other in their commute.

THE STEEL WEB

The shadow population comes and goes, streaming by the thousands into Fort McMurray and the other airstrips scattered across the Patch, catching buses from work camps to board SunJet flights out of the Firebag Aerodrome or commercial planes departing from Fort McMurray airport. Meanwhile, the product of their varied labours flows steadily in just one direction. Suncor's SAGD operation near the aerodrome on the Firebag River, for example, produced more than 180,000 barrels of oil per day in 2015. (This was the lease Ned Gilbert had first acquired for Sun Oil in the early 1950s, the one they mocked as "Gilbert's Folly.") Day after day, those barrels flowed straight from the wellhead fifty kilometres southwest in a dedicated pipeline to Suncor's main plant. There the raw bitumen was upgraded into synthetic crude and pumped into another pipeline, which transported it a short distance south of the Suncor site to a tank farm, the Athabasca terminal—an orderly rank of more than a dozen large, white circular storage tanks on the eastern bank of the Athabasca River. At this point, a barrel of Firebag oil became one of many undifferentiated thousands of barrels of Western Canadian Select produced from multiple sources, all of which waited on a longer southerly journey. The vagaries and calculations of bulk orders and pipeline shipping queues would eventually result in the crude being pumped into the waiting thirty-inch maw of Enbridge's Athabasca pipeline, and from there it entered Enbridge's vast continent-wide network of oil transport pipes, itself part of an enormous steel web of hydrocarbon pipelines that crisscross North America many times over.

The Athabasca pipeline, for its part, carried that random Firebag barrel of oil 550 kilometres south to another tank farm near Hardisty. This small prairie town was established in 1904 on a Canadian Pacific Railway surveyor's map as a good spot for trains to take on water from the nearby Battle River. It was a minor railhead for a hundred years, a tiny urban dot with gridded streets and a population that never exceeded a thousand souls, surrounded by a broad, flat checkerboard of farmer's fields. In the 1950s, as oil pumpjacks started to fill the Alberta prairie, Hardisty was chosen as the western terminus of the first continental pipeline system for the province's oil because of its central location and the salt deposits it rested on, which were easily hollowed out to create subterranean storage tanks. That first pipeline eventually became the backbone of Enbridge's extensive "mainline," and the town was the obvious choice when Enbridge needed a terminus for its Athabasca pipeline, a dedicated pipe to carry oil from Suncor's original oil sands mine, completed in 1999. A decade later, at the peak of the oil sands boom, Hardisty became an even larger oil transport nexus. Seemingly every midstream company in the business descended on the town to build tank farms and map out new pipeline routes—Hardisty to Superior, Wisconsin; Hardisty to Cushing, Oklahoma; Hardisty to the Gulf of Mexico and the Atlantic coast; Hardisty to every point on the compass that might need more oil—and sink hundreds of millions of dollars into rail terminals as the pipelines filled to capacity. By 2015, there seemed to be almost as many mammoth storage tanks on the southeastern edge of town as houses on the streets in Hardisty itself. There are more than seventy of those storage tanks now, an industrial army of them standing stoic on the prairie, filling with synthetic crude and diluted bitumen from oil sands sites through one set of subterranean pipes and sending out shipments across the continent through another.

All told, there is capacity to store more than 26 million barrels of oil and other petrochemicals at the Hardisty terminal. On behalf of clients like Suncor, seven companies store oil here—well-known names like TransCanada PipeLines and Husky Energy, as well as corporate brands like Gibsons and Flint Hills Resources, known mainly in the midstream oil game—but Enbridge remains by far the largest. Enbridge's North American pipeline network, with the mainline out of Hardisty as its backbone, is the largest single petrochemical transport network on earth. Roughly two-thirds of all the oil pumped out of the Western Canadian Sedimentary Basin—conventional oil as well as bitumen—travels to refiners and markets through Enbridge pipes. And it was Enbridge's simultaneous construction of nineteen storage tanks in 2007 that reignited the business in Hardisty and triggered the pipeline expansion mania in Canada's midstream industry.

A long-distance pipeline moves oil in batches, different types and grades sometimes flowing together into a "transmix" that is removed for reprocessing at the far end. Other times the midstream company sends a "pig" down the line, a plastic or steel separator that looks like an outsized bobbin. Pigs also clean pipelines and hunt for leaks. At some point, that Firebag barrel's batch was the next in line for delivery, and it was sent flowing down the Alberta Clipper, chugging along in a sealed chamber thirty-six inches in diameter at around ten kilometres per hour. In just under seven days, it reached Superior, Wisconsin. Some of its batch might have been switched to an Enbridge pipe headed for Chicago or Sarnia, Ontario, but a growing amount of Enbridge's shipments were transferred instead to another one of its pipes, Southern Access, which carried the oil onward to a storage terminal outside Pontiac, Illinois, more than eight hundred kilometres farther southeast.

The pipeline network that snakes across the American Midwest is multivalent. It vectors off to the port of Chicago, or to the pipeline shipping hub of Cushing, or to the refineries in Sarnia. An estimated 2.6 million miles of pipe carry fossil fuels from place to place in the United States,

enough pipe to reach the moon ten times over. The pipelines transport
natural gas and petroleum by-products as well as millions of barrels of
conventional oil and the lion's share of the Patch's daily produce. There
are transfer points and storage terminals and minor refining centres whose
names and locations are well known only in the business, and others—the
port of Chicago, the massive assembly of refining apparatus along the Gulf
coast of Texas—that are far more conspicuous.

There is a major refinery in Pine Bend, Minnesota, on the periphery
of Minneapolis—Saint Paul, specially tooled for heavy oil refining, and
a significant number of oil sands barrels make their way there, traveling
via Hardisty and Superior down a spur pipeline that can carry 285,000
barrels per day. The refinery is owned and operated by Koch Industries,
a family-owned fossil fuel empire based in Wichita, Kansas—one of the
largest privately held fortunes in America and among its most reviled business enterprises. On the American political left and among its allies in the
environmental movement, the Koch brothers are detested for their longstanding support of a range of right-wing causes, including the denial of
the scientific consensus on anthropogenic climate change, and their Pine
Bend refinery is often held up as a symbol of the dark forces behind the oil
sands industry's growth. The Kochs have been refining bitumen since the
1960s, and through their byzantine network of holding companies, they
control leases to great swaths of bitumen-rich but largely undeveloped boreal forest in northern Alberta. They have profited enormously from the
rise of the oil sands—but, then, they have profited enormously from nearly
every major fossil fuel play anywhere in North America for a half century.
(Warren Buffett, a less loathed multibillionaire, also profited enormously
from the oil sands boom, mainly through his purchase of the BNSF Railway, which started moving hundreds of thousands of barrels of bitumen to
ports and refineries as pipeline capacity reached its limit in recent years.)

In any case, a couple of hundred thousand barrels of oil leave Hardisty
bound for Pine Bend each day, and a similar number travel instead to the
Flanagan terminal near Pontiac. After it has passed through a refinery, oil
is among the most fungible of commodities, reaching the market all but

brandless. No one pulls a gas pump from its cradle wondering whether they are filling up with light sweet crude from Saudi Arabia or the Niger Delta, deepwater deposit pumped from two miles under the Gulf of Mexico or an upgraded barrel of synthetic crude from Alberta's oil sands. We ask precious few questions about our oil once it has reached the local gas station.

GET YOUR KICKS ON ROUTE 66

Consider the barrel of Firebag bitumen that arrives at Enbridge's Flanagan terminal on its journey farther downstream. Whatever obscure calculus of market price, available refining capacity, and consumer demand brought it there, it flows out of the Southern Access pipeline's terminus into a storage terminal like most others—a neat phalanx of low, broad white tanks. There are nine large tanks in a three-by-three grid and six smaller ones arrayed two by three at the Flanagan terminal. The facility is located at a rural crossroads in the middle of a wide stretch of flat Illinois prairie, about a mile off Interstate 55, two miles north of Pontiac and a hundred miles southwest of Chicago. The terminal sits in the shade of an artificial hill, the Livingston County Landfill. On the terminal site, there is a cluster of small operations and administration buildings, a parking lot full of pickup trucks, and a general sense of incidental rural industry to the place. It's all built in the style and to the scale of the big grain elevators and farm equipment warehouses that spring from other crossroads across the wide farm-field expanses of central Illinois.

For all of this, the Flanagan terminal occupies a significant crossroads. It stands astride a vital artery of the twentieth-century fossil fuel industry, at the quiet edge of an industrial heartland that has fed American business and global economic growth for nearly as long as hydrocarbons have been burned to make power and do work. Chicago, to the northeast, was the greatest of all the boomtowns born of the industrialization of the American heartland. The city rose out of mean swampland upon completion of the Erie Canal, nearly seven hundred miles to the east, in New York State, in

1825. The canal project transformed the location from the backwoods of the American frontier into a vital hub at the very centre of US enterprise. Wheat, corn, cattle and hogs poured into Chicago's newly built portlands and stockyards. Secondary canals linked the city to surrounding farms, the Great Lakes linked it to the Erie Canal, and the Erie Canal linked it inextricably to the port of New York and an exploding world of global trade. When railroads arose to supplant canals as primary carriers of freight, Chicago became America's premier rail hub. The Pullman railroad car and the American labour movement were both born in Chicago.

Towns like Pontiac now sit beyond the cluster of chain restaurants and service stations at the end of interstate off-ramps, passed by in the blink of an eye at sixty-five miles per hour. But in the first great wave of the oil age's rise, they were bustling towns along magnificent new roadways that grew busier by the day. Pontiac had the good fortune of being situated along an Illinois state road built in the earliest days of motoring, and it was added to Route 66 when the new national highway was first designated in 1926. Though Pontiac wouldn't make it into the song immortalizing certain dots on the highway's map—*Well, it winds from Chicago to LA / More than 2,000 miles all the way*—the town was tightly linked nonetheless to the revolutionary movement in American mobility ushered in by cheap, abundant oil and internal combustion engines. The first gas station opened in town in 1927. Candy making and shoe manufacturing emerged in Pontiac alongside an agricultural sector already thriving amid some of the most fertile farmland on earth. Route 66, passing in a triumphant diagonal slash across the flat, easily navigated centre of America, became a busy trucking route. The American century, fuelled by oil and symbolized by a mass-manufactured private automobile roaring down an open highway, was a myth made real in places like Pontiac.

Nearly a century after Route 66 was inaugurated, oil still arrives in central Illinois in abundance. It comes from halfway across the continent to wait in storage tanks on the plain north of Pontiac for delivery to refineries and ports across another half of the continent. There are barrels of upgraded bitumen among those batches, and, just a little farther down the interstate in Peoria and Decatur, there are Caterpillar factories where the equipment that first made bitumen mining possible was manufactured.

Notwithstanding the colossal physical and ecological footprint of an oil sands mine or refinery complex, the oil business is often like this—everywhere and invisible. Exhaust fumes and subterranean pipes, storage tanks tucked behind landfills, drilling rigs out at sea beyond the horizon and gargantuan trucks past the end of a highway in the frozen forests of northern Canada. Ninety million barrels of liquid crude per day sloshing around the globe unseen.

Some unknown number of barrels from Firebag and the rest of the Patch make their way each day to refineries in the vast industrial lands east of downtown Houston, along the Houston Ship Channel. There they are sold to distant customers and make their way into the reservoirs of hulking oil tankers. The oil shipping business has its own byzantine system of classifying the boats: there are Panamax tankers and Suezmax tankers, very large crude carriers (VLCCs) and ultra large crude carriers (ULCCs)—but all are great floating tubs of steel with long, flat decks and enormous storage reservoirs in their hulls. The Houston Ship Channel is only deep and wide enough to accommodate 900-foot-long Suezmaxes. The larger VLCCs and ULCCs are more than 1,000 feet from bow to stern, longer than aircraft carriers, and the ULCCs are rated for 550,000 tons of cargo. Some of the smaller tankers dock alongside VLCCs and ULCCs more than twenty miles offshore to transfer their oil to the larger boats.

All day and night, oil tankers leave docks in front of refineries along the Houston Shipping Channel. They navigate east, past the San Jacinto Battleground State Historic Site at the channel's mouth, its white memorial towering nearly five hundred feet over the water. From here the tankers turn southeast, crossing San Jacinto Bay and then out its thin mouth into Galveston Bay. There is another narrow channel between the tip of the Bolivar Peninsula and Galveston Island, and the supertankers file through it one by one in a steady line. At dusk in Galveston, the row of bars and restaurants along the seawall fill with tourists, and if they look northeast to the horizon, they'll see a series of beacons low to the surface of the Gulf of Mexico, the lights of oil tankers vanishing into the night as another day's shipments of oil head out to sea.

SEVEN

NIGHT FALLS ON THE PATCH

CRICKET NIGHT IN CANADA

In the early evening on any given day in 2015, the suburban streets of Fort McMurray filled again with white luxury coaches. They crawled down quiet curving streets, dropping off day-shift workers and picking up the night-shift crews. In the colder months, their headlights would illuminate the reflective patches and Xs on the safety vests and coveralls of the waiting workers in the dark. Earlier in the evening, the buses could sometimes be found gathered in groups of three or four or six in the parking lots of schools or the Suncor Centre for the Performing Arts in Timberlea, the drivers chatting and sipping coffee as they waited on start times for evening routes.

Diversified's route 11 ("Suncor—East, West & Mine Ops") is an easy run along an elongated oval suburban street called Timberline Drive in Thickwood, close to Highway 63, the first right after you exit. It runs along the edge of the densely forested river valley that separates Thickwood from Timberlea and gives the community its name. Tall spruces stand at the roadside like a dark row of sentries in the black evening of winter or shine deep green in the bright evening sunlight of summer. Raheel Joseph has seen the forest alongside route 11 both ways many times from the driver's seat of his Diversified bus. The route is among his favourites, navigated quickly, ensuring a fast run out to site and back.

On certain summer evenings, Joseph's mind would turn to cricket as he made his last pickups and drop-offs. The late sunsets of summer in the Alberta north allow plenty of time for outdoor sports, even for a bus driver working an evening route. And in 2015, Joseph's team, the Snyepers, was the best team in the Fort McMurray Cricket Club, and Joseph among its top players. Cricket matches take a full day at minimum—at the highest international level, they can stretch across a whole week—so the club plays on weekends, but there were informal drop-in practices on the pitch at Syncrude Athletic Park in Timberlea on some weeknights. Joseph tried to make it out as often as he could. Finding a cricket club had been a welcome and unexpected change in his connection to his community.

Cricket is a national religion in Joseph's native Pakistan, by far the most popular spectator sport and an honoured tradition at all of the country's schools. It is played in massive stadiums and in dusty back alleys, obsessed over in the press, the nation's pride waxing and waning with its every result against hated neighbouring India.

Joseph played cricket seriously as a teenager back in Pakistan. He was on Islamabad's elite citywide under-nineteen club, a feat roughly equivalent to making a Canadian Junior A hockey team. Soon after he first arrived in Canada, he had his family ship his cricket gear over. It landed in suburban Toronto and then made the trip to Fort McMurray with him. But as he worked long shifts and struggled to hang on in those first years in Canada, he never found time to even find a club, let alone play regularly. Once, back in Mississauga, he stumbled upon a club's practice, and even though he could tell right away the players were nowhere near his skill level, he asked about joining anyway. They explained that the fees were a couple of hundred dollars per month, and so Joseph's gear remained unused for several years more.

One day in 2012, he was driving a shuttle bus on the Suncor site. It was dull work, running workers from plant to mine site and back again, over and over. Hours could go by with few passengers. To pass the time, Joseph was listening to a Bollywood soundtrack on the shuttle bus stereo. At some point a man boarded and recognized the music. He was an Indian expat, and they got to talking. The Indian guy asked Joseph if he played cricket. Joseph said he did, that he'd been looking for a chance to play for a while. The Indian guy explained that he played in a league. It was far from elite—they didn't even have a proper pitch—but Joseph reckoned it was better than no cricket at all. With his steady job at Diversified and a work schedule, finally, that wasn't total madness, he had the time and where-withal for cricket again.

Fort McMurray had been home to a cricket club for more than a decade by that point, but it had only recently started to attract enough players to organize into a formal league with teams, uniforms, a schedule and standings. The energetic head of the league, a bank manager named Irfan Bangash, was bringing a real sense of purpose to the club. In 2013 he persuaded the municipal government to invest a little cash in turn-ing the patch of field out at Syncrude Athletic Park into a more workable cricket pitch, with a groomed strip between the wickets, line markings and benches. In 2015 the pitch was still the only facility at the athletic park without lights for evening play, but at least it was an authentic, permanent pitch. The club had five teams by then, plus a travelling team of all-stars who played (and won) matches with other clubs across Alberta.

One fine June evening, Joseph made it out to a weeknight practice. Ramadan fell in late spring that year, and the Fort McMurray Cricket Club is predominantly South Asian, with many Muslims observing the daytime fast. This is particularly exhausting in June in northern Alberta, with its eighteen hours or more of daylight. Only a handful of players made it to the practice, Bangash and Joseph among them. Bangash took batting practice in his replica Pakistan national team jersey with a cheerful young Trinidadian, while Joseph found a seat on the bench and started strapping on his shin guards.

There was an ease to the scene. The sky above was deep blue, and beginning to fill with the billowing dramatic clouds that so often gather into ferocious evening storms in the Alberta summer. For now, though, there was the warm sun and a lazy cricket practice in the middle of Ramadan. The chatter of beer-league softball rose and fell from the surrounding fields. The cricket practice seemed as workaday Canadian in that subarctic sunlight as the softball players fielding pop-ups and grounders.

Joseph rose once he was in his full cricket gear, looking like a guy who had mastered the scene. When he first arrived in Canada, Joseph's sister had told him, "It's a land of opportunity. If you work hard, you will achieve something." For years, it must have seemed like a false promise. But now he was a very long way from cosmetology school in Brampton and further still from the elite cricket club in Islamabad. And on this lovely evening on the edge of the boreal forest, his sister's prophesy must have seemed fulfilled.

These men had all felt lost in this city not too long ago. They were lone actors drawn to the edge of the earth, so it seemed, in pursuit of high-paying work and a piece of the immigrant's dream of stability and opportunity in a nation that prided itself on providing just that. Bangash talked about how Fort McMurray had for a long time seemed "like a place which is nothing," a cluster of work sites and quiet suburbs, long shifts giving way to dark frigid winter nights that seemed endless. Now they had cricket, and a pitch, and one another.

And this was just a start. Bangash had plans. One day there would be lights, better benches, bleachers. "This is going to be the number one cricket field in entire Canada," he said. That fall, at an Alberta-wide tournament in Red Deer, the Fort McMurray all-stars would dominate so thoroughly that the more established clubs from Edmonton and Calgary whispered of ringers in their midst. How could these guys come out of nowhere and be this good already? Who the hell played cricket in *Fort McMurray?*

The victory and the sense of building momentum for the sport carried them into the winter. Bangash taught cricket basics in an elementary school classroom to immigrant women and girls, many of whom had never been able to play the game in their home countries. Joseph spent his evenings working out at the Keyano College gym, staying in playing shape. The lonely guardhouse and the grinding twelve-hour shifts of motionless boredom were far in his bus's rear-view mirror now.

Across Fort McMurray, if you knew where to look, there were many scenes of a kind of gentle prosperity not generally associated with the term *boomtown*. There were soccer games and wooded paths filled with joggers and cyclists. There was a global village of cultural association celebrations, beloved karaoke nights, a fiddle band drawing Maritimers out to the Royal Canadian Legion Hall down in Waterways. The fresh-paved suburban streets were quiet and safe—Fort McMurray's rates for violent and property crime were not only below the Canadian average but also falling faster than average. All through June, in Kiran Malik-Khan's household and in many others around the city, families gathered in the evening to prepare for *iftar*, the nighttime breaking of the Ramadan fast. Meanwhile, somewhere high above rural Ontario one night later that summer, Nick Martell snoozed away on a flight bound for Fort McMurray, because for skilled labourers like him, there was still no better place in the country to ply their trade.

THE SITE AND THE TRAPLINE

Marvin L'Hommecourt sometimes worked evenings in 2015. Like anyone else working on an oil sands site, his life was dictated by the oft-changing rhythms of the Patch's binary work patterns. L'Hommecourt was a heavy equipment operator at Imperial Oil's Kearl Lake mine, and he'd been at it long enough that the pace felt familiar. Never quite natural, though. Maybe it doesn't feel that way to anyone, but in L'Hommecourt's case, he knew the land too well for too long to confuse driving an outsized Caterpillar bulldozer with anything naturally occurring in the boreal forest.

L'Hommecourt is the rare Patch worker who knew this land before it was his work site. He grew up in a tiny settlement along the Athabasca River called Poplar Point, halfway between Fort McMurray and Fort Chipewyan. He is Dene, a member of the Athabasca Chipewyan First Nation, and this land, from Fort McMurray north to the Peace-Athabasca Delta and up the Slave River to Great Slave Lake and beyond, is still Denendeh to his people, the ones who first named it. The only ones who knew it for centuries, generation after generation, until the Europeans came looking for fur and then the Canadian government came to make and break a treaty and the British Columbia government dammed the Peace River and the oil companies started digging for bitumen. After all that, nothing was the same ever again for the Dene.

You'll meet Indigenous people of Canada who describe their world as postapocalyptic, an alien and hostile place where a stable existence is pieced together, if at all, from the cultural rubble of a cataclysmic conquest. On the far side of two centuries of disruption and oppression on the Canadian prairie—massacred bison herds, the forced assimilation of the 1876 Indian Act and the reserve system, the horrors of the residential schools, and the ecological upheaval of an economy driven by lucrative resource extraction that steadily eroded every way the First Nations of the prairie and the boreal forest knew to live off their land—there is rarely any continuity for Indigenous people with their past, its culture and traditions, and the land that once sustained them.

L'Hommecourt doesn't talk about it that way. But he'd likely recognize the contours of the argument. He lives it every day up at Kearl, where he drives big bulldozers and maintains a traditional trapline just outside the site's perimeter. Kearl is majority owned and operated by Imperial (the Canadian arm of ExxonMobil), and it is among the newest oil sands mines—the first phase started producing oil in April 2013 and the second phase in June 2015, with total production of 220,000 barrels per day. Kearl is also one of the farthest north, deep in what used to be the bush, 130 kilometres from Fort McMurray up Highway 63 and down a long angled northeast access road through forest and muskeg.

L'Hommecourt works twelve-hour shifts at Kearl, ten days or more in a row, in keeping with the industry norm, and bunks at a work camp near the site. And when his stretch of work is done, he often flies back to Edmonton, picks up his truck at the airport, drives three hours home to Cold Lake to spend some time with his family, then drives all the way back to the woods near the Kearl site, 400 kilometres north, to maintain his trapline. He's building a cabin a bit farther upriver at Poplar Point, where he hopes to retire before too long, his retirement plan funded in part by his high-paying oil sands work.

Like all the Dene people, like all the Indigenous people in the region, L'Hommecourt had no say at all in the mine's development or the growth of the industry. He took what opportunities were on offer in order to get by. And now here he was in 2015, driving a bulldozer on Imperial's site, pushing aside thick layers of clay, sand and shale, known in the industry as "overburden," that those mammoth Cat 797s had trucked out of the open-pit mine to get to the bitumen-rich seam. Stacking the soil into neat layers, moving it out of the way to make room for pay dirt. Other times he used the big bulldozer to push oil sands ore onto heaps within reach of the giant shovels—contributing some small portion of the 2.4-million-barrel-a-day flow.

L'Hommecourt drove the big trucks for a time. He's been working in the industry since the mid-1990s, and he's done many different jobs on mine sites. Who would have thought it would lead him nearly all the way back to Poplar Point? It's a tiny stretch of land along the east bank of the Athabasca, not far north of the confluence with the Firebag River. To the Canadian government, it is Chipewyan Indian Reserve 201G, part of the lands granted to the Athabasca Chipewyan First Nation (ACFN) in Treaty 8 of 1899. But who knows how long the Dene have known it, how long it has been a summer gathering spot, a place for hunting and fishing camps? There is a Bureau of Mines report from 1892 noting summer gardens kept near the Dene village there.

L'Hommecourt was born at Poplar Point in 1954. He had a brother and seven sisters. His father built a cabin, one of a half-dozen or so, in

L'Hommecourt's recollection. They had a potato garden and a small ware-house that smelled of dog harnesses because they had a team of sled dogs. As a boy, L'Hommecourt trapped rabbits, and he went hunting with his family for moose and bison.

Like thousands of other Indigenous children, L'Hommecourt was forced at the age of seven to attend residential school, in his case downriver in Fort Chipewyan. "Prior to going to residential school, I didn't speak a word of English," he wrote in a 2009 provincial court affidavit supporting the ACFN's opposition to Shell's expansion of its Jackpine oil sands mine. "When I came out, I didn't speak a word of Dene." But he still spent his summers in Poplar Point, hunting and fishing, listening to his parents and elders talk, so he still retained some understanding of the Dene language.

The residential school only went as far as grade 9, so L'Hommecourt moved on to high school in St. Paul, more than 400 kilometres south. After graduation, he made his way to Calgary and found work repairing freight cars with CP Rail. But he kept coming back to Poplar Point, tried hard to never miss a summer there. In his 2009 affidavit, he compared his connection to the land to the better-known powwow rituals of First Nations on the prairie. "In my culture, we go hunting," L'Hommecourt wrote. "I eat what I kill and live off it, that's the spirituality."

He worked in Calgary for twenty years, until the mid-1990s, when he moved to Fort McMurray after his divorce. Around then, the two original oil sands companies, Suncor and Syncrude, had begun to pursue business partnerships with the First Nations in the region. The ACFN was launching the company that would eventually become Acden—a portmanteau of ACFN and Dene—a diversified oil-field services company with $300 million in annual revenues and an elegant headquarters in the industrial park just north of downtown Fort McMurray, certified gold under the Canadian Green Building Council's green building standards. L'Hommecourt's first job with Acden was hauling trash out of the sites in a pickup truck. In 2000 he applied for a job at Syncrude, and soon he was driving the biggest trucks on-site.

It was a solid job, but the scale and drama of it all didn't do much for

L'Hommecourt. "It's a big truck, but then everything's relative, right?" he says. "It's a big truck, big road, big shovel, big dump. And a big crusher to dump it into, dump the oil sand into."

He found the work tedious, driving an endlessly repeated route in a highly automated vehicle. He wanted nothing to do with operating the giant shovels, which was just as dull and didn't even involve the slight variation of the route back and forth from shovel to crusher. Driving a bulldozer had a bit more variety. Plus there was a vague sense of independence, which had been lacking behind the wheel of a haul truck, each of which is monitored constantly from a control centre on-site. "You stop for anything, they'll know," L'Hommecourt says. But the dozers are left on their own to sort out the loads of overburden the trucks bring. It certainly doesn't compare with the careful craft of skinning a moose in the bush, but there's at least a little creativity to maneouvring the dirt into neat stacks—"lifts," he calls them—three metres high using a bulldozer scoop that could toss bison around by the half-dozen.

Years ago, when L'Hommecourt was working down in Calgary, his mother acquired a trapline. This is a license to trap game along a trail a hundred kilometres long or more in the Alberta bush. The L'Hommecourt trapline is strung through terrain near the headwaters of the Muskeg River, a pretty, narrow stream that meets the Athabasca just north of the First Nations settlement of Fort McKay, where L'Hommecourt's mother grew up. She and her family trapped lynx, beaver, marten, fisher and otter there for years. When his mother got too old to maintain it in the late 1990s, Marvin took it over. During the years after 2000 when he was driving haul trucks and other massive machines for Syncrude, the trapline was a vital escape from the noise and bustle of the mine site and Fort McMurray, where he rented an apartment. L'Hommecourt worked six-and-six shifts in those days, and he would spend his six days off in the bush, either at Poplar Point hunting in summer or out in his cabin on the trapline in winter.

By the time L'Hommecourt filed his affidavit in 2009, however, the peaceful solitude of the place was long gone. A half-dozen oil companies were developing leases along the Muskeg River. To get to his cabin,

L'Hommecourt had to clear a security post at the new Imperial Kearl site. There was a work camp on the site so close by that the workers sometimes snuck out to his cabin to drink because the camp was a dry one. "There's an airport right on the border of my trapline," he wrote, by which he meant the aerodrome for the new Shell Albian Sands site. "There's been forest activity and road building. There are cut lines and drilling all over. You can't swing a frozen rabbit without hitting them."

Fewer and fewer animals came to the forest where he set his traps. "I'm angry," he wrote. "I want to protect my trapline." But when the oil companies came to see him with maps of their leases, they told him they were obligated only to *inform* him of their plans. The trapline license was merely a permission to catch what wildlife passed by; he didn't have the right to deny an oil company its development permit. His oasis lost, L'Hommecourt pleaded in his affidavit to keep oil sands development away from Poplar Point. "It is very important for me to be able to go hunt in that area. If I don't do it, I'll go crazy. It's good to be on the land, that's where the spirit is."

Practicalities intruded on Marvin L'Hommecourt's loftier goals for the land, as they do for anyone. There was never enough money in trapping to make a living at it, and buyers were paying less for lynx and marten pelts every year. Greeks and Russians still wanted those furs, but they had their own money woes. He took the job at Kearl because he could live rent-free at a camp, freeing himself from Fort McMurray's exorbitant rental market. With the money saved, L'Hommecourt bought a house in Cold Lake, where his family has settled. And on many evenings in 2015, he was out at the site, driving a dozer on a twelve-hour shift in the dark, starry boreal night, pushing aside overburden so that bitumen could be mined from the forest surrounding his trapline.

"I don't feel very good about doing that," he says. "But a guy's got to make a living, right?"

To get to his trapline in winter, L'Hommecourt parks his truck at a relative's place in Fort McKay and drives in by snowmobile. He skirts the perimeter of the Kearl site along the way, passing through a "laydown" area outside the site gates—a broad cleared space where oil sands mining equipment is set aside when it's not needed. In winter the shuttle buses are parked there with their motors running all day and night to keep the engines from freezing. L'Hommecourt is thus often obliged to traverse the laydown through the stinging brown fog of exhaust to get to the trail leading to his cabin. There he finds some solace, if not near as much quiet as the place once promised. And if he's lucky, he might still find an animal or two out on his trapline.

Once, a few years back, Imperial was building a bridge over the Muskeg River on the Kearl site. Beavers had built a dam nearby, and it was interfering with construction. The company decided the easiest way to deal with the situation was to trap the beavers, so it contacted Alberta Fish and Wildlife to see who held the trapline license on that stretch of the Muskeg. It turned out to be a heavy equipment operator Imperial already employed, so someone there gave L'Hommecourt a call, and he took a few days off from moving overburden to go down with his traps and clear out the beavers. Because the work was on site, he was accompanied by a security guard and an environmental representative from Imperial and had to follow the company's strict safety guidelines.

"That was the first time I ever went trapping with a life jacket, a hard hat and steel-toed boots," he says. He set four traps and caught the beavers who had built the dam within a few days.

Word of L'Hommecourt's expertise spread among the oil sands companies operating in the region. Since then, he gets an occasional call to help with a beaver lodge or dam getting in the way of someone's operations.

"That's a pretty good job, I think," he says, "so I might do that when I'm all done."

Like countless generations of Dene before him, L'Hommecourt had grown up learning a set of skills to survive sustainably off the land deep in the boreal forest. Those skills had led to contract work in the oil sands industry. He was far from pleased about it, but there wasn't much else to be done along the Muskeg River. "The encroachment is beyond repair now," he reflects. "I mean, we can't put anything back."

Even in the economic doldrums of 2015, the Patch continued to expand northward. There were fewer beds full each night in the work camps along the Muskeg River, but Suncor's Fort Hills mine, downstream from the confluence of the Muskeg and Athabasca toward Poplar Point, remained under construction. L'Hommecourt knew that stretch of the Athabasca north from Fort McKay toward Fort Chipewyan. He knew it as well as someone else might know the street plan of his suburban development. Boating north from Fort McKay on the Athabasca, you passed Shell's Muskeg River mine, and then, after a stretch, there was Fort Hills on your right. Beyond that, the landscape returned to wild forest, and the river might seem to have returned to what it had always been if you didn't know the difference between what a whitefish pulled from the Athabasca tasted like at Poplar Point in the 1960s and what it tastes like today. (L'Hommecourt doesn't eat those fish anymore, doesn't trust them.)

The next major confluence was the Firebag River, but the comparatively small footprint of Cenovus's SAGD operation was far up that tributary from the banks of the Athabasca. Still, a mining company called Teck Resources had a lease to the land on the west bank of the Athabasca right around the Firebag confluence, and in 2015 it was carrying on with the necessary steps of an oil sands mine application: gathering data, producing thick reports, and sending teams of employees to meet and consult with the Indigenous people downstream in Fort Chipewyan. Many of the people there saw the Firebag confluence as the limit of their tolerance for an industrial sprawl they feared had ruined enough of their traplines and hunting grounds and sacred waters already.

On a consultant's map, the proposed new mine site stretched north in parallel to the river until its farthest downstream boundary was all but directly across the river from Poplar Point. This was well beyond L'Hommecourt's personal threshold. There are fifty-seven paragraphs in his 2009 affidavit, and the last one reads: "My grandfather would turn over in his grave if he knew they were developing around Poplar Point. My grandfather would want his kids and grandkids to follow in his footsteps. That's what our culture is all about."

CRIME SCENES

At twilight, dark shadows fall over the Patch. They stretch outward from the city of Fort McMurray in concentric rings until from some angles they appear to encompass the whole earth. There is the city itself, its breakneck growth and the cost of it. The industry, its outsized environmental footprint, the effluent that seeps from tailings ponds, the pollution that blows out an oil sands plant's smokestacks to settle on the land and water all around. Alberta's economy, the whole Canadian economy, the revenues and royalties from millions of barrels of oil. The companies and work sites built on investments made in Toronto or Montreal that employ labourers trained in Prince George, British Columbia, or in Glace Bay, Nova Scotia. Global flows of capital from oil company headquarters and watchful bankers the world over during a long global resource boom that may or may not be ending. The greenhouse gas emissions climbing only higher, all the energy burned to dig the bitumen from the ground and make it into crude, clouds of carbon dioxide adding ton by ton to the ongoing global catastrophe of climate change.

Is this progress? The grand High Modern project begun under a makeshift bubble tent as the Great Canadian Oil Sands in 1967 is a roaring success by the only definition known to everyone who was there that day. But it has come at a significant price to land, water, animals and people, a cost tallied by varying measures over the years and understood to be far too high by those who now articulate a competing definition of progress. Those who subscribe to this competing view tabulate environmental costs not only uncounted but totally unconsidered at the project's launch. They delineate social costs that expand in lockstep with the scale of the Patch itself. And they ultimately assess hydrocarbons as a fuel source of the past and emissions reduction as the sine qua non of any sustainable definition of progress in the twenty-first century.

But however the Patch's value is assayed, the oil still flows in shadow and in darkness, mined and separated and upgraded and refined and pumped twenty-four hours a day, 2.4 million barrels and growing.

On the darkened streets of Fort McMurray in 2015, the immediate local costs were easily identified and largely understood to be well worth paying—not to mention considerably less than the estimates made by many people who'd never spent any time on a Fort McMurray street. No one is trying to pretend there is no downside. Anywhere money is made quickly, you'll find a certain amount of reckless living. Drugs and gambling are readily available up and down Franklin Avenue downtown. Cocaine is particularly prevalent and has been linked with prostitution in the popular image of hard-partying Fort McMurray. A 2011 *Edmonton Sun* headline labelled Fort McMurray the province's "drug, hooker capital." Young professional men will sometimes confess offhandedly to a routine not often spoken about in such casual terms elsewhere: that some nights, after the mock-gladiatorial scene in the city's bars and clubs, they call one of the city's many escort services. And yes, there are perhaps more of those services than the national average.

Debt flows as freely as any other vice in Fort McMurray. The oil sands industry's outsized salaries fuel an inflated housing market, big mortgages and generous lines of credit used to fill driveways with big trucks, huge RVs, and quads and snowmobiles. To work such crazy hours in a place so remote, who could blame someone pulling down the city's generous median salary of $170,000 a year for blowing off some steam with any or all of the above?

The city's frenetic culture spawns real dangers. The province has finally completed the twinning of Highway 63 between Fort McMurray and its intersection with Highway 55 some 240 kilometres south, but in the meantime, the dangerous mix of large industrial vehicles and trucks full of oil sands workers racing south to Edmonton at the end of many long working days on end earned the road an ugly nickname: "Highway of Death."

A boomtown attracts mythic detail with the same careless, random force it draws people, money and resources. Isolated events get blown up into symbols, linked to other isolated events to form trends, all of it amplified by the expanding boom. Fort McMurray was the epicentre of the longest and most emphatic resource boom in the modern history of Canada, and its sins and missteps became glittering layers of detail on the myth. The Highway of Death was one of those, a concise metaphor for the speed and recklessness of the city and its core industry. Traffic had increased rapidly on Highway 63, and accidents and collisions had a headline-making tendency toward extremes of speed and drunkenness and carnage. Dozens of lives were lost needlessly each year. One particularly awful crash in 2012 killed seven people, including a child, adding urgency to an organized campaign called the Coalition for a Safer 63 & 881. (For years, the public had been demanding that the two treacherous opposing lanes be turned into four, separated by a median.) There was little evidence, however, that Highway 63 was a singularly dangerous highway. The five years before the horrendous 2012 accident saw 82 collisions per 100 million vehicle kilometres on the highway, compared with all of Alberta's average of 107 collisions per 100 million for the same kind of two-lane highway.

The local mythology of sin and vice in Fort McMurray was similarly overamped. Visitors expecting a northern frontier town's version of the Vegas strip or Amsterdam's red light district squinted at the Boomtown Casino and the couple of strip clubs along Franklin Avenue and decided that was close enough. And for a time in the first full flush of the boom, circa 2006, the lurid snapshots of a Klondike on the Athabasca were all too easy to take. As a visitor, you never saw a Newfoundlander electrician and his family gathered quietly in their suburban living room or a half-dozen young South Asians sleeping off night shifts in a cramped condo bedroom. But the drug dealers and sex workers plying their trade from the parking lot of the 7-Eleven at the corner of Franklin and Main were like a boomtown billboard, far more brazen in their enticements than the Canadian norm.

When Fort McMurray landed on *Maclean's* magazine's ranking of Canada's "Ten Most Dangerous Cities" in 2010, sitting in the No. 5 spot, it seemed to confirm something about the city's place in the national psyche in a way that leafy Victoria ranking second did not. Fort McMurray was an exotic thing, outside of regular Canadian life, a wellspring of easy money and rumours of hard living, a source of constant political and environmental controversy. Press stories about crime and misfortune there resonated nationally, even internationally. They seemed to confirm something in an ethical or karmic sense. No boom came without grave consequences, no fortune was made without the loss of some vital part of one's soul.

This was a skewed narrative at least as old as the Klondike gold rush, whose fables were mostly unfounded as well. The Klondike's law-abiding reality of hardscrabble survival under the watchful eyes of the North-West Mounted Police exploded into a rollicking myth of fast fortunes and lawless chaos once it was rewritten by American fabulists for movie and TV screens. Even Robert Service, poet laureate of the Klondike, never set foot in Dawson City until a decade after the gold rush was over, and his beloved rhyming yarns of gunplay at the Malamute Saloon cribbed liberally from fables of the California gold rush—in reality, the Mounties had banned firearms from the streets and taverns of Dawson City.

In Fort McMurray, the sensational headlines were often true in a limited sense. Fast oil money did attract purveyors of illicit goods and services, and the Mounties sometimes got their man on Franklin Avenue. Over the years, members of the Hell's Angels, the Mexican drug cartel La Familia, and various Somali gangs were all arrested on drug and violent crime charges with direct connections to Fort McMurray. There is a handful of midrise apartment complexes scattered across the north end of downtown—just off Franklin and not far from the knot of raucous nightlife hotspots like the Oil Can Tavern and Boomtown Casino and that infamous 7-Eleven parking lot—and guns and drugs and even dead bodies had a habit of turning up in one or the other with what seemed like epidemic frequency. A 2012 story in the *Globe and Mail* described "a cocaine-dusted corridor" running from the Somali community in the social housing projects of metro Toronto to those Fort McMurray apartments. More than five hundred Somalis had settled in Fort McMurray by then, and dozens of young Somali men had been killed there and elsewhere in Alberta since 2005. A side note to the notorious crack-smoking scandal of Toronto mayor Rob Ford involved a twenty-five-year-old Somali man who fell six storeys from a Fort McMurray balcony one night in June 2013. The balcony happened to be in the same apartment where police arrested another young Somali who had initially been accused of killing one of the men who appeared in a photo with Ford on the night the video of his crack use was filmed. Scan a few headlines—"Somali man from Toronto killed in Alberta city," "Fort Mac 'drug, hooker capital'"—and it appeared to confirm impressions that big-city crime had descended on a lawless boomtown.

But the data, parsed right, told a more complex story. Responding in part to a spate of high-profile international press that lingered on the lurid details, Fort McMurray's municipal government commissioned its own crime study, conducted at arm's length by criminologist Neil Boyd of Simon Fraser University and published in March 2014. His findings differed sharply from those of Statistics Canada, *Maclean's* and the reporters who bounced in from Britain for a few days to add sensational detail to lurid features. Boyd's primary insight was to calculate per capita crime rates using municipal census data, which, unlike Statistics Canada, counted the city's substantial shadow population of 40,000-plus alongside its permanent resident population. Once Fort McMurray was studied as a city of 120,000, the case for a boom-fuelled crime wave mostly fell apart. Boyd did find ample evidence of the cocaine-dusted part of the tale—the rate of cocaine-related arrests in Fort McMurray was four times the Canadian average. Vehicle thefts in the city were also elevated, nearly twice the national norm. Beyond these two data points, though, Fort McMurray was actually less prone to crime than the rest of Canada, a country in which crime of all sorts—and violent crime in particular—had been declining since the early 1990s and continued to do so as Fort McMurray boomed. The rates of arrest for prostitution and marijuana possession were similar to the rest of the country. Rates for sexual assault and robbery were well below average. Overall, the crime rate in Fort McMurray *decreased* by 44 percent from 2003 to 2012 (it declined nationally by 17 percent over the same period). Largely due to the prevalence of cocaine use, there had been some highly visible incidents of gang-related violence that felt alien and shocking in a city that had been a quiet company town in the woods where everyone seemed to know everyone as recently as the late 1990s. As in the Klondike before it, however, the image of felonious chaos was mostly invented.

Perhaps the rumours of criminal mayhem spread because they gave form to a pervasive unease that lurked in the shadows of the Patch. The sudden wealth, the dramatic shift in power and influence from central Canada to Alberta that came with it, the sheer shocking girth of an oil sands mine—surely there had to be some direct and dire cost to all this. And of course there was, and is. But it is mostly unseen, a smell in the air, the slurry of strange chemicals in the tailings ponds leaching into the groundwater, the clouds of exhaust from upgrader stacks and SAGD boilers causing a slow, steady uptick in carbon dioxide levels in the earth's atmosphere. But here, too, the data sets and fine details have told a story much more complex than the myth of the Patch as "the most destructive project on earth," as the title of a 2008 report published by the Canadian environmental group Environmental Defence phrased it.

Not even the most intransigent of bitumen boosters or the most glib of corporate spokespeople would argue that an oil sands project has no impact at all on the immediate landscape. Some damage has always been self-evident and readily acknowledged, if not always considered a high priority. For the first two oil sands projects—GCOS, which began operating in 1967, and Syncrude, which launched in 1978—the environmental concerns at the industry's birth were those that were the most prevalent at the time. They were local, easily observable, and understood as limited technical problems to be solved over time, alongside measures to minimize damage and avoid disaster in the near term. GCOS operated for four years, after all, before the federal and Alberta governments even appointed their first environment ministers.

"At that time, water and air were free," Clem Bowman, Syncrude's first research director, explained. "So it didn't matter how much water you used; there was no cost associated with it. And the upgrading of the oil, it didn't matter how much carbon dioxide was put off." Still, by the mid-1970s, a handful of environmental issues had begun to emerge, in particular the flaring of "sour gas" (natural gas high in hydrogen sulphide) and sulphur dioxide emissions, both by-products of the bitumen separation and upgrading process. By the time of the next wave of oil sands expansion in the mid-1990s, new technology had reduced both by more than 75 percent.

The most significant environmental issue arising from the first oil sands mines was a messier and more complex problem, one that has continued to trouble engineers and blacken the industry's image well into the twenty-first century. This is the conundrum of the tailings ponds. The necessity of storing and treating mine tailings was well understood from the first days at GCOS. That mine's original tailings pond, an enormous earthen dike on the shore of the Athabasca River, was modelled on similar facilities built for copper mines of the time. The trace amounts of oil, the site's managers assumed, would rise to the surface, where they could be skimmed off. The sand and clay would settle to the bottom of the pond, leaving water that could be treated for contaminants and pumped back into the river, the same as municipal sewage. And then the remaining sand and clay could be trucked away for remediation. The only real concern, in those early days, was to make sure the dike was well constructed, that the great earthen berm would hold strong during the settling process, that it wouldn't give way and spill millions of gallons of toxic tailings fluid into the river. But that was a question answered easily by engineers. Mines the world over managed their tailings this way. Why would bitumen be any different?

The answer, in essence, is a subset of the whole oil sands conundrum. Why had it taken a century to turn this vast oil deposit into a viable commodity? Why was a bitumen mine and processing plant so much more elaborate and complex than a conventional oil well? Because oil sands ore was a stubborn substance, a chemical riddle, sticky in more ways than one. And in time, chemical engineers at both GCOS and Syncrude would be obliged to acknowledge that they'd greatly underestimated the challenge presented by oil sands tailings. This was no simple separation of metal and dirt as transpired at a copper mine. This was, it turned out, one of the most persistent waste problems in the annals of industrial engineering.

The waste stream pumped into tailings ponds at an oil sands mine is often referred to as a slurry, but it is more precisely a colloidal suspension, built on a bond between clay and water that formed over thousands of years and is not easily broken. Colloidal suspensions are a common phenomenon consisting of a solid suspended permanently in a liquid but not dissolved in it. Yogurt, for example, is a colloidal suspension, as well as a demonstration that the "permanence" of such chemical combinations is a relative term. Think of a tub of yogurt left for weeks in the back of a fridge, the liquid beginning to rise to the top as it separates from the milk solids. In conventional mining, this is what happens in a tailings pond. The slurry left over after extracting the pay dirt from the ore is a mix of sand, dirt and clay suspended in the water used in the separation process, and that slurry is held in a settling pond until the solids drop out of the liquid.

Oil sands ore is a sticky mix of sand, bitumen and clay. Over the millennia of its formation, it has developed a common structure in which the sand particles are surrounded by a thin layer of water, which then separates the hydrophobic bitumen from the sand. That water envelope around the sand grains—the "water wetness" of the sand—is vital to the emergence of the oil sands as a profitable business. The hot water used to separate sand from oil exploits the weakness in the mix, prying the two substances apart and washing away everything but the bitumen. But the water envelope in oil sands ore is pregnant with very fine clay particles, a mix of minerals with obscure names like smectite and kaolinite.

GCOS designed its first oil sands mine under the assumption that bitumen tailings would behave like any other tailings. Based on experience in other industries, the overseers of GCOS assumed the tailings pumped into the pond would settle in three years or so. After a year or two, however, there was little in the way of settling out. Instead, the middle layer of the pond was consolidating into a seemingly stable goo, consisting of between 15 percent and 30 percent clay particles and other solids by mass, suspended in water. When oil sands workers described the stuff, they often compared it to the common colloidal suspension it resembled most in density, texture and viscosity: yogurt. And new tailings continued to flow into that first tailings pond at an alarming rate. The earthen berm erected to hold back the tailings, originally built to a height of twelve metres, grew and grew, eventually rising to a hundred metres. As oil sands projects expanded, second and third and fourth tailings ponds would be added to each site. The Mildred Lake Settling Basin at Syncrude's first mine site eventually became, by volume, one of the largest dams on earth. And still the colloidal suspension endured.

In time, the engineers tasked with cracking the oil sands tailings riddle assigned the goo a name—"mature fine tailings" or "fluid fine tailings," often shortened simply to "fines"—and spent years trying to figure out how to make it settle out more eagerly, to consolidate beneath the water layer into a solid that could be dealt with in some final sense. A sample of fines studied at the University of Alberta in Edmonton showed "no consolidation whatsoever" after more than twenty-five years.

In 1973 GCOS hired a chemical engineer named Bill Cary to "solve the tailings problem," as he put it. "What we found," Cary said, "was that this clay layer formed a material like yogurt—about fifteen percent solids, eighty-five percent water. And we showed that it would not settle for, they were talking a thousand years." Beyond a density by mass of 30 percent, the consolidation slowed to a crawl of almost geological timeframe. And in the meantime, the ponds grew and begat new ponds, and they sparkled in the northern sun like lakes. There would eventually be nearly a billion cubic metres of fines beneath the surface of those ponds, converting from colloidal suspension to fluid and solid with agonizing sluggishness. And one April day in 2008, just after a spring blizzard, those 1,600 ducks landed on one of Syncrude's tailings ponds, and the maddening chemical engineering problem the industry had been wrestling with for more than thirty years became its lethal global calling card.

Oil sands tailings, to be clear, are not singularly toxic. Mercury, lead and other toxic chemicals are present in an oil sands tailings pond—all of them found in bitumen ore itself—but consolidating, treating and disposing of such substances is an everyday task in the mining business. There is nastier stuff in the runoff from a copper or gold mine. What oil sands tailings are is singularly persistent. The Mildred Lake Settling Basin is wonder-of-the-world scale because it was built to contain so many years' worth of tailings, not because there are more or uglier chemicals flowing into it. Those unfortunate ducks, after all, were killed by the mats of bitumen on the pond's surface, not the mature fine tailings. But the tenacity of the problem, its unwillingness to simplify, to give the poor engineers a break or yield to a shortcut—it's an apt symbol of the whole industry, really, not just its environmental footprint. It's the resource's original conundrum of abrasive sand unwilling to yield its prize, rewritten as a chemistry problem. And for much of the industry's life, it was the Patch's defining environmental problem as well.

Engineers and chemists have been grinding away at the tailings mess for decades. In corporate R&D departments and in university labs, they've experimented with all manner of additives and processes to accelerate the speed at which the ancient clays will drop out of the water. In the early 1990s, Suncor engineers working to reduce air pollution at their plant discovered that a by-product of their new sulphur dioxide recovery technology—calcium sulfate—could be added to tailings ponds to speed up the process. More recently, Syncrude and Shell have been working with centrifuge technology to accelerate the separation and drying of its fines. CNRL has developed a drying process combining a water separator called a cyclone with chemical thickeners. In 2009, in the wake of the Syncrude duck disaster, the Alberta government enacted a package of more stringent regulations for tailings ponds, referred to by its ominous bureaucratic title, Directive 74. The new directive set hard volume targets

for diverting fines from the waste stream at the processing site and established a timeline for drying and storing the remaining fines. Thirteen of the largest companies in the oil sands, meanwhile, formed a research and development partnership called Canada's Oil Sands Innovation Alliance (COSIA) in 2012 to share technological breakthroughs on all of the industry's most pressing environmental concerns, including tailings.

Perhaps the greatest progress on the tailings conundrum has been made at Suncor. From certain flattering angles, the company has even been willing to claim it has figured out the reclamation strategy that might well lick the problem for good. In 2003, Suncor's engineers began working on developing an artificial additive called a polymer flocculant, a chemical designed to dry out its fines to the point where they form a solid cake durable enough to be trucked away to a long-term containment site. While the technology was still in development, Suncor decommissioned its original tailings pond—the one contained by the hundred-metre-tall dike that first started filling with tailings back in 1967, now known as Pond 1—and launched the industry's first-ever full-scale reclamation of a tailings pond. By 2007, the pond's fines had consolidated just far enough beyond the yogurt stage into a substance comparable texturally to Jell-O that they were able to be pumped away to another part of the mine site for long-term storage—and, the company hoped, eventual treatment with the newfangled polymer flocculant its R&D department continued to develop.

As the fines were being cleared away, thousands of tons of sand from the company's tailings were trucked in to form a solid base and then covered with soil salvaged from overburden excavations on the site. A total of 220 hectares was ready for rehabilitation. Suncor's reclamation engineers formed the soil into hillocks and swales in rough imitation of the natural boreal landscape. In the spring of 2010, a volunteer force of Suncor employees planted 600,000 trees and shrubs, more than 40 native species in all. Reclamation experts filled in the terrain with oats and barley as a "nurse crop" for the tree seedlings. In consultation with local Indigenous experts, Suncor studded the site with tree trunks planted upside down, their old root bulbs providing roosting places for raptors and other birds.

"Mother Nature is going to move back in here," a Suncor engineer insisted in a company video produced in the fall of 2010. The site already looked parklike, and a time-lapse sequence of photos and simulations from 2007 to 2025 depicted a site transformed from toxic tailings and bare dirt to functional wetlands. Everyone understood you couldn't build boreal forest from scratch, that natural processes needed thousands of years to create that lush, diverse landscape. But Suncor's process has yielded a living ecosystem, perhaps even the embryo of a future forest.

By 2015, Suncor had rechristened the site Wapisiw Lookout. Wildlife had begun to visit uninvited, and the project had become part of the company's standard bus tour, a point of beaming pride. Behold a newborn wetland, where not even ten years before, passing ducks would have been in danger of losing their lives if they'd dared to alight in such a malignant place. Man not only develops his world, he *redevelops* it. Rejuvenates it! Creates new life from nothing, from dirty water and mature fine tailings!

That June, the tour guides had to warn visitors to keep an eye out for a black bear that had come roaming through recently in search of late-spring forage. Reclamation had begun by then at another tailings pond, Pond 5, and the engineering team expected to be able to use its polymer flocculant on the fines to accelerate the whole decommissioning process. Sustainability managers and COSIA reps in the industry reckoned that it was only a matter of time before comparatively fast, efficient tailings consolidation and land reclamation was a routine part of an oil sands operation. Executives told crowds at conferences straight-faced that in a hundred years, no one would know there had been a tailings pond or mammoth open-pit mine out there in the woods. Sure, Suncor hadn't met a single one of its tailings targets under Directive 74—no company had—but it was a misguided regulation, designed poorly and in the haste of an emergency PR campaign aimed at erasing the memory of those bitumen-caked ducks. But the larger problem, the long-term solution? The engineers were on it.

The march of progress was sometimes slow but always steady. If the problem wasn't completely solved, it was *solvable*. Put the engineers to work on the right task, and they found a way. What to do about mature fine

tailings? Take a tour bus out to Suncor base site any given day in 2015 and count the birds at Wapisiw Lookout. There's your answer. And if mature fine tailings could be solved? If the most intractable of oil sands messes — this thousand-year yogurty goo that had obliged the construction of some of the largest dams on earth — if that could be solved? Then whatever you might have heard, the industry just knew it was ready for the twenty-first century.

EIGHT

BOOM AND BUST

THE HAUL TRUCK STRUT

In the spring of 2006, the boom in the Patch was fast approaching its peak. Capital investment had raced past the $25-billion mark three years earlier, around the same time the US Department of Energy decided to start counting oil sands reserves as identical to any other proven reserve in its global energy accounting. The reclassification boosted Canadian reserves from 5 billion barrels to 180 billion—third in the world—and provided a massive boost to investor confidence in the Patch. There were soon dozens of companies invested in oil sands development, and new projects were being announced or coming online seemingly every other week. Overall production had grown to more than 1 million barrels a day by 2006, and industry estimates were forecasting 3.5 million barrels by 2015 and more than 4 million by 2020. Delirious boosters sometimes spoke of 8 million or more one day—enough to rival Saudi Arabia for the global production lead. There was no longer much hyperbole in that old "blue-eyed sheik" moniker from the Lougheed days. The muskeg of northwestern Canada was the new Arabian Desert. Alberta was an emerging energy superpower, and the impossibly vast hydrocarbon treasure of the oil sands was its engine. No one had ever seen a boom so explosive.

From 2001 to 2006, nearly half a million Canadians had moved to Alberta from other provinces. In 2006 Alberta's employment rolls were adding new jobs at a fevered clip of ten thousand a month. In Fort Mc-Murray, the newly employed were living in campers in hotel parking lots, renting out backyard toolsheds, and sleeping in tent villages on the outskirts of town. Half of Calgary's swelling homeless population of 3,400 had jobs but nowhere to live. And managing it all with delight from the provincial legislature was Premier Ralph Klein. "King Ralph," they sometimes called him—the blunt, smirking latter-day Calgary cowboy who'd slashed the province's budget, rebooted the oil sands business, and turned deficits into surpluses. Alberta voters had rewarded Klein with his fourth majority in 2004, and he repaid the favour at the start of 2006 by mailing a government cheque in the amount of $400 to every single resident in the province—a "Prosperity Bonus" to remind everyone just how glorious the good times were in Alberta just now.

And so late that spring, when Klein's government received word from Washington that Alberta was being invited to participate in the Smithsonian Institution's upcoming Folklife Festival on the National Mall, it jumped at the chance. The Folklife Festival was a summer tradition in America's capital, an outdoor display of cultural artifacts and pastimes from around the world in the broad green space between the Capitol Building and the Washington Monument. The invitation had initially gone to the federal government, but the feds had passed on it. Well, if they didn't want to strut their stuff in DC, Ralph Klein's Alberta happily would. His government made plans to send dancers and ice skaters and Mounties, plus cooks to make batches of the pierogies so beloved by Alberta's Ukrainian immigrant community. And then someone—it might have been Murray Smith, the Alberta government's liaison at the Canadian embassy in Washington—suggested a haul truck. How could you celebrate Alberta, after all, without a major nod to its energy industries? And what better way to make a statement about booming Alberta today than with a gesture as broad and blunt as a Ralph Klein rebuttal in the legislature? It would even be a sharp nudge to the ribs of any US lawmakers who may have forgotten just who supplied the United States with the largest share of its oil imports.

When the Folklife Festival opened on June 30, 2006, there it was, parked across the lawn from the stately Capitol: a Caterpillar 777F haul truck, its signature bright-yellow shell and two-hundred-ton dump bed gleaming in the Washington sun. It stood there for two weeks, a behemoth looming over an old-timey Alberta chuckwagon and pierogy cooks and the Native American basket makers and Latin dancers from Chicago that other participants had brought to the festival. Klein himself flew down with half his cabinet to launch the exhibit, bringing his Alberta swagger right to the steps of the Capitol, but he barely needed to bother. There was no missing it. One of the world's largest dump trucks inevitably became a focal point.

"It was a tremendous opportunity," recalled Ed Stelmach, who succeeded Klein as premier later that year. As Klein's intergovernmental affairs minister at the time, Stelmach was intimately involved in the festival display. "And I think also others started to pay attention to Alberta, because it was a huge volume of oil, okay? And you didn't have to drill very deep. You know where it is. And so when they heard it's billions of barrels, all of a sudden it got worldwide attention."

A tricky thing about publicity, though, is that it is a chaotic force. It can veer off in unexpected directions and arrive in places far distant from the intended destination, freighted with meaning never anticipated by the people who conceived it. The message the haul truck sent was clear as a prairie sky to an Alberta cabinet minister, bold and unambiguous and true: Alberta is a major force in the oil business now, playing with the very biggest toys. We're open for business, ready to deliver our American neighbours all the safe and secure oil supplies they need. Drop your jaw in amazement—and then join us in this grand project.

This was not how the message was received in some DC precincts, however. In the offices of the Natural Resources Defense Council, for example, it was seen as an affront to the work they were doing and as an insult to the spirit of the festival. The scale of Alberta's oil sands business— and its outsized environmental footprint—had just begun to register on the outside edge of the radar of the American environmental movement, and the haul truck on the Mall served as a jolt that King Ralph's crew never anticipated. The NRDC's Susan Casey-Lefkowitz, then in charge of its Canadian campaigns, told the *National Post* newspaper years later, "It was a pivotal moment. When you bring a tar sands dump truck to the National Mall in Washington, DC, it was like bringing the tar sands into our backyard. For the environmental groups in DC, it was a moment of it sort of being 'They've brought this fight to us.'"

Casey-Lefkowitz spent her frequent festival visits handing out fact sheets on the environmental impact of oil sands production, and the NRDC distributed a scathing press release under the headline "Alberta Tar Sands Feed U.S. Addiction to Oil." But these were small gestures of no real consequence compared with the towering presence of the truck itself. Klein and his crew returned home and swaggered on in the boom's electric glow, the most dizzying ascents in the price of oil still ahead of them. For anyone who read it, however, the press release was an advance guide to the general thrust of the critique that would soon descend on the Patch. The release noted that the oil sands deposits covered an area "larger than the state of Florida" and transformed wilderness "into wastelands." It also claimed that oil sands production created two and a half times as great a volume of greenhouse gases as conventional oil did and had become "Canada's fastest growing contribution to global warming."

Casey-Lefkowitz's pamphleteering and the NRDC press release— these were portents, the first stirrings of a much larger and more direct challenge to the runaway growth of the Patch. And that emerging challenge would turn the very details the big yellow haul truck bragged about against the industry: its awesome scale and engineering might, its rapid growth, its sheer bigness extending beyond truck tires and dump beds to toxic tailings and clouds of carbon dioxide. Two years later, when Ed Stelmach returned to Washington as premier, there would be protesters and placards decrying Alberta's "dirty oil." And not long after that, the NRDC and much of its Washington cohort would join in the movement to make a single bitumen-filled pipeline the front line in a global war against fossil fuels.

BOOSTERS, BACKERS AND PITCHMEN

In Washington, DC, the oil sands seemed like a recent and troubling development, a freakish outgrowth of the skyrocketing price of oil. Back in the Patch, though, it was a dream fulfilled after decades of failed promises and stalled developments. The industry had nearly collapsed completely on so many occasions that when the boom finally arrived, it was celebrated like the payout on a desperate maverick's final long shot bet. Even after GCOS had started pumping out oil at commercial scale, the Patch struggled to find stable footing for another thirty years. And it was only the repeated interventions of a series of champions in the halls of government as well as the executive suites that kept it standing.

The first years after GCOS had staged its grand launch in 1967 had not been kind to the embryonic industry. The new plant was plagued by power failures and equipment seizures in the freezing winter, and sticky, abrasive bitumen wreaked havoc over every inch of the production process. The plant officially produced 45,000 barrels per day, but its operators were discovering the aspirational nature of that target the hard way. GCOS lost $37 million in its first three years of operation and $90 million in its first seven.

"It was costing hundreds of millions of dollars to modify and debottleneck," said George Skulsky, one of the first technicians hired to operate the GCOS plant. "And Sun Oil was throwing money down a well. You couldn't hear it splash. This went on for years. They came so close.

People do not realize how close GCOS came to shutting the plant down totally."

But even as GCOS was barely hanging on, a second consortium marched toward commissioning another commercial-scale oil sands mine. The new partnership, led by Imperial Oil, had christened itself Syncrude and had been pursuing approval for its first project since the mid-1960s. Government sanction finally arrived in 1971, and site planning and preparation began to slowly ramp up. By 1973, the project had gained sufficient urgency that the premier, Peter Lougheed, appeared live on primetime TV across the province to announce that his government and the Syncrude consortium had reached a final deal for the project. When OPEC announced an embargo on oil sales to the United States and Canada as part of its response to American support for Israel in the Yom Kippur War mere weeks later, the timing of the deal seemed prescient. With oil prices soaring and supplies now under political threat, the urgency around the project intensified week by week.

Construction finally began that winter, and by early 1974 Syncrude's Mildred Lake site bustled with 1,500 construction workers. But the deal remained tentative as cost estimates grew beyond the initial $1.5 billion to $2 billion or more and the federal government's new budget arrived with punitive new taxes for oil and gas exports. Then, in the first week of December, one of the Syncrude partners, Atlantic Richfield, summarily quit the consortium, leaving a 30 percent hole in its financing.

A mad scramble ensued in search of a solution. Phone calls pinged back and forth between government officials in Edmonton and Ottawa. Finally, on the morning of February 3, 1975, executives from the Syncrude partner companies and cabinet ministers from the Alberta, Ontario and federal governments met without fanfare and outside the media's brightest spotlights at an airport hotel in Winnipeg to negotiate a deal to save the project. Lougheed and Ontario premier Bill Davis both attended, along with their energy ministers. Federal mines minister Donald Macdonald represented Pierre Trudeau's government, accompanied by Trudeau's ambitious Treasury Board president, Jean Chrétien. Macdonald and Davis, both Upper Canadian patricians in the classic mould, were put off by Lougheed's blunt style. By midday, the Albertans were convinced Macdonald would not be willing to compromise enough to reach a deal. Rumours in Lougheed's camp after the fact had it that over lunch, Chrétien persuaded the mines minister to accept the offer on the table. Two days later, Chrétien rose in the House of Commons to announce that the federal government would be taking a 15 percent equity stake in the Syncrude project, with Alberta owning 10 percent and Ontario the remaining 5 percent. In the coming years, it would be Lougheed, with his steadfast support and multimillion-dollar investments in SAGD, who would be seen as the Patch's great public sector champion. But it was Chrétien, "the little guy from Shawinigan," whose backroom deal-making skills had saved Syncrude.

The emergency deal ushered in the largest construction project in Alberta's history, a $2.1-billion colossus in the Alberta woods. At the peak of construction, Syncrude's Mildred Lake site swarmed with ten thousand construction workers. It sprawled across eleven square miles and required as much electricity as a city of three hundred thousand. Its coking towers rose twenty-one storeys high. The accompanying real estate boom in Fort McMurray brought the town its first suburbs—Beacon Hill, Abasand Heights and Thickwood—as well as its first high-rise apartments. When the Syncrude mine started producing the first batch of its 125,000 barrels per day in July 1978, oil was nearing the peak of a decade-long upward spike, several other projects were in the works, and the entire province was riding the wild waves of a boom without precedent to date—the kind so intense and propulsive it can fool people into thinking it might never end.

The decade after Syncrude began operations would eventually prove even bleaker for the young industry than the one just passed. The boom of the early 1980s busted hard at the end of 1985, as the Saudis glutted the global oil market and sent prices plunging. Investment fell to a standstill, and profits remained slim to none. At Suncor (the GCOS plant, reorganized and renamed by Sun Oil in 1979), more than a thousand workers were on strike. If you kept driving past the site on Highway 63, you reached a grim, ironic monument to the unfounded optimism of the era—a brand-new bridge over the Athabasca, built by Lougheed's Alberta government as part of a package of incentives for a $13-billion oil sands project that had been in the works just before the bust. The oil companies funding the project had backed out in 1982, and locals had taken to calling the orphaned span over the river the Bridge to Nowhere.

Sun Oil was spending $100 million per year to keep its oil sands mine running and barely breaking even in the best years, with no destination of its own in sight. In 1991 the company appointed a new CEO at Suncor, Rick George, and handed him the grim task of deciding what to do with what George himself would later call "an essentially malfunctioning industrial plant." It was costing the company about $20 per barrel to produce oil that frequently sold for $15 per barrel or less. Shortly after George arrived, the plant's operator told him he saw maybe 50 cents per barrel in savings to be reaped from improvements and refurbishments. It was widely understood at the Suncor site that one of George's options was to go to Philadelphia and tell his bosses that the plant should be shuttered.

This, then, was the decisive interval for the Patch, its final teetering moment on the edge of the abyss. Decades later, when the environmental and social costs and outsized carbon footprint of the oil sands came to global attention and protesters by the score would descend on pipeline routes across North America and national capitals around the world to demand an end to the Patch's so-called dirty oil, they were essentially asking the industry's decision makers to reverse a call they'd made in the early 1990s.

Rick George, in any case, chose not to abandon the project. Instead, he hired a miner—or, more precisely, a mining engineer, the first engineer with a mining background to oversee operations at an oil sands plant—and a highly unlikely saviour for the Patch.

As an undergrad at Queen's University in the 1960s, Dee Parkinson-Marcoux was one of the first women to enrol in the mining and metallurgical engineering program. It would be the first of many barriers she shattered in her career. She had chosen mining—joining the "dirt boys," she called it—because she wanted to work outdoors. When she graduated in 1970, women were still believed to be bad luck in a mine and forbidden from setting foot underground. She enrolled in graduate studies instead, wrote a textbook and earned an MBA, after which she found a job at an Esso oil refinery. In the 1980s, she went to Edmonton to run Petro-Canada's refinery, becoming the first Canadian woman ever to do so. And that's where she was when Suncor came calling.

"I understand you like the wilderness," Suncor's headhunter said. "How do you feel about Fort McMurray?"

Parkinson-Marcoux arrived at the Suncor site in the fall of 1991, a new vice president unlike any executive the Patch had ever seen. She was a petite middle-aged woman, a strict vegan and keen amateur botanist. She knew that many of the plant's employees thought she'd been brought in to fire them—maybe even shut down the whole thing. Parkinson-Marcoux spent her first six months focused on listening and watching. Some of the plant's faults and shortcomings were readily apparent to her—the processing plant sat directly downhill from the tailings pond's berm, for instance, and the fire trucks all parked in one spot too close to a rack of pipes carrying volatile process chemicals. These were basic mistakes a dirt boy would never make.

"For twenty-five years, that place had been struggling," Parkinson-Marcoux said. "It was considered the white elephant. It was always considered to just be a disaster. Because the people who ran oil companies didn't understand the process. They had a mine on their hands."

Parkinson-Marcoux soon questioned the wisdom behind the icon of the oil sands industry: the bucket wheel. In the Suncor mine's early days, the company had experimented with using trucks and shovels to dig bitumen from the pit and haul it to the hopper, but the trucks would get bogged down in spring mud or winter snow. They were useful for moving overburden, but the colossal bucket wheels did the digging in the pay dirt. Parkinson-Marcoux figured no one had ever tried building a decent mine road first—"Good mines start with good roads," went the industry cliché—and so she pitched the Suncor execs on a major change: What if they replaced the bucket wheels with big haul trucks and shovels? The cost would be $120 million, more than Suncor spent on an entire year's operations. And this for a facility that half the company still thought should be sold for scrap. It was an all-in bet on bitumen after it had stubbornly refused to pay out for almost a century. This was a risky gamble on the advice of a newly arrived executive from outside the oil industry's boys' clubs, and Rick George took it.

With mammoth trucks and shovels built for the mining industry running in and out of the pit on good roads to feed a processing plant running more efficiently than ever, Suncor slashed its operating cost per barrel by more than $5 in less than a year. In 1992, the year of the $120 million transition, the plant's output increased from fifty-eight thousand barrels per day to a record seventy thousand. The company—and the industry— would never look back. Trucks and shovels, those commonplace miner's tools, had made the dirt pay.

The truck-driven pivot to profitability opened up a path to a possible future for the Patch, but the investment climate remained tepid, and the industry suffered from the diminished profile of a decade of stagnation. By the early 1990s, Syncrude was producing a tenth of Canada's oil all by itself, but its new CEO, Eric Newell, would go to Parliament Hill and draw blank stares when he talked about the oil sands. Once, in a meeting with the editorial board of a major Montreal newspaper, he was asked when his company planned to begin commercial operations. He realized the Patch needed a pitchman.

Newell attacked the role with an engineer's methodical sense of purpose. He convinced the Mining Association of Canada to talk up the industry among politicians, lobbied the federal energy minister and persuaded government and industry players of all stripes to form a task force. He also hit the business lunch and convention circuit. Newell was chairman of the Alberta Chamber of Resources, an industry association for all of the province's resource-development industries, and the office provided cover to take his pitch across the country. He wasn't lobbying for Syncrude, he was advocating for a vital national project, "a new energy vision for Canada." The oil sands was the great untapped economic opportunity of its time, a pool of oil as vast as Saudi Arabia's. It would create jobs nationwide, pour royalties and taxes into provincial and federal coffers. In thirty years, Newell told an audience at the Montreal Stock Exchange, the oil sands could attract $21 billion in capital investments and triple production from 400,000 barrels per day to 1.2 million.

The report of the National Task Force on Oil Sands Strategies came out in May 1995. Its forecast for the oil sands deepened Newell's boast. The industry would bring in $25 billion in the next twenty-five years and create seventeen thousand jobs, while tripling production. By November, the press in Alberta was already talking about "a renaissance in the oil sands" and quoting the steady upward climb in stock prices for Suncor, "the darling of the stock market" since it had split off from Sun Oil into its own publicly traded company in 1992.

In line with the report's recommendations, the Alberta government restructured royalty rates in December 1995, bringing in a generic structure in which oil sands operations would pay just 1 percent of revenues until they had earned back their capital costs, at which point the royalty rate flipped to 25 percent. The federal government, meanwhile, introduced a major tax restructuring called an accelerated capital cost allowance, which let companies investing in a new oil sands project write off their capital investments right away rather than over the decades-long life of the plant. The overhaul of the royalty and tax regimes reinvented the financial climate for the oil sands overnight. New capital investment, which had been at a standstill, roared into the Patch. And the industry's erstwhile champion, Jean Chrétien, who was now the prime minister of Canada, gathered his partners in industry and government for a celebration in Fort McMurray that was dubbed the Declaration of Opportunity.

When he'd last set foot in Fort McMurray to turn sod at the launch of construction on the Syncrude plant in 1976, Chrétien was a cabinet minister in Pierre Trudeau's loathed Liberal government, which held no seats in Alberta. Chrétien arrived at a local curling rink packed with well-wishers on June 2, 1996, as the first Liberal leader to win seats in Alberta in a generation. The crowd for his lunchtime speech was estimated at 1,800. Chrétien was joined by Premier Ralph Klein and Alberta's energy minister, Pat Black. Also onstage were eighteen oil company CEOs and the grand chief of the Assembly of First Nations, Ovide Mercredi, who lauded Syncrude's record as an employer of Indigenous workers.

Chrétien was always better at blunt backroom talk than oratory, but the audience cheered his message heartily all the same. "It's difficult for me to believe today that the oil produced here is competitive with conventional oil production," the prime minister said. "I will relate I didn't think it was to be possible." It was a hunch he'd shared for years with an entire wary industry. "It's fantastic because we have more oil here than in Saudi Arabia. So for the security of the nation, it's something."

Eric Newell was one of the oil executives onstage that day in Fort McMurray as Chrétien echoed his pledge. He had wondered at times if it was too ambitious. After all the Patch had been through, all the false starts and setbacks, would $25 billion really come raining down now in twenty-five years? Newell was right, in a sense, to doubt the numbers. The first $25 billion in capital was invested in the next eight years. And by 2008, just twelve years later, investment would reach $20 billion *per year*.

MR. STELMACH GOES TO WASHINGTON

In the final months of 2007, the price of oil rose above $80 per barrel, a threshold it had never before breached. It stayed there for days on end, spiking from $83 up to $93, dropping down to $88 and then racing back up to $96 or $98. Oil prices had been rising steadily since Brent crude last traded below $20 per barrel in February 2002, but the rally of late 2007 was a wild ride all its own. Each plateau seemed freakish, almost impossible, and then it would be cleared and become the new baseline for another crazy run. Finally, on the second of January, 2008, the price of oil briefly traded above $100 per barrel. Never mind that in inflation-adjusted dollars, the price of oil had hit $101.70 in 1980, at the outbreak of the Iran-Iraq War—this was a staggering precedent. Brent crude closed slightly below $100 that day, at $98.45, fell back below $90 for a few weeks, and then resumed its vertiginous climb. The price closed above $100 for the first time ever in late February and then roared on to $120 in May and $140 in June. On Thursday, July 3, 2008—the eve of American Independence Day, when there would be no trading on US exchanges—it closed at $143.95, the latest all-time high in week after week of record-breaking prices.

Throughout 2007 and on into early 2008, the long boom that had roiled and rocked through Fort McMurray and Calgary and everywhere else connected to the Patch built to something like mass delirium. New arrivals to Fort McMurray were sleeping eight or ten or a dozen to a two-bedroom condo and still there was not enough room in town. From Walmart to Tim Hortons to the local fish-and-chips shop, no one could keep their businesses sufficiently staffed even at the highest wages in the country. Commutes expected to take fifteen minutes could stretch into hours in traffic that had far outgrown capacity. Scenes of similarly manic growth played out across Alberta. Edmonton and Calgary were the fastest-growing big cities in Canada, and had been that way for years by the start of 2008. Alberta felt, for the first time ever, like the very centre of Canadian life.

And overseeing it all, improbably, was Alberta's thirteenth premier, Ed Stelmach, a soft-spoken former grain farmer from a Ukrainian community east of Edmonton. Stelmach had none of his predecessor Ralph Klein's swagger or bluster—the press called him "Steady Eddie"—but the honour of an official trade visit to Washington, DC, fell to him nonetheless.

In January 2008, in the midst of the glorious, worrisome chaos of the boom, Stelmach made a formal visit to the US capital. It should have been a triumph, a sort of confirmation that Alberta had truly arrived as the energy superpower. Weren't these—despite the dark clouds and gripes of a province bursting at the seams from its growth—weren't these good times? There had never been a boom quite like this one, never such a sense of importance to the province's business. And here came Steady Eddie, the farm fields of eastern Alberta far behind him, landing in the capital of the world's reigning superpower.

Stelmach had his sustainable resource development minister, Ted Morton, in tow, along with a small retinue of other provincial officials. There were to be two days of working luncheons and congressional meetings, capped by the exclamation point of a one-on-one meeting at the White House with the vice president of the United States. The meeting was so important, and Dick Cheney's security so tight, that the details hadn't even been confirmed until after premier's delegation had landed in Washington. Stelmach didn't know how many premiers of Alberta or anywhere else had ever had White House meetings with vice presidents, but he was sure it wasn't routine. This was the big leagues.

Stelmach had lunch the first day with US energy industry officials and then addressed an energy forum on Capitol Hill. He met privately with the chair of the House Select Committee on Energy Independence and Global Warming, briefed a room full of congressional members, and hosted a reception at the Canadian embassy. The second day, Stelmach mainly talked up Alberta's agriculture sector and reassured Washington officials that Alberta's beef was free of mad cow disease, which had roiled the cattle business on both sides of the border a few years earlier. In the evening, he watched his hometown Edmonton Oilers lose a nail-biter to the Washington Capitals in overtime.

And then, on the morning of Friday, January 18, 2008, Stelmach set out along with Morton and Alberta's Washington envoy, a former Progressive Conservative cabinet minister named Gary Mar, for perhaps the most important meeting of his professional life. Certainly a career highlight, a photo op for the provincial archives — they were off to a meeting with Dick Cheney at the White House.

Alberta premiers had been trying to finagle face time with the vice president for years, and Cheney had been all set to come to Alberta himself in 2005 until the Hurricane Katrina catastrophe swept those plans aside. Stelmach was well aware he was on his way to meet a veteran oilman

and political titan. Cheney had landed his first White House staff job before he was thirty and served as secretary of defence through the first Gulf
War. Between government jobs, he had spent five years as CEO of the
global oil-field services company Halliburton. Stelmach could not help
but be aware of the power imbalance. Five years earlier, while Cheney was
helping to plot the invasion of Iraq, Stelmach had been the Member of the
Legislative Assembly for Vegreville-Viking.

The ritual was in some sense nearly as old as the oil industry itself: the
foreign vassal comes to the world capital to pay tribute and seek favour.
Agents of the Russian czar went to Paris in the 1880s to secure a loan from
the Rothschilds, that legendary French banking dynasty, in order to bring
a vital pipeline to the shores of the Black Sea and liberate their landlocked
oil fields. In the early 1950s, seemingly half the US State Department and
any number of senior British officials could be found in the better hotels of
Tehran, waiting on the whims of Iranian prime minister Mohammed Mos-
sadegh, whom they referred to as "Old Mossy" and who met with them in
pyjamas, reclined in his bed at the royal palace. In the wake of the first
OPEC crisis in 1975, a Soviet delegation to Washington spent a weekend
killing time at Disney World as the guests of Gulf Oil while its members
waited for Richard Nixon's White House to mull over the possibility of
cutting a deal for Russian oil. And President Jimmy Carter bade farewell
to 1977 at a New Year's Eve celebration with the shah in Tehran, toasting
Iran as "an island of stability" in a troubled region.

Still, Stelmach was clear on his goals. His message was the same as it
had been for the members of Congress, the energy forum audience, his
seatmates at the hockey game: Alberta was a stable, safe and secure supplier of oil. A stable democracy, not a dictatorship. A safe country, not a
hive of terrorists. A secure resource exporter, not a country that would use
its oil production to seize political advantage. Canada was not, in short, the
Middle East. The United States was its biggest customer, nearly its only
customer. And Canada was America's single largest source of oil, supplying
about 40 percent of all US imports, nearly four times Saudi Arabia's share.
(This was a longstanding fact that always surprised American audiences.)

America's next-door neighbour and closest ally. Stable, safe and secure. Stelmach's job security may have rested to a significant extent on his ability to maintain and strengthen this trade with the United States—if all of Canada's economic health wasn't riding on the oil boom, the rhetoric in Ottawa and Edmonton alike sure made it seem like it was—but that didn't make the message any less self-evident. If Cheney was the gatekeeper of the global oil game's big leagues, Stelmach came bearing an emerging energy superpower's impeccable argument for entry.

The morning was chilly and grey. Washington was a stoic blur of monumental stone through the smoked glass of the visiting dignitary's requisite Lincoln Town Car, which the Canadian ambassador had loaned the premier for the occasion. At the White House, Stelmach and his colleagues spent half an hour passing from one security post to another. Outside Cheney's office, they were informed of the meeting's precise protocol. They would enter alone, just Stelmach, Morton and Mar; their own security detail would wait outside. They had fifteen minutes to state their case to the vice president. Then a phone would ring, Cheney would answer it, and that would be their signal to leave.

When they entered the office, the first person Ed Stelmach saw was the largest soldier he'd ever laid eyes on. Was he a marine? A Green Beret? Whichever he was, this guy was a monster. His arms were crossed in a way that made Stelmach think of his neck snapping like a scene in some action movie. There were armchairs facing a desk, and Cheney was seated behind it. The Albertans sat, and they talked. Cheney was an oil guy, so there was no need for explanatory preamble. He knew the game. He'd written some of its rules, pretty much. Stelmach made it clear that Alberta would supply as much oil—a *stable, safe, secure* supply—as America would take. Sending it southward as efficiently as possible, Stelmach explained, was a top priority. A streamlined approval process for pipeline projects would be a huge help. Cheney brought up the potential for greater domestic production from shale. Stelmach reaffirmed that Alberta's government was as committed to free trade as anyone anywhere. Its environmental regulations were second to none. Stelmach told Cheney about investments they were making in carbon capture and storage and reducing the carbon footprint of a barrel of bitumen. Cheney had been to Alberta on a hunting trip, so he and Ted Morton chatted about that. When the phone rang, the vice president picked it up briefly and said something short and quiet into the receiver and put it back down. They kept talking. The meeting stretched longer than half an hour. That felt like an accomplishment in itself.

Afterward, Stelmach faced the Alberta press corps that was traveling with him and ran through the highlights. He was certain the United States would remain a welcome customer for oil sands production. Stelmach's Washington visit had been hounded a little by protesters—there were maybe forty of them outside the Canadian embassy the night of the reception, waving their placards about dirty oil—and so he told the press he had reassured the vice president that the oil sands industry was hard at work on reducing its environmental impacts and shrinking its carbon footprint. This was a delicate topic for a PC premier—there were members of his own caucus who considered climate change an overhyped distraction based on questionable science.

"The vice president is very aware of the province of Alberta in terms of a very stable, safe, secure supply of oil," Stelmach said, "and also is aware of the environmental practices that we're applying in developing those resources."

The Washington press corps never asked for Dick Cheney's thoughts on the meeting—but then again, the vice president was not a man who felt obliged to chat with them or anyone else.

DISTANT EARLY WARNING

One week after Ed Stelmach returned to Edmonton from his historic Washington meeting with the vice president of the United States, he unveiled his government's new climate change plan. It committed Alberta to reducing greenhouse gas emissions by 14 percent from 2005 levels by 2050. The goal was far weaker than Canada's Kyoto Protocol pledge—6 percent below 1990 levels by 2010—and well out of step with other provincial plans. At a meeting of Canada's premiers in Vancouver a few days later, Stelmach tabled his plan and left early, leaving his environment minister to carry on the discussion. He was the only premier no longer in the room. But then, none of them had a rollicking boom to manage, and Alberta was less than six weeks from a provincial election.

In mid-February 2008, as Stelmach campaigned for reelection, the advocacy group Environmental Defence released a scathing report, *Canada's Toxic Tar Sands*. The subtitle, *The Most Destructive Project on Earth*, appeared on the cover in even larger type than the title, splashed over a dark-hued photo of an oil sands plant spewing smoke and steam. Statistics and graphs were scattered throughout the pages within, but the tone was more polemical than technical. "With the Tar Sands, Canada has become the world's dirty energy superpower," Executive Director Rick Smith wrote in the introduction. The report detailed diseased fish and strange cancers downstream from the oil sands mines. It accused the Alberta government of having "outsourced" environmental monitoring to the industry and allowing the boreal forest to be turned into a "toxic moonscape" of open-pit mines and tailings ponds full of "toxic sludge." There were sections on airborne emissions that might be causing acid rain and greenhouse gases contributing to climate change. The concluding section appeared under the headline "Clean It Up or Shut It Down."

The Environmental Defence report made national headlines and obliged a response. Stelmach was on the campaign trail in Fort McMurray when the story broke. He dismissed the report as the work of "silk-suited environmentalists" from Toronto spreading falsehoods, and he argued that the air quality right there in the capital of the oil sands was better than in many other Canadian cities.

"My job," Stelmach told the press, "is to protect this province, to protect the prosperity of Alberta and make sure the correct information gets out."

The premier was clearly catering to Alberta voters, for whom the combative response no doubt played well. But it was a dangerous misreading of what would prove to be a mounting and durable line of critical attack on the Patch. Environmental Defence's report was a lone cannon shot over the bow of the boom's great roaring industrial vessel, an attempt to bring some small, momentary attention to the costs of the Patch's growth as well as the benefits. The demand to "Shut It Down" had no real weight behind it; it could only initiate a real discussion about the "Clean It Up" side of the equation. But for too long, Alberta had been abused and ignored by Ontario elites, a definition that extended to Toronto environmentalists, even if they were rarely seen in silk suits. Stelmach reacted not as the leader of a newly muscular energy superpower but as the cornered premier of a perennial underdog and also-ran in the messy hierarchical politics of Canadian Confederation. It was a long-established instinct in Alberta, but in this case it was the wrong one, and it would send the national— and later global—debate about the ecological cost of the oil sands down a rough, mean path to intractable conflict.

Scalding as the rhetoric in the *Toxic Tar Sands* report was, there was still a conversation to be had, a way for the Alberta government and the oil sands industry to engage their critics and potentially begin to stake out some middle ground. Mere weeks before the report came out, the Patch's own most prominent environmental voice, the Cumulative Environmental Management Association, would urge the government to declare a temporary moratorium on new oil sands leases until the region and its regulators could catch up with the pace of the boom. CEMA was no band of silk-suited Torontonians—its forty-seven member organizations included Suncor, Imperial Oil and many other oil companies, as well as the Canadian Association of Petroleum Producers, numerous environmental groups, First Nations, and the municipal government of Fort McMurray. It had been formed by Ralph Klein's government in 2001 to conduct joint research on the environmental footprint of the oil sands. And in early 2008, it was telling another PC government that the Patch's growth was beginning to spin out of control. A 2007 provincial government report on Fort McMurray's strain under the boom had led to nearly $400 million in emergency spending, which was welcome but nowhere

near enough to cover the $1.2 billion in infrastructure shortfalls the mu-
nicipality had identified.

A blue-ribbon economic panel, meanwhile, had looked at Alberta's
management of its revenues (also at the government's behest) and concluded in January 2008 that the province "needs more fiscal discipline,"
that it couldn't expect to "forever live off its natural resources." The Heritage Fund, set up by Peter Lougheed to store the riches of the fossil fuel
industry, had stagnated and become an emergency cover for provincial
budgetary woes. If the Alberta government had continued to put the
30 percent per year of non-renewable resource revenues into the fund that
Lougheed had mandated, it would have contained more than $125 billion
at the start of 2008; instead it held just $16 billion. Oil companies were
getting rich off the boom, but this did little for the tax bases of Calgary and
Edmonton and Fort McMurray, which had only property taxes to rely on
as they welcomed tens of thousands of new residents each year.

Environmental monitoring had begun in the air and water around
the oil sands mines, but it was spotty and inconsistent, with no baselines
to work from and no rigorously established thresholds of human or environmental health to warn against. The provincial government's Energy
Resources Control Board, established in a different century and resource
era from the one that now reigned in the Patch, continued to review each
new project as diligently as it knew how. But it had no authority to control
the *rate* of growth, which was the crux of the current problem.

Stelmach was in the midst of an election campaign that seemed closer
than it turned out to be, and some precincts of the oil and gas sector were
still spitting mad over the previous year's royalty review. He would not
anger the beast further. There would surely be time, after re-election, to
rebalance the overheated economy and the stressed environment. Perhaps
Stelmach couldn't have known how soon the window would close. The
industry's image—and the province's—would soon vanish into the maw of
a global media and activist machine that didn't care about provincial election cycles or the stresses on small-town Alberta politicians. But in any case

what he said was that his government didn't think it should be "touching the brakes" on the boom, and there was no one else who could. And so onward it careened.

BUSTED

Ed Stelmach and the PCs returned to power in March 2008 in an unexpected landslide. In the midst of the boom's upheavals, ecstasies and anxieties, Albertans clung to the political status quo. Stelmach hosted his first post-election Premier's Dinner in Edmonton on April 24. The dinners were a longstanding PC tradition, a chance for deep-pocketed donors and long-time supporters to eat conference-hall steaks with their political allies, rub shoulders with a few cabinet ministers, maybe even bend the premier's ear for a few minutes on a pressing matter. The April 2008 edition was hosted at the main ballroom of the Shaw Conference Centre before a packed and triumphant crowd. Thirty-seven years after Peter Lougheed launched it, the PC dynasty remained unstoppable, able to win handily at the polls even with the helm in the hands of a widely second-guessed, small-town farmer whose political acumen many of the party's faithful had once doubled.

Stelmach took the dais to sustained applause. A placard on the podium read "New Ideas, New Approach."

"Friends, this is a real celebration," he began. Suddenly a black-clad figure descended on a wire from the ceiling, lowering a broad black banner that read "$telmach: the best premier oil money can buy." The bottom-right corner had a sort of logo reading "Stop the Tar Sands," next to an outline map of the province. At bottom left was the well-known trademark of the environmental group Greenpeace. After the activist reached the floor and was hurried away by security, Stelmach carried on with his recitation of his government's accomplishments. The incident was relatively novel—Greenpeace had only opened its first Alberta office in Edmonton the previous summer—but it registered only a minor blip in the day's news cycle in Alberta and then was gone.

Five days later, as Stelmach and his caucus were getting ready for the day's afternoon legislative session, they received word that a flock of ducks had landed on a Syncrude tailings pond and got themselves stuck in the tarry bitumen residue. The news arrived in abbreviated and inconclusive form at first. It was a dozen ducks, maybe a few dozen. Before long, it was hundreds. Within days, everyone in the legislature and seemingly half of the world would learn that more than 1,600 migrating ducks perished, dragged under the surface and drowned in a toxic pond.

In the immediate aftermath of the incident, confusion reigned. Government officials, asked by the press to comment on the disaster, often had the same information the media had. Syncrude was slow to respond and unforthcoming at first. In retrospect, some blame would fall on the company's new management. For decades, Syncrude's senior executives had been long-time oil sands veterans like Eric Newell and Jim Carter, who had lived for years in Fort McMurray and had close, direct connections with the provincial government. If this relationship could sometimes seem too cozy, it also meant that efficient communication and coordination could be counted on in an emergency. The company had been quasi-governmental in its early days and still saw itself as intimately connected to the province and its leadership; Syncrude managers were sensitive to local concerns and potential political impacts. But Tom Katinas, a career ExxonMobil refinery operator, had taken over the company in 2007 on behalf of its lead partner, the Exxon subsidiary Imperial Oil. Under Katinas, Syncrude's response to the duck incident seemed overly opaque and lawyer-driven in the Exxon style. As press coverage mounted and the public recoiled in horror at the images of bitumen-soaked ducks struggling for survival, the public relations costs spread beyond Syncrude and its failure to deploy deterrent cannons, condemning first the whole industry and then the entire province. And Stelmach's government, made to answer for Syncrude's oversight, flailed in the larger spotlight. A week after the story broke, Stelmach was still citing statistics to the press about how many birds were killed annually by wind turbines in the United States.

"No matter what we did, you couldn't get ahead of the story," Stelmach said years later. "And that was the first time that I think the oil industry, you know, the CEOs, started to realize, 'Uh-oh, we can't take things for granted.'"

Guy Boutilier, Fort McMurray's Member of the Legislative Assembly at the time, was shocked at the bungled communication. "All of the good work of corporate social responsibility, of the things that we had been doing for the twenty years prior to that, seemed to go out the window very quickly," he said later. The government had just passed a budget with $25 million earmarked for a three-year marketing campaign aimed at rebranding the oil sands industry internationally in the face of the emerging dirty-oil message. Syncrude's carelessness at its tailings pond and its clumsy response, in effect, had just launched that campaign worldwide, prematurely, with images that powerfully reinforced the negative image.

Boutilier had been mayor of Fort McMurray in the 1990s and provincial minister of the environment in the early years of the boom. Back then, he'd have heard right away about a major environmental incident at Syncrude, and the person on the phone would have been not just a Syncrude executive but also a concerned neighbour. It was, in a sense, an unintended consequence of the boom itself, the downside of energy superpower ambitions. The Patch was no longer an overlooked outsider backed by local boosters. It was a global force in the oil business, and its missteps now had global consequences.

While the Alberta government plotted its oil sands PR campaign and Environment Canada began an investigation that would eventually lead to charges against Syncrude for the duck disaster, the environmental movement spent the summer of 2008 in meetings and conferences that would turn out to be the beginnings of a sustained international campaign against the oil sands.

That July, Michael Northrup of the Rockefeller Brothers Fund, a major philanthropic organization based in New York, convened a conference call for a small group of environmental non-governmental organizations (NGOs) to talk about the oil sands. The Rockefeller fund's endowment had been created by heirs to John D. Rockefeller's Standard Oil fortune. Northrup's PowerPoint pitch to the group was entitled "A Globally Significant Threat." Michael Marx of the San Francisco activist group Corporate Ethics International laid out a modest strategy to "change the debate" about oil sands development in the near term before pushing for a moratorium on new development and advocating with oil sands customers to stop buying bitumen. In an irony even greater than that of the meeting being led by handlers of Standard Oil money, Marx had become interested in oil sands advocacy as director of the International Boreal Conservation Campaign, a partnership between the conservation group Ducks Unlimited and the Pew Charitable Trusts, a philanthropic organization founded using J. Howard Pew's Sun Oil largesse. The heirs of the corporate godfather of the oil sands were, in a sense, bankrolling the movement for its demise. Also present on the call were Susan Casey-Lefkowitz of the NRDC (who had opposed the haul truck parked on the National Mall in 2006) and Dan Woynillowicz of the Pembina Institute, an Alberta-based energy watchdog.

Informal information sessions among NGOs happen all the time, and the "Globally Significant Threat" discussion was no more consequential than any number of others that surely happened that year among environmental groups with similar areas of interest. This meeting was significant only in retrospect, as an early sign that the global energy superpower had begun to attract unwanted attention and embryonic opposition far beyond an uninvited guest or two at a premier's dinner in Edmonton. Pembina's presence was indicative of the changing nature of the Patch's opposition as well. Pembina had been founded in 1985 by rural Albertans whose lives and agricultural livelihoods were being threatened by sour gas leaks from natural gas wells across the province. Over the years, it had morphed into a think tank with a gentle but firm advocacy arm, seen within the industry as an often frustrating but ultimately friendly local critic. Dee Parkinson-Marcoux, for example, met routinely with Pembina's founding executive director, Rob Macintosh, during her tenure at Suncor in the early 1990s for lengthy, informal discussions about emerging environmental issues in the oil sands. Pembina's public calls for tighter regulation of the industry and a less reckless approach to growth grew sharper and more frequent as the boom took hold; no newspaper feature on the wild west of Fort McMurray circa 2006 was complete without a cautionary quote from a Pembina spokesperson. If the audience for Pembina's rigorous research was now as likely to be an American activist as a Suncor VP, then the conversation about the oil sands that initiatives like Stelmach's three-year PR campaign hoped to recalibrate might already have been spinning beyond anyone's control.

The following month, Fort Chipewyan hosted a three-day conference called Keepers of the Water that would prove similarly significant as a catalyst for later opposition to the oil sands and its pipeline proposals. This was the third annual Keepers of the Water meeting, and its agenda stretched beyond the oil sands to any industrial activity posing a threat to the sacred waters of the Canadian North, from dams and pulp mills to urban growth. But oil sands were particularly central to the discussions at the 2008 event. The Athabasca Chipewyan First Nation was the host, and its chief, Allan Adam, had grown impatient with the official channels of redress for the rise in rare cancers and the prevalence of deformed fish in his community. Dr. John O'Connor, who'd first raised the alarm about Fort Chipewyan's cancer cluster, was the keynote speaker. A deformed fish that appeared to have two mouths, pulled from Lake Athabasca the week before the conference, shocked attendees and attracted national media attention. The event also provided the first meetings between Dene elders and Norwegian activists worried about the recent oil sands investments made by Statoil, the oil company partially owned by the Norwegian government. In the coming years, the prominence of oil sands opposition on the agendas of European environmentalists would trace its roots in some measure to those three days under the boreal sky in Fort Chipewyan.

NINE

DOWNSTREAM

MIXED BLESSINGS

From the point of view of its European settlers and nation builders, Canada has long maintained a paradoxical relationship with its immense wilderness. The natural bounty was the lure, the emergent nation's raison d'être—it was a treasure trove of resources to exploit—but it was also a national endowment to be protected and relied upon for survival. The fur trade's voyageurs were both skilled wilderness explorers and harvesters of animal pelts. Cod fishermen had to intimately understand the sea and its raw, brutal power in order to pull fish from it by the boatload. Loggers in the British Columbia wilderness, western settlers living off of and clearing prairie land to prepare it for farming, gold prospectors in the Klondike, oil sands pioneers punching holes in the boreal forest—all of them became intimate with Canadian nature and dependent upon it even as they transformed it from ecology to commodity. The tension of this dual role, its intrinsic unsustainability, has always been clearest with regard to Canada's relationship with the Indigenous people who were given no voice whatsoever in either the exploitation or the stewardship of the resources, and who were left out of the national story in general for hundreds of years.

In the Patch, environmental concerns and Indigenous relations alike were an afterthought in the long decades of experimentation and the first years of the commercial industry. Environmental issues were not even described as such until the mid-1970s, and environmentalism remained a distant movement, focused mainly on scrutinizing the makers of insecticides and the butchers of whales. Canada's First Nations, meanwhile, were treated as a nonexistent political force entirely under the sway of the federal government's authoritarian Indian Act.

The industry saw its greatest challenges in core engineering questions: how to cut the cost of digging and refining bitumen, how to keep steel-toothed bucket-wheel excavators and conveyor belts operating in the deep freeze of the boreal winter. Even the tailings pond issue was initially an engineering problem, a question of dike size and integrity. And so by the time the industry began to really bear down on the environmental problems that had first been identified in the 1970s—sulphur dioxide clouds, mature fine tailings, immediate regional concerns of that sort—a very different story about the nature of the oil sands had already begun to be told by those left out of its business lore.

This dissonant oil sands narrative began, as so many dark oil sands tales do, with a tailings pond. In the winter of 1982, Suncor's Pond 1 leaked into the Athabasca River. Water from the pond had been seeping into the groundwater constantly at levels below a threshold later deemed "safe" by the provincial government since the plant first started operating in 1967, but this was a far more significant spill. There wasn't much in the way of monitoring or emergency environmental response in the industry in those days, so little hard data remain from the incident. What is known is that a large volume of bitumen residue and tailings fluid flowed into the Athabasca, which carried it away downriver.

The nearest settlement downstream of the first Suncor mine is Fort

McKay, an Indigenous community on the banks of the river less than thirty kilometres north with a population, at the time, of about four hundred. Owing in part to the water pollution coming from the two oil sands plants upstream, Fort McKay trucked in its potable water and stored it in two large tanks as a matter of course. But the winter of 1981–82 was a ferocious one even by northern Alberta's standards, and it had played havoc with Fort McKay's water supply. The propane heater on one tank broke in the cold and caught fire in December, burning down the entire apparatus. The following month, the other tank froze solid and cracked apart as the ice expanded. The residents were obliged from then on to use river water for drinking and everything else.

The bitter cold triggered equipment failures and fires at Suncor that winter as well, causing the tailings spill in late January, among other problems. Suncor reported later that it had tried to notify the chief of the Fort McKay First Nation, Dorothy MacDonald, about the spill by phone after the Alberta government ordered it to do so, but according to the company, it wasn't able to reach her. In any case, the people of Fort McKay weren't informed about the state of the river until more than three weeks later, when Suncor employees visited the community in person. For three solid weeks, the residents of Fort McKay drank and bathed in water awash in oil sands mining effluent. Remarkably, there was no serious illness or injury as a result, but the incident galvanized the community and turned Chief MacDonald into an angry activist overnight.

"Where the hell was the government when all this was going on?" she demanded at a press conference in March 1982. "How foolish can you be to allow a company like Suncor to conduct its own monitoring? Do bank robbers turn themselves in after they've done the job?" MacDonald petitioned Alberta's Environment ministry to take action against Suncor. The company was eventually charged with multiple violations of the federal Fisheries Act and the provincial Clean Water Act, but the case faltered and Suncor was acquitted.

Back in Fort McKay, the community's attitude toward industrial development in the boreal forest had changed for good. In 1983 Chief

MacDonald led a blockade of the main road through the reserve. This was primarily in protest against big, fast-moving trucks hauling lumber from a logging operation farther north, but it also made trouble for oil sands workers passing through Fort McKay on their way to new projects being developed. The blockade ended in a reluctant compromise, with the Fort McKay First Nation agreeing to allow the traffic through the community but at a greatly reduced speed. And the complacency and cooperation of the region's First Nations, however reluctant they had been all along, could no longer be taken for granted.

Prior to the Suncor tailings spill, the Patch's pioneers paid little mind to the First Nations of northern Alberta. As scientists and engineers gathered bitumen samples from the banks of the Athabasca River and experimented with rudimentary processing plants in the first decades of the nineteen hundreds, the vast majority of the region's Indigenous peoples continued to live as they always had. Or they attempted to, pushing back against the federal government's establishment of protected parks where they could no longer hunt and reluctantly surrendering their children to government-run residential schools. In 1967, as GCOS began mining bitumen at commercial scale, Cree traders were still bringing their pelts by dogsled to the bridge over the Athabasca in Fort McMurray to trade.

When Dorothy MacDonald and her Fort McKay kin began to challenge the industry's environmental record in the early 1980s, this was all they had to build on: a "community" in Fort McKay composed of three disparate peoples (the Dene, Cree and Metis) with distinct cultures and different mother tongues; a treaty whose most basic legal foundations had never been mutually understood; and nearly a century of marginal citizenship under a patrician federal government that had shown little but contempt for the language, culture and traditions of Canada's First Nations. There is a sort of duality to the Indigenous people's relationship with the Patch—as with Canada itself—and it is coherent only in the context of this grim, fractious, highly contested history.

What happened next, after the Fort McKay First Nation's blockade of

the road through its land in 1983, was in practical terms a kind of mutually beneficial cooperation with the oil sands industry. The fur trapping
business in northern Alberta was in steep decline, due in large measure to
a sustained and enormously successful campaign by environmental organizations around the world to discourage people from buying and wearing
fur clothing. In 1986, the last year of Dorothy MacDonald's tenure as chief,
the band council began negotiating with the provincial and federal governments to form the Fort McKay Industry Relations Corporation and explore
business opportunities for her band in the Patch. "She saw that we couldn't
really stop industry, but we could have an impact and a say," MacDonald's
daughter told a reporter many years later. (MacDonald died in 2005.)

The new relationship began with a single contract to provide janito-
rial services. Under a new chief, Jim Boucher, elected in 1986, the Fort
McKay First Nation soon became an ambitious partner in the growth
of the oil sands industry. As new mining projects came to encircle Fort
McKay from the late 1990s onward—first Syncrude's Aurora mine, and
then Shell's Albian Sands and CNRL's Horizon—the contract work begat
the Fort McKay Group of Companies, which grew into a diverse oil-field
services conglomerate. By 2013, it had a half-dozen divisions, more than
four hundred employees—including more than sixty Indigenous residents
of the community itself, a quarter of the employable population—and
more than $100 million in annual revenues. Fort McKay Group subsidiar-
ies rent heavy equipment to the surrounding oil sands mines. They maintain and repair on-site vehicles, deliver fuel and supplies, haul waste. The
First Nation owns and operates its own work camps and an industrial park,
and it has become a catalyst for local entrepreneurship.

In 2015 Fort McKay was among the wealthiest Indigenous communities in Canada, with average annual household incomes of more than
$100,000 per year and unemployment below 5 percent, as it had been
for years on end. Owing to a 1987 land claim case, finally settled by an
agreement with the federal and provincial governments in 2004, the First
Nation controlled 23,000 acres of the land surrounding the community, including an estimated 8,200 acres resting on high-quality oil sands

deposits. From time to time during the booming decade that followed the land claim settlement, the band investigated the idea of developing an oil sands project all its own. In the meantime, the band council had built a daycare centre and elders' centre, and it provided more than a hundred new three-bedroom homes to band members at below-market prices. Jim Boucher—still chief nearly twenty years later, most recently re-elected in the spring of 2015—draws a reported salary of more than $600,000 per year serving as chairman of the Fort McKay Group of Companies as well as head of the band council. In 2008 he received a National Aboriginal Achievement Award for his business acumen. To the oil sands industry's boosters, facing a mounting wave of international news about Indigenous protest and environmental destruction, Boucher and his community were the very model of harmonious partnership with First Nations communities. Boucher once told a reporter that his approach to the industry was to "take the good with the bad." Some days in Fort McKay, with late-model pickup trucks filling the parking lot in front of the smart new band council office and business bustling for all those oil-field service companies, the good side was not hard to find.

Consider Birch Mountain Enterprises, an oil-field services company that operates out of the Fort McKay First Nation's industrial park just south of town. Birch Mountain is one of more than a hundred companies owned by First Nations in northeastern Alberta—Dave Tuccaro, a Mikisew Cree originally from Fort Chipewyan and one of the most successful Indigenous entrepreneurs in the region, has called them "our new traplines." Out at Birch Mountain's equipment yard, there are a couple of big maintenance warehouses sided in bright blue and white aluminum, a row of parked trucks—midsize tanker trucks smaller than eighteen-wheelers, for delivering water and fuel, steamer trucks for cleaning the mammoth equipment vehicles out at the site—and the requisite cluster of interconnected ATCO trailers to serve as the business office. Inside, the reception area and hallways are decorated with the successful small business's standard range of practical gear and ceremonial bric-a-brac, framed thank-you photos of smiling minor hockey teams and plaques from local business associations, a Keurig coffee machine and boxes of giveaway pens with the Birch Mountain logo etched on barrels made of animal horn.

On any given day in 2015, Chris Wilson might have been in his office between work calls. The sign on the door said *President*, but Wilson still looked like the shift-working oil sands mechanic he once was—hair cropped hip-hop short, muscled torso wrapped in a tight Harley-Davidson T-shirt, a maze of tattoos running up his exposed lower arms. He'd been working as a heavy equipment mechanic at Syncrude for more than a decade back in 2005 when he decided he wanted to start his own business. He knew there was always plenty of work for a mechanic—both at the oil sands sites and back in the fast-growing industrial park in Fort McKay.

Wilson bought himself a big Ford F-450 and ordered thousands of dollars' worth of tools. The day he launched his business, though, the tools hadn't arrived; his brother raced into Fort McMurray and bought a few of the most crucial ones at Canadian Tire. It was an anxious start, but the business was soon roaring along and Wilson's brother quit his Syncrude job to join Birch Mountain. A Fort McKay friend, Ivan Boucher, signed on not long after that, and they quickly built a bustling little contracting business as mechanics in the Patch. Then an idea struck Wilson as he waited for a steam truck to arrive to pressure-wash the oil sands muck from a haul truck he was working on. Clearly there weren't enough of these steam trucks around. This was a bigger investment—a steam truck costs nearly $200,000—but the Patch was booming all around them and the opportunity was there waiting. One steam truck was soon seven, and Birch Mountain's business snowballed from there. It doubled in size in 2008, even as the global economy plunged. Today, the company has a staff of 250 that is more than 50 percent Indigenous—a veritable model of the second generation of young, ambitious entrepreneurship Jim Boucher dreamed about back in 1986 when he decided the First Nation would profit from the oil sands rather than fight back endlessly.

"The projects are here, get on board—that's the way I look at it," Wilson said. "Don't fight it, because I think it's a lost cause to fight it."

Some days, no doubt, that fairer side of Fort McKay's "good with the bad" relationship to the Patch isn't hard to find. Other days, though, the wind blows a certain way, and nobody knows exactly which oil sands site it comes from or precisely which chemical process has occurred, but the air will stink. People report that their eyes sting just from being out in it. And who knows what causes it or what it might do to people, but on those days, the people of Fort McKay are all too aware of the darker side of their relationship with the production of bitumen.

There are government reports and scientific studies that will tell you the air quality in Fort McKay is not above any dangerous threshold. Sometimes those same reports point out that the monitoring is uneven, or that it hasn't been looking for all the chemicals that might be in a cloud blowing over from an oil sands operation, or that the "safe" thresholds sometimes verge on arbitrary. But anyway there's evidence—if not enough, not yet—that there's no cause for alarm. They've been monitoring air quality closely for fifteen years in the Fort McMurray area. There are little white trailerlike boxes crowned in spindly detection equipment and surrounded by chain-link, eighteen in all, operated by the Wood Buffalo Environmental Association. You can go online any time of the day or night and read the data in real time. Hydrogen sulphide and ammonia and ozone in parts per billion, particulate matter in micrograms per cubic metre. There's one of these monitoring stations just north of Fort McKay itself.

There are further reassurances. The provincial government produces reports, and the industry reps invariably say they're all for more of them— more monitoring, gather all the facts—and the band council pushes for more. One study looked at 172 air-quality complaints in Fort McKay from 2010 to 2014 and found "few examples of dangerous short-term releases," but it also noted "technical gaps" in the monitoring regime. Another study has proven that the mines release secondary organic aerosols—SOAs, part of the fine particulate matter counted by those monitors—but not much is known yet about their effect on human health. Another found polycyclic aromatic hydrocarbons (PAHs), known carcinogens, at twenty-three times preindustrial levels in lake beds thirty-five kilometres from any oil sands site, which is farther from several oil sands operations than Fort McKay sits.

The industry's shadow falls heavy and dark over the community. And even if no one knows every single detail about what it all means, everyone knows this land is not the land their grandparents walked. That land is gone forever, and the smell some days reminds everyone in Fort McKay of how much has been lost. And in the meantime, the good keeps coming and so does the bad.

In April 2016 Chief Jim Boucher announced that the Fort McKay First Nation was pursuing legal action against the provincial government for giving permission to an oil sands company to go ahead with an application to develop a project near Moose Lake, one of the few wild places near Fort McKay where band members can still hunt and trap game. Two months later, Boucher announced the First Nation had begun looking into oil sands extraction of its own on a less valued piece of its traditional land. And a few months after that, Boucher said the First Nation would buy a 35 percent stake in a Suncor tank farm for $350 million to serve the company's new Fort Hills mine, still under development north of Fort McKay. These do not represent changes in the chief's disposition toward the industry, nor the First Nation's. This is just what comes to pass when one of the largest engineering projects on earth sets up across the river from a tiny Indigenous community in the boreal forest without permission. You take the good with the bad. You count your blessings, but they're always mixed.

BASELINE DATA

Farther downstream in Fort Chipewyan, on the shore of Lake Athabasca 175 kilometres north of Fort McKay, the same complex, conflicted scene unfolds. Both the major Indigenous groups in the community, the Athabasca Chipewyan First Nation (the ACFN, who are Dene) and the Mikisew Cree First Nation (MCFN), operate diversified oil-field services companies that generate hundreds of millions of dollars in revenue each year. (The community's Metis population negotiates separately with the industry through the local chapter of the Metis Nation of Alberta.) Both band councils nonetheless staunchly oppose the northward expansion of the industry. And the hard science tracking the industry's impact on its downstream neighbours remains murky, working from limited data to reach uncertain conclusions that invariably lead to calls for further study.

Fort Chipewyan is remote even by the region's standards, accessible only by air or boat from the south until the Athabasca River freezes and the ice road to Fort McMurray becomes navigable. In the first decades of oil sands development, it remained far enough afield that it barely registered in the industry's internal calculus of risks, impacts, consultations and partnerships.

Fort Chipewyan's relationship with the Patch first came to national prominence in 2003, when its fly-in doctor, John O'Connor, told the press he'd discovered a cluster of rare cancers among the community's nine hundred residents. Lymphoma and cancers of the bile ducts and the blood were all occurring at elevated rates. He called it a "public health crisis." In response, provincial health authorities dithered and the provincial government obfuscated while the Patch boomed. In 2007 Health Canada slammed O'Connor with charges of causing "undue alarm" and several other misconduct complaints, all of which were later dismissed.

Meanwhile, in the boom's lengthening shadow, the cancer cluster issue drifted from accusation to veritable certainty in the eyes of Fort Chipewyan residents, even as the research remained tentative and inconclusive. A 2009 study by the provincial government confirmed higher rates of cancer in the community—fifty-one cases in the twelve years from 1995 to 2006, when provincial averages would have predicted thirty-nine—but the sample sizes were so small for each individual type of cancer that it was impossible to determine whether the anomaly was a simple statistical outlier or evidence of an emerging epidemic. Back in Fort Chipewyan, where Indigenous people's concerns had been routinely neglected by every level of government for generations, the uncertainty became prima facie evidence of a cover-up, a scandal.

The renowned biologist David Schindler of the University of Alberta, whose pioneering research on environmental hazards such as phosphates and acid rain had led to international regulations on industrial polluters, soon entered the fray. After O'Connor's alarm call, Schindler embarked on studies of toxins in the lakes and snowpack near oil sands mines. His first papers on the topic came out in the journal *Proceedings of the National Academy of Sciences of the United States of America* in 2009 and 2010. Schindler discovered elevated levels of thirteen substances listed as "priority pollutants" by the US Environmental Protection Agency (EPA), including arsenic, mercury, lead and PAHs, a wide-ranging category of carcinogenic compounds released when fossil fuels are burned. The oil sands industry had long argued that the presence of such chemicals in the Athabasca River was due to the natural seepage of bitumen—which contained a great many of those harmful substances—into the water. But Schindler's report found the levels were higher in samples taken closer to the oil sands mines than in samples from farther away, suggesting local contamination from industrial sources.

In an effort to convince industry and government officials of the issue's urgency, Schindler joined with a handful of scientists, doctors and community leaders from the Fort Chipewyan and Fort McKay First Nations—including Dr. O'Connor—to present his findings to the nation's media at a press conference in Edmonton in September 2010. In addition to the dry data in the report, Schindler paraded deformed fish pulled from Lake Athabasca in front of the cameras, grotesque whitefish corpses covered in tumours and lesions of unknown origin. The shock tactic worked. The alleged environmental and health crisis in Fort Chipewyan soon supplanted the plight of bitumen-coated ducks as the default protest issue in the Patch.

Within days, a global media spotlight descended on Fort Chipewyan far greater in size than Schindler likely imagined. In the last week of September, the movie director James Cameron, widely regarded as one of the most powerful people in Hollywood, paid a visit to the Patch. The timing was coincidental, but with deformed fish so fresh in the public mind, Cameron's arrival amplified the sense of crisis. Cameron was born in Canada, and he began to take a special interest in Indigenous environmental issues in the wake of the 2009 release of his movie *Avatar*. The

multibillion-dollar blockbuster was a sci-fi fable about a distant planet covered in pristine rainforest wilderness being rapidly laid to waste by a rapa-
cious mining company digging up a mineral that has become humanity's
primary fuel source back on earth. The planet's rainforest is inhabited by
an Indigenous humanoid tribe called the Na'avi, who fight back against
the mammoth machines of the miners. In April 2010 Cameron attended
a meeting of the United Nations Permanent Forum on Indigenous Issues,
in New York, and screened *Avatar* for the attendees. In a press interview
ahead of the meeting, he described the oil sands as a "black eye" on the
image of his native Canada, lamenting its pursuit of "a dead-end paradigm, which is fossil fuels." At some point around then, the ACFN invited
Cameron to visit Fort Chipewyan. Serendipitously, the director landed in
the Patch just two weeks after Schindler's press conference.

Cameron arrived in Alberta at the very peak of his Hollywood mogul-
dom. In the years after the 1997 global megahit *Titanic*, Cameron had
reinvented deep-sea exploration for a documentary and induced a step
change in 3-D special effects to make *Avatar*. The striking similarities between the film's colossal mining gear and the Cat 797s on an oil sands
mine site, as well as the analogous position of the Na'avi and the Dene in
their path, were lost on no one. When news of the impending visit reached
the provincial legislature in Edmonton, Premier Ed Stelmach cut short a
working trip to Quebec to meet with Cameron.

On Tuesday, September 27, Cameron arrived in Fort McMurray.
With a media retinue in tow, he attended a morning technical briefing
and chatted with the provincial environment minister. He toured a reclaimed wetland on Syncrude's Mildred Lake site and a well pad at Cenovus's Christina Lake in situ facility. Then he boarded a plane to Fort
Chipewyan and spent the rest of the day meeting with band officials and
elders. In the evening, there was a feast of stew and bannock and a hoop
dancing display. The next day, Cameron flew to Edmonton to meet with
the premier. The *Edmonton Sun* greeted him with a front-page image of
his own face in a green Syncrude hard hat and a one-word headline—
"Dipstick!"—in extra-large type. ("Hollywood phoney James Cameron

will help take Alberta to court over oil sands," read a subhead, erroneously.) Cameron's discussion with Stelmach was by all reports much more amicable. The director and the premier bonded over their shared farm-boy roots—Cameron in northern Ontario, Stelmach in a prairie community southeast of Edmonton—and agreed to disagree about some of the merits of oil sands development.

At a final press conference, Cameron provided significantly more nuance to his take on the oil sands than he had when he spoke of Canada's "black eye."

"It will be a curse if it's not managed properly," he said. "It can also be a great gift to Canada and to Alberta." He warned that the project's pace needed careful management, that the downstream environmental costs should be taken much more seriously. "The people in Fort Chipewyan are afraid to drink their own water, they are afraid to eat the fish, and they are afraid to let their kids swim in the river. The idea of that is appalling to me, and for a community to live in fear like that, we need to look into this."

Cameron had come to the Patch with an engineer's eye for improvement and at least a partially open mind. The premier saw the value in his visit, even if the *Edmonton Sun* never would. Perhaps Cameron couldn't have known, but his whirlwind tour would soon become a template, and subsequent visitors would prove less interested in the complexities of the scene.

In the meantime, the science of the oil sands and its environmental footprint carried on. It began from less certain assumptions than are often the case in such studies, in part because the farther north you go in the boreal forest, the less science has been done. Schindler and other researchers found elevated levels of a range of heavy metals and other oil sands–connected toxins in the water near Fort Chipewyan, but there are essentially no preindustrial baseline studies of the Peace-Athabasca Delta's aquatic chemistry.

The delta is a massive wetland on a scale similar to the Mississippi Delta. It is a labyrinth of rivulets and streams, low forest and muskeg, enormous lakes and countless tiny ponds. The water levels in the delta rise and fall, and sometimes whole lakes and marshes disappear for decades in response to the flow of the two great rivers that wind down from the Rocky Mountains, meeting in the delta to slosh together and continue north to the Arctic as one. En route to the delta, the Peace and Athabasca Rivers flow past coal-fired power plants and pulp mills and through intensively cultivated farm country. The banks of the Athabasca and many of its tributaries are studded with bitumen outcroppings that deposit oil sands into the river. And the Peace has roared through terrain rich in conventional oil and natural gas development since 1918, long before oil sands entered the equation. The two rivers meet in the Peace-Athabasca Delta, a wilderness like nothing else on earth—a UNESCO World Heritage Site anchored by a massive protected space, Wood Buffalo National Park, which is two-thirds the size of New Brunswick. Until recently, almost nothing was known about the water that covers it.

Starting around 2000, a research team that included scientists from the University of Waterloo, Wilfrid Laurier University, the University of Manitoba and the University of Regina began some of the first studies of the historic hydrology and aquatic chemistry of the delta. The initial research was spurred by a lawsuit against BC Hydro, the provincially owned hydroelectric company that had first dammed the Peace River in 1967.

The W. A. C. Bennett Dam was a 3,000-megawatt High Modern engineering triumph of its day. It was also the single greatest disruption to water flows and Indigenous life the delta had ever seen. In the first few years after the dam's completion, the delta ran dry and Lake Athabasca's water level plummeted as the massive reservoir filled behind the new dam. With no water to travel on in summer and no ice to cross in winter, Indigenous hunters, trappers and fishers were unable to provide for themselves. For many Dene, the dam's construction marked the first permanent exodus from the bush to the town of Fort Chipewyan. BC Hydro had funded the Waterloo research team to determine the fine details of the dam's long-term impact on the delta, so that it paid out only for the damage that could conclusively be tied to its activities.

The original research team included Roland Hall of the University of Waterloo and Brent Wolfe of Wilfrid Laurier University, who carried on with their research after the lawsuit had been settled. It was rare in their fields—aquatic biology and ecology, respectively—to find an ecosystem of such scale and importance where so little primary research had been conducted. As part of the BC Hydro study, they had gathered sediment cores from lakes in the delta—chunks of sandy debris from the lake bottoms, some of them three hundred years old—to establish baseline readings of the aquatic system's chemistry. Some of the cores came from lakes that had filled with flood water before the oil sands mines began operating and had never since reconnected to the waterways flowing northward from the Athabasca. These provided snapshots of the composition of water in the delta before industry arrived, which could be compared to more recent samples to see what had changed after large-scale oil production began in the region.

Their findings were preliminary, their research ongoing. Still, in 2012 and again in 2014, Hall, Wolfe and their colleagues published papers showing no significant spike in pollution in the delta since the first oil sands mines started operating. The 2012 study noted that volumes of airborne heavy metals and arsenic in their core samples peaked in the 1950s and 1960s. (The smelter at the Giant gold mine north of the delta in Yellowknife released as much arsenic every day in the 1950s as the oil sands industry had in its lifetime.) The 2014 paper argued there was "little to no evidence of pollution by the oil sands development" downstream as far as Lake Athabasca and beyond. "Notably, our data show that the Athabasca River has been a source of metals to the Athabasca Delta for centuries before oil sands development, equivalent to that measured in recent years."

Wolfe and Hall readily acknowledged that the chemistry of an ecosystem as vast and complex as the Peace-Athabasca Delta and the full ecological impact of an industry as enormous in scale as the oil sands were in no way fully explained by a couple of scientific papers. The Peace and Athabasca Rivers flow past coal plants and pulp mills, through cities and towns. The eastern shore of Lake Athabasca was for decades home to a major uranium mine. The tailings ponds upstream near Fort McKay still leached toxins into the groundwater around them, and the coking stacks still sent carcinogens into the air to settle in lakes and snowpack in the immediate vicinity. Nevertheless, the industry's longstanding assertion that natural bitumen seeps were the source of whatever contamination was found in the water farther downstream turned out, according to best available evidence, to be plausible.

Of all the major scientific studies and blue-ribbon reports on the environmental impact of the oil sands published in the years after the boom began, few received as little attention as these ones. The delta's story—and the Patch's—had veered off in other directions, carried by a narrative arc about how to measure progress in the twenty-first century that was moving too fast to wait on the slow, steady accumulation of all the data.

THE PRICE OF FAME

When James Cameron visited the Patch in 2010, neither he nor his hosts fully understood the magnitude of the opposition to oil sands development soon to arrive. The largest American climate change activism campaign in a generation was just beginning to mount, and its chosen target was a new pipeline project proposed by TransCanada PipeLines to carry eight hundred thousand barrels of bitumen per day from central Alberta to refineries on the Gulf of Mexico. The pipeline's name—Keystone XL—would soon become a catch-all term for the entire global industry's failure to act on climate change.

The oil sands had been clear and prominent on the radar of the international environmental movement well before Cameron brought the world's media spotlight to Fort Chipewyan for the first time. Canadian environmental groups had been issuing backgrounders and reports about the ecological destruction in the region and the Alberta government's apparent lack of regulatory oversight on the pace and scale of its growth for years. In 2008 the Canadian arm of Environmental Defence published its thirty-page report calling the Patch "the most destructive project on earth."

Months later, Syncrude's duck disaster made worldwide headlines, and images of ducks covered in tailings pond scum and open-pit-mine moonscapes began to appear on billboards in Europe and in environmental reports in Washington.

But all this was mere prelude. In December 2009 the world's politicians, climate policy experts and environmentalists met in Copenhagen, Denmark, for COP15—the fifteenth UN Climate Change Conference, or Congress of the Parties—which was a desperate effort to save the coordinated global response to climate change that had begun with the first summit in Rio de Janeiro, Brazil, in 1992 and the introduction of the Kyoto Protocol in 1997. COP15 was an unmitigated disaster, a near-total collapse of the entire climate treaty process. It left climate activists thoroughly demoralized—especially in the United States, where a cap-and-trade bill on greenhouse gas emissions, President Barack Obama's signature piece of climate legislation, died in the Senate a few months later.

Hunting for a climate campaign they could win, American activists settled on the Keystone XL pipeline project, which had already been attracting opposition from ranchers and other landowners in its path in Nebraska. The choice was not arbitrary; Keystone XL made an attractive target. It was a single issue, a stand-alone project that could be approved or cancelled by executive authority of the president alone. It could be protested and blocked in a manner familiar to environmental groups that had built their reputations saving stands of old-growth forest from chain saws and pods of whales from harpoons. It was self-contained and tidy, readily reduced to a declarative hashtag—#NoKXL—on social media. And the oil to be carried by the pipe came from an industrial project few had heard of that was readymade for placards and billboards, a mammoth open-pit mine site that looked like someone had built *Avatar*'s mining operations on the Mordor stage set from *The Lord of the Rings*. There was even an Indigenous population, a real-life Na'avi, ready to host visiting celebrities.

This was the momentum building behind James Cameron's oil sands tour, and the campaign roared on after he was long gone. The people of Fort Chipewyan—the thousand Dene and Mikisew Cree and Metis residents of the village and the surrounding reserve—were used to being ignored, and so they made the most of the media spotlight when it fell upon them. The Mikisew Cree took their case to the United Nations, petitioning UNESCO to reclassify Wood Buffalo National Park as a World Heritage site "in danger," which would put pressure on the federal and provincial governments to bring in special protections for the region. And the ACFN became world famous. Celebrity tours of the oil sands soon became almost commonplace, the superstars arriving in northern Alberta one after another: actor Leonardo DiCaprio, rock legend Neil Young, Archbishop Desmond Tutu and Bill Nye the Science Guy. Each toured the oil sands mines north of Fort McMurray by helicopter. And many of them also flew into Fort Chipewyan to pose with the ACFN's media-savvy chief, Allan Adam, standing together to denounce the industry, calling on the world to stand with this brave Indigenous community and stop the pipeline—stop the whole oil sands project—before there was nothing left for the Dene or anyone else. Reports of their visits often featured stock footage of Suncor's production plant or Syncrude's tailings pond, clouds of smoke belching into the sky. Cut to pristine forest, Dene dancers twirling in vivid blue and red robes, Chief Adam and some megastar shoulder to shoulder, looking noble and grave.

The nuance of the fledgling science and the uncertainty of its conclusions vanished from the discussion. Local health and environmental issues were conflated breezily with the outsized carbon footprint of oil sands production and the entire mounting planetary climate crisis. The oil sands were killing people in Fort Chipewyan now. And it was a pending climate catastrophe that could kill us all. It had to be stopped.

"The fact is, Fort McMurray looks like Hiroshima. Fort McMurray is a wasteland. The Indians up there and the Native peoples are dying." That was Neil Young on Capitol Hill in Washington, DC, in 2013. Director Darren Aronofsky, who visited Fort Chipewyan with DiCaprio, published a journal of his visit on the Daily Beast website under a headline calling it "The Climate War's Ground Zero." Archbishop Tutu described the oil sands as "filth" after his tour of the Patch, "emblematic of an era that must end." Bill Nye said his tour was "depressive" and that he found the environmental impacts "astonishing and overwhelming."

Hiroshima. Mordor. The most destructive project on earth. The visitors came and went, and the howl of protest built month by month. Meanwhile, Obama's decision on the Keystone XL project waited on a new State Department environmental impact assessment or another engineering report. By 2015, all the data points and all the momentum—economic, political, environmental—pointed in the wrong direction for the Patch. Oil prices plunged below $50, triggering project cancellations and layoffs and nerve-wracking analyst reports suggesting that whatever came after this bust might not look anything like the boom just ended. US approval of Keystone XL, once described by Prime Minister Stephen Harper as a "no-brainer," appeared questionable, and then it started to seem unlikely. Harper's party lost its re-election bid in October, and finally, in November, Obama rejected the proposal outright.

Then came COP21 in Paris in December, another round of climate talks. The conference was expected to achieve little after the collapse in Copenhagen and the dissembling in the years since. But somehow a wildly improbable new climate deal became reality, signed by the formerly intransigent United States and China as well as the new Canadian government. And so 2015 closed with a sharp rebuke of the definition of progress that had held sway for more than half a century and sanctioned an oil patch in the woods of northern Alberta.

"The world will depend on oil for decades to come," a Bloomberg reporter wrote on the eve of the Paris summit. "But 2015 may very well be remembered as the beginning of the end." It was a message that seemed particularly grave for those 2.4 million barrels of bitumen still flowing into the marketplace each day—among the most expensive and emissions intensive of the entire global supply, an economic marvel turned necessary evil while the Patch's business and political leaders were still trying to figure out how they had become the target of such ire.

When the chorus of opposition to oil sands development first began to rise, there was a default response to such chatter ready and waiting in the

Patch. The industry's executives and boosters, its rank and file, heads of Chambers of Commerce and Rotary club stalwarts across Alberta, politicians at every level of government—they knew how to reply to these critics. How did James Cameron's private jet get itself airborne and fly all the way from Los Angeles to Alberta, anyway? Didn't everyone—critics and boosters alike—use their product every single day? Oil was a commodity in high and increasing demand. If someone wants to point a finger, point it at the tailpipe of the car in their garage. Ask them if they want to go back to the age of horses and buggies. Not to mention that Alberta's industry was about as tightly run as they come. Talk to an oil guy who'd been to Saudi Arabia or the Niger Delta or the deep jungle of Ecuador about what kind of environmental oversight you found there, how much the government worried about its per capita emissions footprint. One day, sure, maybe there would be another way to do things, solar panels on the roof and an electric car in the garage or who knows what, hyperloops or jet packs or a million bikes in every city, like those crazy Dutch and Danes. But today? Today, everyone still needs oil.

"If I honestly believed we could meet the needs of our customers, employees and shareholders and the general public by switching from petroleum to solar, wind, biochemical or any other energy source, we would be out of the oil sands tomorrow," wrote Rick George, former Suncor CEO, in his 2012 memoir *Sun Rise*. "It's not going to happen, however, and I would like people to understand the true role of the oil sands in meeting a vital need before they insist the world would be a better place without them." In George's chapter on "The Challenge of Global Warming," he contrasts the Patch's greenhouse gas emissions with humanity's global carbon footprint. "Canada is currently responsible for 2 percent of GHG emissions, and oil sands production in turn is responsible for 5 percent of Canada's total emissions. Put those numbers together, and you get about one-tenth of 1 percent of global emissions." The following chapter, which addresses the industry's critics, begins, "Thanks to my training as an engineer . . . I tend to value facts over speculation." Later in the chapter, George notes the total square footage of the three homes in Malibu owned by James Cameron.

There was a kind of provincial politician you met at industry functions during the boom years, a regional fundraiser for this or that charity, an awards banquet put on by the Canadian Association of Petroleum Producers to congratulate some oil sands company for planting so many trees. He—it was always a *he*—would be the representative from some small town or rural region, Brooks or Sundre or the Peace Country or a dozen other places no one outside of Alberta has ever heard of. Places where there had never been anyone but a Progressive Conservative representing them in the legislature as long as the guy sitting there had been alive. Places where winning the PC nomination was the whole race, where the winner was sent to the legislature in Edmonton with 60 or 70 percent of the vote, and if he did that two or three elections in a row, he might well be the minister of the environment sitting there. He might listen to a little after-dinner chat about climate change and sustainable business, he might even nod along. But ask him what should be done?

Well, you need to understand. You go out to Brooks or Sundre and start talking about *reducing emissions* or *the low-carbon economy* or whatever that speaker was on about? That is *not* what the voters in those parts elected you for. They weren't thinking about that—they might not even know what it means. Or they might even think all that was some UN nonsense spread by liberals and socialists and charlatan scientists chasing easy funding for another level on their ivory towers. Just like Trudeau and his damn National Energy Program. You stopped by a PC rally during the boom years, you were pretty much guaranteed to see a bumper sticker on more than one pickup truck that said, "Protect the West," and then it listed the three worst threats to western Canadian liberty, which were the wheat pool, the Liberals' godawful gun registry, and the Kyoto Protocol. No, these people didn't want to hear about their *carbon footprint*. And if you went around as their stalwart PC representative forcing that talk down their throats, pretty soon you were out of a job yourself.

This is what they said in government circles in Alberta, in private, pouring another glass of wine after a banquet hall dinner. It's what they said right up to the day in May 2015 when their leader, Jim Prentice,

stepped up to that podium at the Metropolitan Centre in downtown Calgary and conceded the election to the left-wing NDP.

DELTA BLUES AND GREENS

In September 2015, with oil stuck at $45 a barrel and former US secretary of state Hillary Clinton declaring her opposition to the Keystone XL pipeline from the campaign trail, a helicopter circled Fort Chipewyan for several days in a row. The helicopter was a Bell JetRanger II chartered out of Fort McMurray. It was dark red with a white belly and floatation pontoons affixed to its landing skids. It lifted off from the small airstrip just north of town a couple of times each morning and a couple more each afternoon. Once airborne, it traced a lazy, squiggling loop north from Fort Chipewyan, circling westward over the Peace-Athabasca Delta.

The sky in the delta at summer's end is often cloudless and sighing blue. The landscape unfolds across the horizon in broad belts of deep green, gold, dusty brown, and aqueous blue, low scrub coniferous trees alternating with tall grass and muskeg, all of it encrusted with lakes and bogs and rivulets, seemingly too many to count.

As the helicopter made its trip across the delta, it set down in an erratic pattern at various stretches of open water and swampy bog. It eventually followed the Slave River roughly southward and then came in low over wide, shallow Lake Claire and Lake Mamawi, which opens out into Lake Athabasca itself. As the helicopter passed by the Fort Chipewyan waterfront, it stopped, hovered, and set itself down on the lake's surface, a few hundred metres offshore. Three figures emerged from the passenger seats, as they had at more than a dozen other aquatic spots along its route. They squatted down on the pontoons to dip big plastic water bladders and probes into the water. And then the chopper lifted off, ran quickly over the town, and set back down at the airstrip to unload its cargo.

The crew on each trip, in addition to the pilot, consisted of either Roland Hall or Brent Wolfe; a graduate biology student from the University of Waterloo named Casey Remmer; and a volunteer, usually a park ranger

from the Wood Buffalo National Park office in Fort Chipewyan or an elder from the Dene or Mikisew Cree nations. Each time the helicopter
set down in the delta, this ad hoc research team would gather five litres
of delta water. Four litres went into a carboy, a generic name for the soft-
sided, collapsible plastic water bladders preferred by field researchers in
aquatic chemistry. Another litre filled a Nalgene bottle of the sort people
bring to the gym, and a small additional sample was scooped into a small
laboratory vial. Readings were also taken using a device the research crew
referred to by its brand name—the YSI, a handheld digital sampling tool
attached to a long, black metal wand that, when submerged, provided
readings of depth, temperature, pH, turbidity, oxygen level and a handful
of other physical details.

At the end of each trip through the delta, the researchers loaded their
samples into an old minivan they'd borrowed and drove back to the main
drag in downtown Fort Chipewyan, where they were staying in a vacant
house owned by Parks Canada, next door to the Wood Buffalo National
Park office. They stored the water samples in a couple of big industrial
refrigerators in a storage shed in the yard.

Wolfe and Hall had set up a makeshift laboratory in the basement to
conduct some initial testing on the samples. All day, while one of them
was out in the chopper, the other was in the basement, working through
the meticulous analytical steps with one sample after another. During
a week of field research, they would gather samples from seventy-three
sites—sixty-two lakes and eleven river locations—and process dozens of
them of them before their departure.

The basement lab sprawled across every available surface in the
house's laundry room. Boxes of disposable filter screens and bags of sy-
ringes and small sample bottles sat on top of the washer and dryer. On the
counter next to them, surgical tubing snaked from a mechanical pump to
a series of graduated flasks. Long into the evening, Wolfe and Hall ran the
water samples through several different filtering processes. They poured
water from bladders into graduated flasks, ran the pump to force the water
through screens, gathered the debris-covered screens and wrapped them

in aluminum foil. A folding side table was filled with little envelopes of foil and small plastic bottles of treated water, each with a coded series of numbers and letters written in Sharpie on the side to indicate the date and location and the kind of filtering it had undergone. After the research trip concluded, the filtered samples would be sent to various university and commercial labs to be analyzed for a range of parameters including chemistry, types of algae present, and the amount of particles suspended in the water. The data set that the whole process yielded would add another small window on the truth of what was in the water in the Peace-Athabasca Delta and how it got there. Three times a year, Wolfe and Hall and their colleagues returned to the delta to add new data sets to this larger picture slowly emerging.

The first research project Wolfe and Hall embarked upon had aimed to determine how much damage the building of the W. A. C. Bennett Dam in the headwaters of the Peace River did to the delta's delicate, complex hydrology. They had barely unlocked the delta's larger riddles, though, and so they carried on with the research through a variety of federal scientific funding agencies. Along the way, Wolfe received a Northern Research Chair position from the Natural Sciences and Engineering Research Council of Canada (NSERC, Canada's premier scientific funding program).

Wolfe and Hall soon saw ways to use the data they were gathering from sediment cores to reconstruct the history of water pollution in the delta, which could address mounting concerns about the impact of the Patch just then beginning to boom. They applied to an NSERC program for new funding, but to their surprise, the program's review committee told them their research was so obviously valuable to industry that they should seek funding that way instead. After all, the world's wealthiest commodity business had deeper pockets and far fewer kinds of research to fund than NSERC did. Through their contacts at BC Hydro, Wolfe and Hall were eventually put in touch with a lawyer at Suncor. They were piloted through the company's internal bureaucracy in fits and starts. In 2010, more than four years after their initial NSERC application, Suncor agreed to back their work in the delta. As their research ramped up in the years after that, other industry partners (BC Hydro and CNRL) provided support, as well as the Alberta government, NSERC and a handful of other federal funding bodies.

With financial backing in place, Wolfe and Hall and their graduate students began their triannual visits to Fort Chipewyan—in late spring, summer and early fall. The samples they gathered allowed them to see the way the water changed across a full season, as well as year to year. Comparing their results with the historic information revealed in core samples, Wolfe and Hall aimed to uncover crucial evidence about how and when the delta's water was contaminated. It wasn't enough to say there were carcinogenic PAHs or traces of arsenic in the water at a particular level; when and how they got there mattered. To tell that tale, the research investigated both the chemistry of the water and the overall hydrology of the delta—the movement of the water across the land over time.

"There's no doubt that there's pollutants that are getting into the river," Wolfe said. "It's just, are they in measurable quantities compared to what is already there? We know there's pollution. We're just trying to characterize it."

Let's say a researcher discovers a concentration of a particular contaminant in a delta water sample. As pure chemistry, this is a single reading, a volume per millilitre of water. The samples processed in the basement lab in Fort Chipewyan revealed that kind of information, as did previous studies reporting "elevated" levels in the region of contaminants such as heavy metals and PAHs associated with oil sands production. That data can be compared with environmental regulations and safety guidelines, deemed acceptable or not. But it can't speak to when or how the contaminants got there. So Wolfe and Hall expanded their research in pursuit of reliable baseline data. And they used their sediment cores to look at how the water has changed over time.

"The sediment core studies are just completely instrumental in going back in time and looking at what those concentrations were like prior to the 1960s, when oil sands development began," Wolfe said.

He and Hall also sent off those extra little vials of delta water they gathered to find their distinctive isotope signatures. Water is water—a molecule consisting of two hydrogen atoms bound to one oxygen atom—but rare forms of water can have two additional neutrons in one of the oxygen atoms or one extra neutron in the hydrogen atom. This reveals the water molecule's isotope, and it provides a kind of fingerprint. The isotope signature explained where the water sample had come from—revealing, for example, whether the lake it was drawn from had recently been inundated with flood waters and how much evaporation had taken place there. All of this helped to map the extent of flooding in the delta and fill in some of the missing information needed to figure out how it had changed over the years.

As diligent scientists, Wolfe and Hall always describe their work as in progress and their conclusions as open to dispute. Still, they have found to date that the contaminants in the delta's water aren't connected to the rise of the Patch. "When you get that far downstream to the Athabasca Delta," Wolfe said, "we have these studies that suggest that we cannot detect any evidence of pollution or contaminants above the background levels."

The financial support Wolfe and Hall received from Suncor became a portentous asterisk in some press reports when their research began to confirm what the oil sands business had long claimed, which was that the contaminants in the delta's water found their way there primarily through natural bitumen seepage. But they publish their data and analysis in peer-reviewed science journals, not corporate reports. A sediment core doesn't care who paid for the chartered helicopter that enabled its extraction—it simply provides an ancient snapshot of the water's composition before industry of any sort began in the region.

There is no question the delta today is not the delta that once was before oil was mined from bitumen, coal burned and uranium unearthed to make electricity, trees mashed into pulp at riverside mills. Fish routinely come out of the water in the delta on a gill net with lesions and tumours. Elders from Fort Chipewyan all the way down the Slave River to Yellowknife and beyond report fish and game that seem off somehow, the flesh too soft or the flavour not right. Everyone in Fort Chipewyan knows there is less water in the lakes than there used to be. Everyone knows someone who has cancer or who had a family member die of cancer. Everyone is anxious about the water, what's in it, what it might be doing to them. But the Lake Athabasca shoreline receding, the people of Fort Chipewyan swearing off fish or worrying over their water—this is not evidence of culpability, for the oil sands or any other industrial project whose effluent and clouds of hydrocarbon smoke have invaded the ecosystem in the last hundred years.

This is the grunt work of science, the tedious heavy lifting: hundreds of samples, gathered and analyzed and labelled and sent to labs for further testing, three times a year, year after year, until a pattern emerges. This is how you determine exactly what toll the oil sands operations takes on their environment, not by way of a protest slogan or corporate press release. The total emissions created in producing a barrel might be 17 percent more than the average barrel of crude (as the EPA determined) or three times as much (as some activists claimed). Or it might be somewhere in between. When there are definitive numbers to answer such questions—if there are—they will emerge from the hard work done by scientists in the manner of Hall and Wolfe.

The people in Fort Chipewyan have legitimate questions, and they have been asking them in vain for years. On the subject of the Patch and what it's doing to the health of the planet, people all over the world have legitimate questions. But there are few definitive answers. The studies to date inevitably conclude with more suspicion than certainty. A 2007 study of contaminant concentrations in delta water noted they were elevated and appeared to be rising but lamented the "paucity of data." The provincial government, responding to repeated calls for more information, established the Peace-Athabasca Delta Environmental Monitoring Program (PADEMP) in 2008. Wolfe and Hall were charter members, and they and their colleagues gather in Fort Chipewyan every February to compare data. They consider input from eleven Indigenous groups in the region, each of which has a seat on the program's steering committee. They review data measuring everything from carcinogenic PAHs at thirty-three sites to methylmercury levels in delta invertebrates. There are presentations about the health of white sucker fish and contaminants in wood frogs. Water flow rates and muskrat DNA give clues as to the ongoing changes in the delta, the impact of dams and oil sands mines upstream. The findings are generally preliminary, the long-term studies ongoing. One presenter after another at PADEMP acknowledges the extraordinary dynamism of the delta ecosystem, its mysteries deepening in complexity with each spring melt and winter freeze. There is no doubt the landscape, the water and the animals have been altered by human hands here, but unraveling the varied fingerprints of hydroelectric dams and pulp mills and agricultural runoff and uranium mines, differentiating all of it from the oil sands activity just upstream that is the near and present danger that brought everyone to this February meeting in Fort Chipewyan—this is a project barely underway.

This debate finds its mirror in the ones about exactly how much more carbon dioxide is produced by a barrel of bitumen than by a conventional barrel, how much more greenhouse gas would be added to Canada's substantial per capita footprint if this pipeline or that project expansion was approved, and whether that per capita footprint even matters—and if it does, then how much does it matter when the global footprint is so much larger and growing so fast itself? Every politician and business spokesperson in the Patch can tell you unequivocally, just like Rick George did, that the oil sands represent less than 10 percent of all of Canada's emissions and just 0.1 percent of the world's. So why are the seventy annual megatons of carbon dioxide from these 2.4 million daily barrels—less than 3 percent of global demand, a share growing far more slowly than the share from America's fracking operations—why are these the ones that can't be tolerated?

These are all difficult and important questions, the ones about aquatic chemistry and climate politics alike, and they deserve to be answered. The final answers won't fit on placards or bumper stickers. But there are interim answers, and those have already been shrunk to slogan size, the waters muddied by the entrenchment of opposing camps.

In some sense, all the confusion and suspicion are by-products of the Patch's own reversal of fortune. The oil sands went from marginal experiment to roaring success at such breakneck speed that it was a colossus by the time the industry's minders had started to figure out how to answer the most rudimentary questions about the ecology of it all—an issue which, to be sure, was far from a top priority for Alberta's industry-friendly government. What was in the water and how did it get there? How do you remediate an oil sands tailings pond? How much carbon dioxide is the Patch adding to the province's or the world's carbon footprint? Where is this all heading, and is this where the province or the country or the world wants to go?

No one exactly knew, and there was no time to answer it. There was a boom on. The great High Modern engine was racing half blind into the frigid boreal night. All you could do was ride along.

TEN

SPOILED PATCH

COPENHAGEN BLUES

In the bureaucratic argot of the United Nations, the global climate conference in Copenhagen, Denmark, in December 2009 was officially known as the fifteenth Congress of the Parties to the United Nations Framework Convention on Climate Change. Most of the attendees just called it COP15—the number counting the years since the climate treaty negotiated at the 1992 Rio summit went into force in 1994, and COP rather handily serving as an acronym for the conference and an abbreviation of the host city. There was much fanfare to COP15, a certain amount of hope and an even larger measure of desperation that the conference would salvage the stagnant Kyoto Protocol, which had committed 192 of the world's nations to greenhouse gas emissions cuts but had spurred nowhere near enough action. The United States was one of the few countries that hadn't ratified the Kyoto treaty, and with Barack Obama now in the

White House, bureaucrats and activists alike hoped to see a truly global agreement emerge.

COP15 was a brash pageant of international climate change activism and advocacy. Alongside the formal proceedings, an activist-led People's Climate Forum attracted fifty thousand people. There were alternate protocols issued on behalf of Pacific island nations in danger of vanishing into the rising sea and protest demonstrations in support of Indigenous rights. Inside the conference hall, meanwhile, Obama and his delegation appeared ready to make a deal. As the negotiations stretched over days, however, progress ground to a halt, and the bureaucratic version of chaos reigned as the Chinese delegation—aided, on occasion, by India and a handful of African nations that serve as Chinese surrogates in such forums—sabotaged the COP15 draft declaration, deleting specific language in favour of vague promises and setting it up for a failure that could be blamed on the United States. "China gutted the deal behind the scenes and then left its proxies to savage it in public," wrote environmental journalist Mark Lynas, who attended the proceedings, in the *Guardian*.

The Canadian delegation at COP15, led by Prime Minister Stephen Harper, was notable for its intransigence. Though Canada was still a signatory to the Kyoto Protocol—a commitment made by Jean Chrétien's government in 1997—Harper had made no effort to hide his contempt for climate summits and their declarations. As an opposition MP in 2002, he'd dismissed Kyoto as a "socialist scheme." COP15 was Harper's third UN climate conference, and his government's delegation was now routinely singled out for the "Fossil of the Day" award bestowed by the activist community upon the government deemed least helpful to the proceedings.

To observers from afar who, if they pay any attention to UN confabs at all, expect them to end in bureaucratic stalemates and vaguely stated good intentions, COP15 was a routine boondoggle. But to many in the international environmental movement, it was a catastrophe, a final grim hope of salvation—or at least some semblance of it—cruelly torn to shreds on the conference floor. This was especially true for American activists, who had toiled through the grim years of swaggering oil-business cronies George W. Bush and Dick Cheney in the White House dreaming of a president who would arrive at an event like COP15 willing to actually take action.

In a blog post for *Mother Jones* mid-conference, environmental writer and activist Bill McKibben—who had written one of the first mainstream books on climate change (1989's *The End of Nature*) and founded an international climate action network called 350.org—wrote about his grief while attending a special church service at COP15, where both the Archbishop of Canterbury and Desmond Tutu spoke. "This afternoon I sobbed for an hour, and I'm still choking a little," McKibben wrote. The service had begun with a procession of artifacts symbolizing climate change's wrath—bleached coral, desiccated ears of corn—and McKibben found himself overcome by the sense of futility they represented. "I've done everything I can think of, and millions of people around the world have joined us at 350.org in the most international campaign there ever was. But I just sat there thinking: *It's not enough. We didn't do enough.*"

For American climate change activists, this sense of futility and despair was widespread and rapidly deepening. Earlier in 2009, the US House of Representatives had narrowly passed a bill to bring in a cap-and-trade system that would put a price on greenhouse gas emissions across the United States. It was a compromised piece of legislation, but after the policy vacuum of the Bush years, it became the flagship not just of Obama's climate policy ambitions but of the entire mainstream environmental movement's hopes for real action, finally, on what was understood to be the defining environmental issue of its time—if not a potentially existential threat to the whole project of human civilization. By COP15, however, the cap-and-trade bill had stalled in the Senate, and in the early spring of 2010, it was clear the Democrats lacked the support to pass it. Ultimately, they never even put it to a vote. A quarter century after the climate change crisis had emerged, the movement to do something about it had ground to a desultory halt in the capital of the world's number two emitter of greenhouse gases. This was in part because of the meddling of the world's top emitter—China—but also due to deep intransigence in the United States itself. The climate action movement appeared to be going nowhere.

The reasons for the bouts of stagnation and the slow, lurching nature of what action has been taken on climate change—not just in the United States but worldwide—are as complex and varied as the whole enormous contraption of industrial society. But a significant factor for the environmental movement was that it had evolved to fight much different battles from one as pervasive and multivalent as climate change. The loose web of institutional NGOs, grassroots protest groups, think tanks and lobby groups that define the movement was built on the structure and logistics of discrete campaigns. Conservation groups in the early nineteen hundreds—the earliest antecedents of the modern environmental movement—arose to demand protection for particular stretches of treasured wilderness. (The model for advocacy in that era, John Muir's Sierra Club, was named for the Sierra Nevada mountain range it fought to preserve.)

The basic concept—and, in the case of the Sierra Club, the organization itself—carried on through the reinvention of conservation as environmentalism in the postwar years. Rachel Carson's 1962 book *Silent Spring* and the ensuing campaign to ban the pesticide DDT created the new prototype. Carson's book was an alarm call not just about the damage DDT was wreaking on birds' eggs but about the ecological blind spots of an entire industrial order. The response, though, was narrowly focused, specific and measurable: ten years after the book first hit shelves, DDT's production and use had been banned in the United States.

There soon emerged something like a standard structure to the life cycle of an environmental issue in the years after *Silent Spring*. A problem would be identified as significantly acute and urgent, often by scientists or environmental groups or both in concert. Public awareness was then raised through protest, publicity stunts and media campaigns. Government officials were persuaded of the necessity to act. New regulation was proposed, debated, drafted, passed. Affected industries were obliged, often reluctantly, to comply.

There was a symmetry to it. A rogue Greenpeace boat blocks a whaling ship's harpoons, the subsequent media attention plants "Save the Whales" in the public consciousness, and in due course an international moratorium on commercial whaling is enacted. Industrial phosphates pouring into the Great Lakes are identified as the cause of biodiversity-killing algal blooms, and toxic chemicals known as PCBs are found leaking into waterways. Their use and disposal become tightly controlled. Sulphur dioxide emissions from power plant smokestacks, clear-cut logging, a refrigeration chemical destroying the atmosphere's vital ozone layer—one after another, specific environmental contaminants and pollution streams are identified, campaigns mounted, and problems reduced, if rarely solved completely. If the ground-level reality of such campaigns was often much more precarious and complex, the entirety of it was nonetheless fixed in time and place. Environmental crises were discrete phenomena that could be assessed, addressed, contained.

When climate change emerged from the halls of academia in the late 1980s as a major public policy issue, it was assessed at first as another campaign—very likely bigger than any previous one but subject to the same basic rules of nature and the same modes of politics. All the old environmentalist tools of mass protest, awareness building, and media manipulation were brought to bear on the issue. Within a few years of the first congressional testimony on the science and public threat of climate change, delivered in June 1988 by NASA climate scientist James Hansen, the issue's vast scope and generational timeframe had been well enough understood to make it the core focus of a series of international conferences hosted by the UN. The Kyoto Protocol that emerged from those meetings was modelled on the hugely successful 1987 Montreal Protocol on Substances That Deplete the Ozone Layer, which had ushered in worldwide controls on the production of the refrigerant chemicals known as CFCs (chlorofluorocarbons) that had blown a hole in the ozone layer.

Climate change, however, could not be tackled in any fundamental way merely by demanding that a few companies manufacturing a single pollutant cease and desist. Greenhouse gases were emitted by virtually everyone, everywhere, all the time. They were the smoke pouring from the engine of all of industrial society. The culprit was more than 85 percent of the energy used by humanity each day. Virtually everyone on earth was culpable, and the consequences were slow in arriving and distant in both time and space from the source of the pollution, creating changes that were incremental and largely invisible. A whole subgenre of behavioural psychology emerged to explain how ill-suited the human animal was to assessing the risk of climate change and acting in any meaningful way to avoid it.

And so, a quarter century after the first alarm bells, while the ineffectual collective process of climate change action fell moribund in a Copenhagen conference hall, the world's carbon footprint still grew with terrifying speed and persistence. In the months after COP15, some American environmentalists came to believe that the whole lunatic discussion begged for a reboot. It needed some kind of catalyst, a focal point for collective action, a discrete campaign like the ones that had done away with DDT and saved at least some of the damn whales. What was needed at this dire moment was a symbol whose scale could at least approximate the enormity of a whole planet in peril. Something colossal, at the very outside edge of the capabilities of human engineering. Something distant from most people's daily lives, largely unknown and poorly understood, easily recontextualized as otherworldly and insane.

Something that looked just like an oil sands mine.

THE CARBON BOMB

In June 2011 James Hansen—the NASA scientist who first informed Congress of the climate change threat— circulated a white paper to his colleagues in the climate sciences. It was a succinct two-page memo titled "Silence Is Deadly." Its subject was the proposed Keystone XL project, "a huge pipeline to carry tar sands oil (about 830,000 barrels per day) to Texas refineries unless sufficient objections are raised." Hansen expressed cautious, highly qualified optimism for the prospect of phasing out enough of the world's coal-fired power plants to stabilize the planet's climate, but "if the tar sands are thrown into the mix," he wrote, "it is essentially game over." Alberta's bitumen deposits, Hansen explained, contained 400 giga-tons of carbon dioxide, enough to raise atmospheric concentrations by 200 parts per million all by themselves. Given that the climate change crisis had been brought on by two hundred years of global industry that had only raised carbon dioxide concentrations by 100 parts per million, this was a shocking data point. Hansen called on his fellow scientists and activists to raise objections to the project with the State Department, which would soon be deciding whether to approve it.

The letter came to the attention of Bill McKibben, who recognized Keystone XL as the kind of catalyst the climate change movement had been tragically lacking. Here was a single project, subject to the approval of the State Department, which meant ultimately that the president alone could accept or reject it with one stroke of a pen. The companies that would profit from it most were Canadian. The source for the pipeline's oil was unknown outside hardcore activist circles, which meant the American public in need of persuasion had few established opinions about it.

McKibben rounded up ten other prominent activists as cosignatories and redrafted Hansen's white paper as an open letter and call to action. "To call this project a horror is serious understatement," the letter read. "The tar sands have wrecked huge parts of Alberta, disrupting ways of life in Indigenous communities." The pipeline would also create the risk of an oil spill in the massive, vital Ogalalla Aquifer beneath the American plains. But the pipeline's worst impact, the letter explained, was what it would do to the earth's climate. The letter restated Hansen's assertion that Keystone XL would create a situation that was "essentially game over" for stopping climate change. "The Keystone pipeline," it continued, "would be a fifteen hundred mile fuse to the biggest carbon bomb on the con-tinent, a way to make it easier and faster to trigger the final overheating of our planet." The letter called for weeks of civil disobedience with the express intent of being arrested in Washington that August. If the protests and arrests occurred in sufficient number, McKibben and his colleagues hoped, it could convince the Obama administration to reject the project.

"Winning this battle won't save the climate," the letter concluded. "But losing it will mean the chances of runaway climate change go way up."

That August, as promised, the letter's signatories and hundreds of others gathered outside the White House intentionally committed acts of trespassing and were arrested. The protests didn't lead to a rejection of the Keystone XL pipeline—Obama's State Department continued to delay a final decision—but it galvanized the environmental movement across North America. Finally, there was a single villain, a focal point for action, a way to measure victory. And a pair of phrases—*the biggest carbon bomb, game over for the planet*—that reduced the staggering scope of the climate change problem to the scale of a campaign's concise slogans.

On the first of February 2010, Canada's environment minister, Jim Prentice, delivered a lunchtime speech at the Palliser Hotel in downtown Calgary. This was home turf for Prentice, a Calgarian and long-serving local MP who had taken on the most thankless role in Stephen Harper's cabinet. Less than two months earlier, Prentice had endured a grim trip to Europe for COP15, where he delivered the federal government's bland talking points about balancing action on climate change with the economic health of "our energy sector." Prentice and everyone who heard him speak at COP15 knew that was code for the so-called dirty oil of the Patch. Prentice braved the jeers of protesters, "Fossil of the Day" awards, and a false press release in his office's name, issued by the notorious activist prankster group the Yes Men, that purported to pledge new and hugely ambitious emissions reduction targets for Canada. A smart, experienced politician and one of the least malleable figures in Harper's cabinet, Prentice evidently took little pride in the work; though often a forceful, fiery orator, he fell into a flat, bureaucratic tone for much of his official speech at COP15, reading off the paper on the podium in front of him for long stretches. But he also took time before the conference began to meet with representatives from Canada's Youth Climate Coalition. More than many politicians of his stature, Prentice was interested in why his critics opposed his positions, and he was one of the sharpest internal critics of his government's foot-dragging on climate policy.

Back home in Calgary, Prentice addressed a far warmer crowd. The ballroom at the Palliser was full of old colleagues, business associates and party loyalists. Up and down the Plus 15s that snaked away from the hotel throughout the city, there was little but praise to be heard for the Conservative government. The near collapse of the global economy had been a gut-churning swoon for everyone, but Canada, its tightly regulated banks having skipped out on most of the debt-trading mayhem that had fuelled the crisis, had bounced back quickly and emerged as one of the strongest economies in the world. Billions of dollars were pouring back into the oil and gas sector already. Alberta was ascendant, Calgary triumphant. Sing to us of our energy superpowers, Jim!

Prentice would have been forgiven for catering to the hometown biases and basking in easy applause after the humiliation of Copenhagen. Instead, he took the opportunity to puncture the room's smugness. Some in the Patch might have wanted to pretend there was nothing to those "Fossil of the Day" awards but the bleating of environmentalists and socialists who didn't understand business, but Prentice was more observant and thoughtful than that. He'd sensed a much more serious shift in the mood at COP15. He knew the Patch was now a global target. You heard the same thing from oil sands developers with European ties. When Shell Canada launched an expansion of its mining operations a couple of years earlier, for example, its president, Neil Camarta, spent as much of his time in the Netherlands reassuring the parent company's brass about greenhouse gas emissions as he did talking about revenues and profits.

"It is no secret," Prentice told his Palliser audience, "and should be no surprise, that the general perception of the oil sands is profoundly negative. That is true both within Canada and internationally. We need to continue the positive work of industry, with investments in environmental technologies that will show the world how environmental responsibility and excellence can be taken to new levels. Absent this kind of Canadian leadership, we will be cast as a global poster child for environmentally unsound resource development."

The boom's extraordinary powers of collective amnesia, however, had already regained a strong hold over crowds like the one at the Palliser that day. Their guy was in charge in Ottawa, oil prices were climbing upward again, and whatever gripes they might have in Copenhagen and the Hague, the world still couldn't ever get enough oil to sate its needs. Thanks for the talk, Jim, but there are higher priorities here in the Patch.

In April 2010, two months after Prentice's cautionary speech, a blowout at a BP offshore drilling rig in the Gulf of Mexico triggered an uncontrolled oil spill. Day after day, the blown well gushed crude into the sea. Cable news networks provided live coverage as hapless repair crews attempted to cap the leak, seemingly making up solutions on the fly. Failure compounded failure. The spill continued for weeks. The well's self-aggrandizing name—Deepwater Horizon—and the self-involved laments of BP's dreary CEO became world famous. The viewing public saw the awesome scale and audacious engineering prowess of the offshore oil business in the worst possible light.

Deepwater Horizon was of a piece with Caterpillar's heavy haul trucks and SAGD's wizardry, a push to the very limits of the industry's technological abilities. It was the deepest oil well ever drilled, standing in water nearly a mile deep and drilling another thirty thousand feet below the sea floor. And now it was a catastrophe. The oil business appeared live on TV for days on end as a study in reckless incompetence, and Deepwater Horizon provided a vivid new frame of reference for the dire cost of the world's oil addiction for the first time since the *Exxon Valdez* oil tanker spill in 1989. Finally, on July 15, a BP repair crew managed to stop the spill and cap the well, and company lawyers were left to sort out the mess and pay out billions in damages.

Ten days later, a pipeline operated by Enbridge that was carrying dilbit across Michigan to waiting refineries in Sarnia sprung a leak and started to gush its contents into a creek feeding into the Kalamazoo River. The pipe had sustained a rupture about six feet long, which caused pressure inside it to drop and trigger an alarm at Enbridge's control centre back in Edmonton. The safety systems built into oil pipelines can readily stop the flow of oil and seal off a ruptured section of pipe. But for reasons never adequately explained, Enbridge waited until it received a phone call seventeen hours later from an official on the scene in Michigan before shutting off the flow.

The magnitude of Enbridge's Kalamazoo spill was nowhere near that of the Deepwater Horizon disaster. A few dozen residents in the area of Enbridge's spill had to be temporarily evacuated, and the weight of the heavy crude caused it to sink to the bottom of the river, making for a slower and more complicated cleanup. But by the end of September, 90 percent of the oil had been recovered, at a cost to Enbridge of about $1.2 billion. In all, the pipe poured about 840,000 gallons of bitumen—roughly twenty thousand barrels—into the river. Deepwater Horizon bled as much oil into the Gulf of Mexico every eight hours of its eighty-six-day uncontrolled release, en route to about five million barrels in total, nineteen times larger than the *Exxon Valdez* debacle. The damage to the Gulf's ecology was beyond measure and is still being felt. The total cost to BP would eventually exceed $60 billion, without counting intangibles like the brand equity lost by having its name rendered synonymous with catastrophic incompetence.

For the Patch, though, Enbridge's mess was nearly as difficult to contain. It came in the wake of Deepwater Horizon at a moment of maximum public interest in the risk of oil spills, just as opposition to oil sands pipelines was starting to build to a frenzied pitch. The Patch's pipeline boosters would spend the next few years attesting over and over again that their pipes would be safe and almost entirely spill-free, and that whatever minor spills did occur over the decades-long life of a pipeline would be readily contained by foolproof emergency systems. And there, looming over them, would be images of the soiled Kalamazoo River, the great question mark of why Enbridge's technicians did not respond to the emergency alarm, the National Transportation Safety Board's characterization of the company's response as "Keystone Kops." The following year, as American activists began talking about a carbon bomb that could mean game over for the climate, there would be ample recent evidence of uncontrollable disaster in the country's collective memory.

UNSPUN

As the oil sands industry rose in prominence and its critics grew more numerous and strident, there was a particular line that often emerged from the Patch's boosters in discussions of its failures, downsides and potential catastrophes. *We just need to tell our story better.* The case for the oil sands was self-evident, so the line implied, if you just knew the whole story. The reliability of Canada as a trading partner, the stringent environmental regulations in the Patch, the tailings ponds and mine sites already being turned back into wetlands, the jobs attracting workers from across the country and around the world—these were decent people providing the vital energy that fuelled the good life. If you'd seen awful pictures of bitumen-soaked ducks or moonscape open-pit mines, well, that was because the Saudis or the Venezuelans or the Russians sure weren't inviting reporters to hop into helicopters and circle *their* energy industry's sites.

Calgary is self-consciously proud of its reputation for optimistic entrepreneurship and friendly can-do community spirit. The signature event of its largest annual festival, the Stampede, is a series of free pancake breakfasts hosted by businesses and community groups across the city every morning. The preferred ritual for visiting foreign dignitaries is to "White Hat" them, which refers to a hokey ceremony where the VIP is presented with a big, white Smithbilt cowboy hat—a tradition that emerged out of the fan base of the Canadian Football League's Calgary Stampeders.

The city's civic culture lent the same tone to the Patch as it grew. Here was another plucky outsider in need of cheerleading, a hard-luck enterprise that would surprise everyone and change the whole country with just a bit more support. Under attack, that boosterism could easily turn to rote dismissal, a strident defensiveness that verged on shrill, or braying rah-rah public relations spin. Or, as was the case for the Patch as criticism pressed in on all sides, a dangerous mixture of all three.

As Jim Prentice warned against becoming the world's poster child for climate disaster and the international news filled with stories of catastrophic spills, the Patch responded by trying harder than ever to tell its story better. The provincial government, for example, embarked on a marketing campaign. In the fall of 2010, visitors to Times Square in New York and Piccadilly Circus in London might have noticed an LED-screen banner with the Alberta government's logo on it, enumerating the oil sands industry's virtues—"Responsible," "Carbon capture and storage," "strict regulation"—and then urging onlookers to "Tell it like it is." Stephen Harper's government in Ottawa, meanwhile, dispatched cabinet ministers one after another to New York and Washington to pitch high-profile think tanks and forums full of congressional staffers on the virtues and rewards of investing in the oil sands and approving that Keystone XL pipeline. The cheerleader diplomacy culminated in the prime minister's September 2011 visit to New York for the opening of the UN General Assembly, at which a Bloomberg reporter asked Harper about Keystone XL approval, and Harper responded that it should be a "complete no-brainer." The glib phrase would stick for years to come.

Shortly before the Alberta government started spending hundreds of thousands of dollars on billboard ads in Times Square, eight environmental NGOs—including Corporate Ethics International, which had been rallying support for action against the oil sands among its allies in the environmental movement since 2008—pooled resources to launch a billboard campaign of their own. The ads, which appeared in cities across the United States and Western Europe, showed images of oily ducks stuck in tailings ponds alongside images of flailing pelicans caught in the Deepwater Horizon spill. The campaign was called "Rethink Alberta," and it branded the oil sands as "the other oil disaster," urging tourists to boycott the province.

The Patch's boosters responded with shock that was at least partially genuine. The industry was not used to being treated as the bad guy on an international stage. "We have all been caught off guard by the scope of the anti-oil campaigns," a spokesperson for the Canadian Association of Petroleum Producers told the *Edmonton Journal* in the summer of 2010. The campaigns they launched in response were pitched almost exactly to the same scale and tone as the "Rethink Alberta" campaign—roughly the same level of precision and sophistication you'd encounter in a collegiate debate or in the partisan jousting during Question Period at the Alberta Legislature. The environmentalists' clumsy, overwrought points could be countered and disproved, and *our story* told better and through bigger megaphones. This would prove to be a catastrophic miscalculation of the kind of media and political game in which the Patch now found itself.

The concerns being raised about the oil sands industry's real and pervasive environmental problems went well beyond its media image, and they were being raised in forums far larger and more consequential than billboards and Question Period debates. Starting in the fall of 2010, for example, the European Union began proceedings to reclassify Alberta's bitumen as a separate grade of higher-emissions fuel under its new Fuel Quality Directive, which could result in an effective ban on bitumen imports. Though Alberta sent virtually no bitumen to Europe at the time, the official sanction as "dirty oil" could easily spill over into other jurisdictions and would set a dangerous precedent as the industry sought to expand its exports into markets in Asia and beyond. The federal government spent the spring of 2011 lobbying furiously against the directive. A German EU representative would later tell a *Globe and Mail* reporter the vehemence of Canadian lobbying had "no equal" in his experience. (The full-court press would pay off, as oil sands barrels avoided the separate labelling.)

Pushback against the Patch now seemed to be rolling in from every direction. Pressure was mounting on Norway's government to force Statoil to sell its oil sands assets—a protest effort aided by connections made between Alberta First Nations and Norwegian activists and Indigenous groups at the 2008 Keepers of the Water conference in Fort Chipewyan. In London, British activists opposed to oil sands investments stalked BP and Shell shareholder meetings. And then in the fall of 2011, Barack Obama called Stephen Harper to inform him he would be delaying a decision on the Keystone XL pipeline until after the 2012 election. The no-brainer had become political poison. Bitumen was not a thing a president wanted stuck to him during an election year.

Perhaps even more significant to Obama's decision than the Keystone

XL protests and threats of European Union sanction was that the United States was hosting an oil boom of its own. In a few short years after the American economy's vicious downturn in the fall of 2008, technological breakthroughs in hydraulic fracturing had combined with Obama's generous stimulus program to ignite the biggest increase in US domestic oil production in half a century. Nearly everywhere where major deposits of oil-rich shale could be found—central Pennsylvania, near the original Rockefeller-era oil strikes; the foothills of Colorado; the plains of Oklahoma and West Texas; and especially the Bakken formation in North Dakota—there were now thousands of new oil wells producing fracked crude cheaper and faster than Alberta's bitumen could get to market. The shale threat had stalked the Patch for nearly its entire history—Karl Clark's colleagues fretted over it in the 1950s, and Peter Lougheed worried in the 1970s that Colorado shale would eliminate the market for bitumen if in situ deposits weren't developed. And now the feared shale boom had arrived. While activists mounted noisy campaigns against the eight hundred thousand barrels of oil Alberta producers wanted to ship to the United States via Keystone XL, American shale producers increased domestic oil supply by more than two million barrels per day from 2010 to 2013 alone. And the bonanza meant that Barack Obama had more wiggle room by the day to delay a verdict on the pipeline. The urgency was gone. The Patch had lost much of its leverage.

In the wake of Obama's decision to delay approval of the pipeline, Stephen Harper's government went on the attack. It would prove to be another major miscalculation, perhaps its greatest one. Harper had never been a fan of the Obama administration and hoped to see a Republican president more enthusiastic about pipelines come to power in the 2012 election. In the meantime, the prime minister decided to push hard for a pipeline to the Pacific coast and a stronger oil export relationship with China—both because the industry's leaders had been keen on reaching Asian markets for years and because it might shock Obama's administration into recognition that it still needed Canada's oil as badly as Canada's oil needed Keystone XL.

The first sign of the shift in tone and strategy came early in January 2012, when Harper's natural resources minister, Joe Oliver, published an open letter at the ministry website. The letter landed just as the National Energy Board was about to begin hearings on Enbridge's proposed Northern Gateway pipeline, which was intended to ship bitumen due west from Edmonton to Kitimat on the northern coast of British Columbia and from there to Asia-bound tankers. Oliver's letter opened with talk of "an historic choice" facing Canadians about whether "to diversify our energy markets away from our traditional trading partner in the United States or to continue with the status quo." But Oliver quickly moved on to his real focus: the "radical ideological agenda" being promoted by environmentalists using "funding from foreign special interest groups" to sabotage the Canadian economy. "Unfortunately," he wrote, "there are environmental and other radical groups that would seek to block this opportunity to diversify our trade. Their goal is to stop any major project no matter what the cost to Canadian families in lost jobs and economic growth. No forestry. No mining. No oil. No gas. No more hydroelectric dams."

Oliver's letter received widespread media coverage and was broadly seen by the environmental activist community across Canada and beyond as a declaration of war. It would soon be accompanied by nuisance audits of environmental NGOs funded by specially earmarked funds handed to Revenue Canada in the spring 2012 budget. The same budget gutted environmental research funding and rewrote numerous laws to ease the regulatory hurdles and environmental oversight on pipelines and other oil and gas projects. Harper, meanwhile, embarked on a trade mission to China, during which he informed a new audience that Canada was "an emerging energy superpower." In an apparent dig at Obama, Harper added, "We need to sell our energy to people who want to buy our energy." Afterward, he asked a member of his delegation, "Do you think the Americans were listening?"

Harper needn't have asked. Americans were paying attention to Canadian energy issues as never before. But unfortunately for the prime minister, his message was not the one they were most interested in.

#NOKXL

By the time of Joe Oliver's combative letter, the conversation about Keystone XL and Alberta's oil sands in activist circles had already moved far beyond the reckoning of a lone cabinet minister. The pipeline, once a symbol of the larger climate change fight—a necessary first skirmish for the beleaguered American troops—was becoming the whole war.

Opposition to Keystone XL did not begin with international climate campaigners like Bill McKibben, and its growth relied on informal regional networks and alliances as much as on the high-profile civil disobedience of McKibben and his colleagues in Washington. In fact, it's possible, perhaps even likely, that the antipipeline movement would have stalled quickly if it were simply a question of the carbon footprint of bitumen. But it began as a vicious fight over land rights in Nebraska ranch country, and that made all the difference.

In 2010, well before James Hansen's "Silence is deadly" letter launched the wider campaign against Keystone XL, a fledgling progressive political engagement group called Bold Nebraska stumbled on the pipeline project almost by accident. Bold Nebraska's founder, Jane Kleeb, had been told by an environmentalist friend to check out a public hearing on Keystone XL. She was reluctant to go—"I didn't know what the tar sands was," she later told a reporter—and was surprised to find a small-town meeting packed with ranchers opposed to the project. Though the State Department had not yet approved the pipeline, TransCanada was already beginning to make eminent domain claims on property in Nebraska. This sparked an unlikely alliance of a progressive political group and mostly conservative-leaning ranchers, forming the first pillar of the opposition to Keystone XL. And it became a fixed pillar with astonishing speed—by 2011, the TransCanada name inspired spontaneous jeers from the crowd at a University of Nebraska Cornhuskers football game when the company's ad ran on the scoreboard.

Around the same time, First Nations activists in Canada—particularly Clayton Thomas-Muller of the Indigenous Environmental

Network—started discussing the pipeline with Indigenous groups along the Keystone XL route. Rather than talk up greenhouse gas emissions, Thomas-Muller focused on the threat the pipeline posed to the land and water in the region and the Ogalalla Aquifer. By the time climate action groups entered the fray, a loose but effective opposition to the pipeline's local impacts had already formed.

The civil disobedience in Washington in the summer of 2011 started to shift the focus of national environmental groups to Keystone XL and the oil sands carbon bomb, but the movement really found its legs the following summer, when McKibben published an article in *Rolling Stone* magazine called "Global Warming's Terrifying New Math." The math combined the 2-degree-Celsius threshold—the change in global average temperature that climate scientists had long regarded as the maximum allowable warming if catastrophe was to be avoided—with a "carbon budget" of 565 gigatons. That second number was the volume of carbon dioxide emissions that a major study had calculated as the maximum permissible to stay below 2°C. The third number in McKibben's *Rolling Stone* piece was 2,795 gigatons, the volume of carbon dioxide that would be released if all the proven reserves on the balance sheets of all the world's fossil fuel companies were extracted and burned. McKibben never mentioned Keystone XL specifically, but the article did suggest that a goal should be to "keep those carbon reserves that would take us past two degrees safely in the ground."

The *Rolling Stone* article caught the attention of Tom Steyer, a California-based hedge fund billionaire who had become a major financier and organizer of progressive political campaigns. Steyer flew out to meet McKibben at his home in rural Vermont. Over the course of a long hike in the Adirondack Mountains, they discussed the article, its implications, and an alliance. Back in California, Steyer organized a retreat with his political contacts to work through tactics and strategy. The movement against the carbon bomb now had a very deep-pocketed ally, and the political groups working with Steyer, whose connections included senior members of Secretary of State Hillary Clinton's 2008 presidential campaign team, would adopt McKibben's priorities. In social media shorthand, they would all work together to ensure there would be #NoKXL. "The goal is as much about organizing young people around a thing," Steyer's climate adviser Kate Gordon told the *New Yorker* in 2013. "But you have to have a thing."

After Obama's re-election, which had been backed heavily by Steyer's network of political action groups, the president's tone on Keystone XL shifted. The pipeline would not be approved, he said, if it was shown to "significantly exacerbate the problem of carbon pollution." If, in other words, the carbon bomb argument held weight. Obama also scoffed at the inflated job creation figures the pipeline's proponents were throwing around—which ran as high as twenty thousand—noting that those claims were only remotely plausible during the construction phase of the project, with a hundred permanent jobs at most remaining once the pipeline was up and running. In March 2012 Obama had quietly expedited approval for Keystone XL's southern leg, which was entirely within the United States, after TransCanada split the project into two separate permits. (The southern leg has been transporting hundreds of thousands of barrels of bitumen from Oklahoma to the Texas coast every day since it was completed in early 2014.) In the wake of the election, the protests and Steyer's lobbying, however, Obama appeared to be souring on the value of the northern leg.

By 2013, the pipeline's approval had become something far greater than the project itself. It was being transformed into something like a litmus test for a politician's commitment to action on climate change. Or for anyone else's.

STREET FIGHT

Political movements are unpredictable, often haphazard affairs. What looks in retrospect like brilliant strategy and flawless coordination is often an accidental admixture of luck, timing and the strange loose momentum of a political idea. *#NoKXL. Shut Down the Tar Sands. Defuse the Carbon Bomb.* By whatever formal and informal means—through email lists and Facebook posts and countless other digital channels—these messages pinged across the continent and around the globe until every local environmental protest seemed to be at least partially a demonstration against the Patch.

For Helen Yost of Moscow, Idaho, the campaign began in the spring of 2010, when she learned that ExxonMobil would be trucking enormous oil production equipment through her town. The Exxon name was pure terror to Yost. She had left home in Nebraska as a teenager and hitchhiked across the country, making her way eventually to Alaska and falling in love with the wilderness along the way. She was in Alaska when the *Exxon Valdez* disaster occurred in 1989, and her grief over the damage led her to the University of Montana to study resource conservation. Now the company's destructive force was coming to the quiet, outdoorsy town in upstate Idaho where Yost had settled. She decided, with that unshakeable conviction that has fired activist movements the world over, that she would refuse, bodily, to let it pass. This was how Yost became an expert in the logistics of the "megaload" shipping business and a committed anti–oil sands activist.

In technical terms, *megaload* refers specifically to the weight of a transport truck's cargo. Shipments of a certain weight and size need special megaload permits to be transported on highways, often employing meandering routes to avoid overhead obstacles and middle-of-the-night timings to keep from causing traffic chaos. Police escorts are sometimes required as well, especially when a megaload passes through a town of any size. In upstate Idaho in 2010, megaloads mostly meant one thing: oil sands plant modules bound for the Kearl Lake project being built by Imperial, an ExxonMobil subsidiary, north of Fort McMurray. These massive components of an oil sands processing plant—turbines, heat exchangers, sections of coking tower, some of them weighing nearly a million pounds—were assembled in factories in eastern Asia, shipped across the Pacific to Portland, Oregon, and then transferred to freight barges and hauled up the Columbia River to Lewiston, Idaho. From there they were loaded on their outsized trailers and carried the rest of the way by some of the biggest freight trucks on earth.

Yost and some like-minded locals formed an activist group called Wild Idaho Rising Tide in early 2011. The "Rising Tide" name indicated its affiliation with a global network of grassroots climate change action groups that traced its origins to Dutch protests at the 2000 UN Climate Change Conference in the Hague.

"We could only turn out a few people in more rural areas, and people just thought we were ridiculous," Yost said. "But I was like, 'No, we're going to hound them until they stop.' Because at that point it was more about the tar sands. And it was also about activists being directly confrontational instead of trying to fight things from their desk at conservation organizations."

By 2013, nearly every megaload that passed through Idaho and Montana en route to the Patch was met with protest. Yost's group had found allies across the region—environmental groups in the college town of Missoula, Montana, direct action organizations from the Spokane area that had cut their teeth on local Occupy Wall Street solidarity protests, and Indigenous rights groups from the nearby Nez Perce Reservation, as well as occasional visitors from reserves farther afield and First Nations activists from Canada.

Most often, a small knot of protesters would physically block the megaload's route through town, filling a quiet intersection in the middle of the night to stop the truck until local police arrived to break up the demonstration. At the first protests, the police most often simply removed the protesters from the scene. But as the protests persisted, arrests became common. In 2014 some of the protesters received calls from the FBI, evidently exploring links between the megaload protest groups and a more radical sabotage group called Deep Green Resistance.

On their websites and blogs, the participants meticulously documented their campaign, which they frequently framed as an effort to stop "the largest, most environmentally destructive, industrial operation on earth." Stopping the oil sands industry was no longer a symbolic step toward a greater goal but an end in itself.

From region to region, the pattern repeated itself. On the other side of the country, for example, oil sands opposition became the rallying cry in a local fight about harbour-front development in South Portland, Maine. Portland Pipe Line Corp. (a pipeline operator jointly owned by Imperial, Shell and Suncor) had applied for a reversal to its pipeline in the region in 2009 without fanfare, but the company hadn't taken action yet and was required to renew the application in 2013. The pipeline pumped fuel from South Portland to Montreal, but the company now wanted to bring the Patch's heavy oil from Canada to the port for international shipment. The new arrangement would require two smokestacks to be installed on the South Portland waterfront as part of the apparatus needed to move heavy oil from pipeline to oil tanker.

The NRDC brought the application to the attention of local grass-roots activists, who began organizing opposition based on local air quality issues and the visual intrusion on the small city's pretty waterfront, where docks lined with bobbing sailboats and a vintage lighthouse flank the small industrial port. The Conservation Law Foundation, a regional environmental lobby organization, joined the fray, spurred in part by news of Enbridge's Kalamazoo River spill in spring 2013.

"What started off as a small group of concerned neighbours in a living room then grew to become Protect South Portland, which then grew to become the largest grassroots group probably ever in the history of South Portland," says Taryn Hallweaver, a local environmental activist who helped organize the campaign against the pipeline. The pipeline question became a central issue in South Portland's municipal election that November, with opponents canvassing citywide in favour of a waterfront protection ordinance intended to block construction of the heavy oil smokestacks. The ordinance was rejected by a few hundred votes, but it had become such a contentious issue the new city council quickly passed new legislation to accomplish the same goal.

In South Portland, as in the Pacific Northwest, activists had found a local and immediate way to push back against the Patch and all it represented. For environmentalists in those first years of the climate change era, the news was a daily barrage of horrors, stories recounting damage beyond measure and giving vague shape to a calamity beyond anyone's ability to grasp, biblical in its size and import. But in the face of all they couldn't control, they had found a simple gesture, a lever that could be taken in hand, a way to *do something*. Whatever else, here no oil shall pass. It won't flow. We will stop it. We can win.

Back in Canada, the gathering momentum of the movement against the Keystone XL pipeline and the oil sands in general brought new purpose and resolve to environmental groups across the country. Enbridge's proposed Northern Gateway pipeline project—intended to thumb the industry's nose at Obama's intransigence by opening a direct trade route to China—provoked especially strong pushback. This was in part because the pipeline terminated at the tiny British Columbia port town of Kitimat, which, if connected by pipe to oil sands terminals in Edmonton, would bring supertanker traffic to a long, narrow channel through the Great Bear Rainforest—a majestic wilderness of towering old-growth cedar, salmon streams and a rare species of white-coated black bear known locally as "spirit bears." But Northern Gateway was also a rallying point because the proposed pipeline route traversed the traditional territory of dozens of British Columbia's First Nations that, unlike their Alberta counterparts, had never ceded their land to the Canadian government by treaty. Legal cases had been strengthening the land claims of British Columbia First Nations in the region for years, culminating in the 2014 case of *Tsilhqot'in Nation v. British Columbia.* In what the *Globe and Mail* called "the most important ruling on aboriginal rights in Canadian history," the Supreme Court of Canada overturned the doctrine of *Terra nullius* and granted the Tsilhqot'in First Nation in central British Columbia full legal title to their traditional territory. This was nothing like the fuzzy, easily manipulated "duty to consult" that oil sands companies encountered in Fort McKay and Fort Chipewyan. Even if the National Energy Board approved Northern Gateway—which it eventually did, in 2014—the project promised to vanish into the courts for years. Keystone XL remained the industry's preferred route to tidewater.

The Northern Gateway resistance spurred substantial and lasting connections between Indigenous people and environmental groups across the country. And the Gateway protests merged seamlessly with larger resistance to the excesses of the Conservative government on a dozen other fronts in 2012 and 2013—protests against the muzzling of scientists, the dismantling of Department of Fisheries libraries, the defunding of the Experimental Lakes Area in northern Ontario where basic research had

the marketing budget of its Natural Resources Department seventyfold from 2010 to 2013, took out full-page ads in magazines like the *New Yorker*, and built a glossy web portal of its own called Go with Canada. The site, laden with links to fact sheets on Keystone XL, pipeline safety and environmental regulations, touted Canada's "responsible resource development" and branded the country "America's best energy partner."

To follow the alternating sharp and flat notes of the Keystone XL debate in the press as it built toward a crescendo was to watch an industry and political class that hadn't bothered to absorb the tone of their own stories. The prime minister or an Alberta cabinet minister might sign off on millions in advertising and speak in calm, reasonable language about the industry's environmental challenges at a Council on Foreign Relations meeting in New York or a congressional forum in DC, but the public face of the Patch was more often combative and sneering. The press coverage showed TransCanada bullying Nebraska ranchers with eminent domain and spending hundreds of millions of dollars on Washington lobbyists. Enbridge's communications and consultation efforts with Indigenous groups along the proposed Northern Gateway route became infamous within the industry for their crass tone and cluelessness about the cultural and political differences between Alberta and B.C. First Nations, talking about money to be made and jobs to be had by signing off on a project with bands who had never ceded their sovereign right to the land. Peter Kent, Harper's environment minister, was in front of TV cameras within hours of returning to Ottawa from the 2011 UN Climate Change Conference, withdrawing the Canadian government from the Kyoto Protocol. When the prominent University of Alberta scientist David Schindler published a report on water pollution in the oil sands region, Alberta's environment minister replied glibly to reporters that the contaminants Schindler had discovered were "not a concern and are of insignificant levels." (Ed Stelmach appeared in the press the very next day to soften the tone of his minister's dismissal.)

Oil sands sites are corporate enterprises, and Keystone XL was a private sector project, but the predominant tone of Patch boosterism belonged

nevertheless to Stephen Harper's federal government. Approval was a political calculation in Washington, and Harper's Conservatives had invested an
enormous share of their political capital in getting oil and gas projects built
in pursuit of energy superpower status and a booming economy. In marked
contrast to the federal government's $200,000 full-page New Yorker ad, there
was Canada's US ambassador, Gary Doer, ranting about the unwelcome
opinions of "California celebrities" in a September 2013 New Yorker feature
story on the anti-Keystone movement. "You can't own five homes and drive
around in a corporate plane and then claim to be some Buddhist purist,"
Doer told the magazine. "It is an interesting thing when you have people
going to Copenhagen saying, 'I've weaned myself completely off of all fossil
fuels,' which begs the question, How long is that kayak ride from Malibu to
Copenhagen?" This line of argument would, to be sure, play for chuckling
applause at an Edmonton Rotary Club meeting. But in the pages of the
New Yorker, it confirmed the growing sense of a government and an industry
deaf to its critics and profoundly indifferent to the real concerns being raised
about the environmental costs of oil sands production.

And then there was Harper himself, playing host in June 2014 to Aus-
tralian prime minister Tony Abbott, whose government was, if anything,
more hostile to climate change action than Harper's own. The Keystone
XL debate raged ever stronger, and even oil executives had started to call
for more robust climate policy from the feds, but Harper lauded Abbott's
leadership in repealing Australia's carbon tax. For years, Harper and his
caucus had hurled the phrase "job-killing carbon tax" at their parliamen-
tary opponents pushing for stronger climate policies. With Abbott at his
side for a joint press conference in Ottawa, Harper lectured the world's
governments on the hollowness of their good deeds. "No matter what they
say," Harper said, "no country is going to take actions that are going to
deliberately destroy jobs and growth in their country. We are just a little
more frank about that."

The Abbott visit served as a sort of bookend to a communications strategy
that had begun two and a half years earlier with Harper's natural resources
minister painting the oil sands industry's opponents as radicals beholden to

foreign money who had no goal other than crippling the Canadian economy. For better or worse, the Canadian government held the same line it always had on the industry's environmental record—good enough, and better than, say, Venezuela's—and waited on President Obama's final verdict. In the meantime, on Harper's watch, the Patch became a pariah. The rallying cry of #NoKXL transformed from opposition to a particular pipeline into blanket condemnation of an entire industry. Canada's international reputation for environmental leadership, built over decades of work on major global issues like ozone depletion and acid rain, eroded away to nothing in a few short years. Well-meaning Cenovus ad campaigns and cynical government PR schemes alike became costly exercises in futility. The ranks of "radicals" opposed to breakneck oil sands expansion and the pipelines to serve it expanded to include everyone from scientists marching in their lab coats in the streets of Ottawa to First Nations from Quebec to Vancouver Island to the mayor of the Vancouver suburb of Burnaby. In the mountain towns of Idaho and Montana and in the harbour cities of New England, on the streets of Washington and Ottawa, in plazas fronting parliaments in Oslo and Brussels—everywhere, it seemed, that climate change was being debated, KXL and its oil sands sponsors were the universal villains, the climate criminals, Public Environmental Enemy No. 1.

Calgary mayor Naheed Nenshi, a political moderate first elected in 2010 and beloved by progressives across Canada as the antithesis of dismissive Stephen Harper, travelled to the World Economic Summit in Davos, Switzerland, in January 2013, to talk up the virtues of Alberta's dynamic oil capital. He was shocked at the vitriol and misinformation levelled at the industry. "What I learned," Nenshi told the local press upon his return to Calgary, "is that we have not done a good enough job as industry and as Canadians in making the complicated case for this pipeline." It was a lament he would return to again and again, as the vehemence of criticism in Davos in 2013 built into a worldwide cacophony of arguments against the Patch.

"For some reason," Nenshi told CNBC more than two years later, "that one-metre pipe has been asked to bear all the sins of the carbon economy."

ELEVEN

FOOTPRINTS IN THE SANDS

NUMBER GAMES

The culture of a place—and an industry—often endures even in the face of radically changed circumstances. A company town still sees itself as intimately connected to a long-departed industry, a business sector moves from margin to mainstream (or vice versa) without embracing its changed role. The oil sands were an underdeveloped subsector at the margin of the global oil industry, situated deep in the hinterland, far from centres of economic or political power. Calgary was a scrappy business town of ranchers and wildcatters, not a political capital or financial hub, in a province long treated as the hick prairie cousin of Confederation. The Patch emerged on the margin of a margin of a margin. It boasted of energy superpower status even as it still felt, at its core, like a risky frontier dream in constant danger of failure. This was a place and a culture profoundly unprepared to fight a twenty-first-century media battle over the complex challenges of climate change.

254

In Keystone XL, climate change activists thus found a uniquely convenient target, slow-footed and ill-suited to the international arena of symbolic politics it had stumbled into. The Patch seemed almost a willing poster child for a movement against an environmental disaster that had for years seemed inchoate and intangible. It was a climate villain for all tumultuous seasons. And so the proximate target became the enduring proxy for the wider debate, and the proxy became the vessel into which, as Calgary's mayor put it, the entire carbon economy's sins were stuffed.

This was the tactical nature of the movement against Keystone XL and the industry that spawned it. But what were the facts of the case against the oil sands and its one-metre pipe? What villainy did the Patch's opponents charge it with committing?

There was, above all else, the carbon bomb, a horrific threat at the full scale laid out by James Hansen and Bill McKibben. But Hansen's carbon bomb math grew less terrifying the closer you looked at it. The most thorough rebuttal came from University of Alberta energy economist Andrew Leach just weeks after Hansen published his original white paper in the spring of 2011. Beginning with Hansen's claim that 400 gigatons of carbon dioxide would be released by the full exploitation of the oil sands resource, Leach broke down the emissions calculations behind that figure in a lengthy blog post. He acknowledged off the top that the 700,000 or more barrels per day that would travel down the proposed Keystone XL pipeline represented a significant potential source of greenhouse gases. Using the 0.616-tons-per-barrel figure that US environmental groups assigned to bitumen over its life cycle, from extraction in the boreal north to a motor vehicle's tailpipe—the "wells to wheels" footprint of the fuel, as climate policy wonks call it—Leach determined that Keystone XL's annual contribution to the world's fossil fuel bonfire would be 157 megatons of emissions, "equivalent to those of all the cars and trucks on the road in Canada." On the surface of it, then, Hansen and McKibben and everyone who'd rallied around the cause of defusing this carbon bomb had a point—even if it was predicated on the dubious notion that none of those

700,000 barrels per day would be mined and delivered to gas stations by some other means if Keystone XL was rejected.

Leach's real problem with Hansen's carbon bomb math, though, was the 200 parts per million of carbon dioxide that Hansen claimed the oil sands would release into the atmosphere. It was an accurate figure, Leach explained, but it referred to the entire known bitumen resource in Alberta—all 2.4 trillion barrels of it—not the 166 billion barrels of proven reserves that could be extracted at a profit with present-day technology and market conditions, or even the 2 million barrels per day then being produced. Even at 5 million barrels per day—roughly where the industry thought it might expand to by 2030—it would take more than 1,300 years to extract and burn all 2.4 trillion barrels and hit Hansen's 200-parts-per-million figure. Hansen's argument, Leach concluded, exaggerated the climate threat of the Keystone XL project by "somewhere between ninety and five hundred times," depending on how generously you bent the calculations in its favour. If this was a carbon bomb, it was far smaller than Hansen had suggested.

Hansen eventually nudged his figures downward in a 2012 *New York Times* article, "Game Over for the Climate," to 240 gigatons and 120 parts per million. He added that deposits of "tar shales" in the United States, a "close cousin" of oil sands not yet under production, could unleash another 300 gigatons of carbon dioxide. In testimony before a Senate committee in March 2014, Hansen said his original numbers had been "misinterpreted," that he was arguing simply that oil sands represented "that first big step into unconventional oil," which would send humanity down the road to likely climate catastrophe.

This was already a more nuanced argument than the Keystone XL protesters generally allowed, and it ignored the inconvenient fact that the first step had already been taken in the Patch at least a half century earlier and many more had been taken since. One of the hallmarks of Keystone XL opposition in the United States, in fact, was its imprecision on this front—its suggestion that oil sands production in general hung in the balance of the pipeline verdict, that oil sands mines would cease operating or else weren't up and running yet, that only the fuse of the Keystone XL carbon bomb would set the whole disaster in motion. (In his 2014 Senate testimony, Hansen said that "a lot of that tar sands will never be developed" if the pipeline wasn't built.) This conveniently overlooked the massive expansion of oil-by-rail terminal capacity that had accompanied the booms in both bitumen and fracked shale oil. In the years between 2009 and 2015 when Keystone XL was being fiercely debated, American shale producers added more than 4 million barrels per day to domestic production, shipping it often as not by rail. At least half the oil from the Bakken shale formation in North Dakota, for example, left the region by train—as many as 800,000 barrels per day. The single greatest oil transport disaster of the time was the explosion of a train laden with Bakken shale oil in Lac-Mégantic, Quebec, in July 2013, which killed forty-seven people and reduced the town centre to rubble.

A 2012 analysis by University of Victoria climate scientists Andrew Weaver and Neil Swart in the journal *Nature Climate Change* shrunk the Patch's carbon bomb even further. Looking only at proven reserves, Weaver and Swart calculated that extracting and burning all 166 billion barrels would increase average global temperature by 0.02 degrees Celsius. And if "only the reserve currently under active development were combusted," they wrote, "the warming would be almost undetectable" on a global scale.

"We wanted to address the carbon-bomb question," Weaver explained. "And frankly, these numbers aren't as big as I thought they would be."

Although the oil sands industry might have been less explosive than critics implied, that certainly didn't mean it was anywhere near benign on the climate change front. The "dirty oil" moniker stuck to the oil sands in part because it was broadly accurate. Of all the ways the 90 million or so barrels of the world's oil were produced each day, few released as much greenhouse gas per barrel as Alberta's bitumen did. Industry defenders could point to certain heavy oil deposits in Venezuela and California as marginally more carbon-intensive sources of oil, but that in no way diminished the size of the oil sands barrel's footprint.

Here again, though, bias and hyperbole clouded the facts. Pipeline opponents, for example, frequently claimed that bitumen created two or even three times as much carbon dioxide per barrel as conventional oil. This was roughly accurate if you limited the frame of reference only to the extraction process. Bitumen production, requiring either enormous trucks and shovels or vast quantities of steam generated by burning natural gas, as well as energy-intensive upgrading, has a much larger carbon footprint than pumping Saudi crude from a conventional well. But the figure that actually matters to the planet's health is total emissions—from wells to wheels. Numerous studies over the years have attempted to calculate the definitive average difference between the emissions from oil sands and conventional crude, yielding a range from roughly 8 to 37 percent. The benchmark most widely adopted, 17 percent, was originally determined by the US Environmental Protection Agency. A 2009 University of Calgary study of wells-to-wheels impacts, meanwhile, found that between 60 percent and 85 percent of the life-cycle emissions required to move a car one kilometre down a highway occur at the tailpipe, depending on the emissions intensity of the source. In other words, the overall difference between the least polluting sweet crudes and the most carbon-intensive in situ bitumen was 100 grams of carbon dioxide per kilometre at most, while the vehicle emits 212 grams more during that kilometre of travel regardless of the fuel source. The figures lent some credence to the argument made by many industry leaders in the Patch that attacking climate change exclusively on the supply side of the equation would be of limited effectiveness until there were dramatic changes on the demand side. As long as people still burned all those millions of barrels per day to drive to the office and fly off on vacations and get fresh produce shipped to their local supermarket out of season, it wouldn't matter too much to the planet where the oil had come from.

Still, the Patch remained a legitimate target for opposition on climate change grounds. It was, in particular, by far the most significant *new* factor in Canada's national carbon footprint. Year after booming year through the first two decades of a new millennium coming to be defined by the challenge of climate change, oil sands production was the single largest source of new greenhouse gas emissions in Canada. By 2015, oil sands production generated about 70 megatons of greenhouse gases per year, more than 9 percent of the country's total emissions, up from just 34 megatons in 2005. Politicians pandering to Alberta voters liked to point out this was barely one-tenth of 1 percent of global emissions, but for the vast majority of Canadians who believed action was needed to reduce the country's footprint, this mathematical sleight of hand was irrelevant. At a time when other provincial governments were phasing out coal plants and introducing carbon taxes, Alberta was the national laggard, its emissions ticking steadily upward with each year of wild growth in the Patch. The smirking contempt for Kyoto targets and carbon pricing from lawmakers in Ottawa and Edmonton only exacerbated the tension. Even without the added force of the carbon bomb protests from south of the border, the Patch was bound to wind up a target of climate change advocacy in Canada.

In 2015, new governments at both the federal and provincial levels took measures to slow the growth of the Patch's carbon footprint and remove Alberta from the ranks of climate villainy. Under Rachel Notley's left-leaning NDP, elected in May, the Alberta government enacted a comprehensive climate change policy plan, formulated in part by a panel chaired by Andrew Leach, who had deconstructed Hansen's carbon bomb argument. The new plan included a phase-out of the province's coal-fired power plants, an across-the-board carbon tax, and a hard cap on oil sands emissions of a hundred megatons per year.

In effect, the oil sands emissions cap was a generationally scaled buffer for the industry, a recognition that decades of investment and development couldn't be abandoned overnight. The Patch could continue to build out at least some of the projects already underway, but it wouldn't be able to grow much beyond that without substantially reducing its emissions intensity. This was already a source of pride for some in the Patch — on average, the industry had reduced its greenhouse gas emissions per barrel by more than 25 percent from 1990 to 2014, and pacesetters like Harbir Chhina at Cenovus liked to talk about a day not so far off when barrels of bitumen would be produced without generating any emissions at all. A recent study noted, however, that much of the reduction in emissions intensity was accomplished by 2005 and overall emissions per barrel have risen since then.

In the meantime, Alberta's government went to the Paris climate talks in 2015 as an eager participant alongside Justin Trudeau's new Liberal government. Canada had recommitted to real action on climate change at home and on the world stage after a decade of intransigence. The oil sands, long a rebuke to climate negotiations, were reintroduced to the world as a source of the wealth needed to build the infrastructure of a low-carbon economy. The message of the world's climate change advocates had been heard, and the new tone was a welcome one. Many critics inside Canada and beyond soured on it quickly, however, when Trudeau's government began approving pipeline projects months after it rolled out its national climate change plans. To many activists, the industry could never be part of even an interim plan. *Keep it in the ground* had become a non-negotiable maxim. The years of poor communication and mostly insubstantial action to resolve environmental concerns had taken their toll. There was little in the way of middle ground. The camps would remain divided.

As the opposition to the Patch deepened and scrutiny increased, a more substantive critique of the industry emerged, one that spoke in terms of precise emissions targets and timelines as well as capital expenditures and balance sheets. The foundation of this argument was the 2°C threshold, which had emerged as the baseline measure of serious planning for coordinated climate change action. The place of an emissions-intensive fuel source like bitumen in a world where warming was kept below 2°C had been in question for years, but the issue crystalized in early 2015 around an influential study in *Nature* by British researchers Christophe McGlade and Paul Ekins of University College London. The paper examined what had become known as carbon budgets: the precise amounts of oil, coal and natural gas that could be burned between now and mid-century within the 2°C limit. In their study, McGlade and Ekins examined a range of scenarios regarding price and emissions intensity. They foresaw a future in which a third of the world's oil reserves, half of its natural gas reserves and more than 80 percent of its coal reserves could not be burned.

"Regarding the production of unconventional oil," they wrote, "open-pit mining of bitumen . . . drops to negligible level after 2020 in all scenarios because it is considerably less economic than other methods of production." Without economical carbon capture and storage, they added, "all bitumen production ceases by 2040." One data point in particular made headlines across Canada: as much as 85 percent of Alberta's bitumen reserves would have to stay in the ground.

It was a stark conclusion, and it seemed to confirm what the industry's opponents had been saying for years—that the Patch was fundamentally incompatible with a stabilized global climate under any circumstances. There was another statistic from the study, however, not mentioned in the alarm-raising headlines: 75 million. This was the total daily oil supply worldwide in 2050 under McGlade and Ekins's carbon-constrained 2°C scenario. That data point featured prominently in a post by Andrew Leach for *Maclean's* magazine under the headline "Are oil sands incompatible with action on climate change?" The precise nature of the oil supply in a world still burning 75 million barrels of oil every day was, Leach argued, highly uncertain. The conclusion that 85 percent of bitumen was to "remain unburnable" to meet the 2°C target, he wrote, was "simply not supported by their results—it's an outcome of their model, but not a necessary condition." It *could* be the case, in other words, but it wasn't *required* in order to stay within the world's carbon budget as they'd delineated it.

Oil analysts knew that simply keeping global supply from falling off a cliff as conventional supplies dried up in the coming decades would require millions of barrels of new production. Who knew where those barrels would come from or what technological breakthroughs might shift the profitable barrels from one source to another? Certainly no one sinking billions into oil sands projects in 2005 anticipated the extraordinary explosion in the production of low-cost shale oil that began just four years later. Many in the oil sands in the early 1990s hadn't expected their own dramatic vault to profitability to happen as soon as it did. And this was without mentioning that even after the Paris climate conference in December 2015 yielded a major breakthrough, there was still not a single nation on earth with the policies in place to hit its targets in a 2°C scenario, let alone the 1.5°C target that emerged from Paris. It was a technocratic variation on Mayor Nenshi's theme: Why again was bitumen being asked to be the first to atone for all the world's climate sins?

DIRTY PATCH

Beyond its carbon footprint, the tally of the Patch's environmental costs is well established, long understood, tabulated as neatly as the sections in an environmental group's damning report. What's less clear is the full scale and extent, the root causes and the effectiveness of possible responses. The industry has had an enormous, pervasive, lasting impact on the boreal forest ecosystem in which it operates and many others through which its products flow. But for every pointed attack on its environmental record, there is a credible—or at least potentially credible—response from the industry. And for every one of the industry's defences of its record, there is an equal and opposite caveat. Everyone agrees the Patch is, to some extent, a dirty business. Few agree on just how dirty.

A case in point, and the most common criticism of the Patch beyond its greenhouse gas emissions, is the spill risk posed by oil pipelines. Spills are undeniably a part of the oil and gas business, and they are startlingly frequent. In Alberta alone, the industry as a whole—not just the oil sands but conventional oil in all its forms—has yielded an average of two crude spills *per day*. The overwhelming majority of these, however, are minor in scale, a few cubic metres at most from an overflowing tank or a small leak in a pipeline seam. In its defence, the oil and gas sector in Alberta likes to point out that the frequency of those incidents has been declining even in the boom years. Still, spills haunt the industry constantly, and the truly disastrous ones—like that Enbridge pipeline dumping bitumen into the Kalamazoo River—often make international headlines.

In the Patch, as is so often the case, the spill issue is complicated by the singular and unknown properties of bitumen itself. About 40 percent (mostly from mining operations) of the Patch's 2.4 million barrels of daily production is upgraded and shipped to market as synthetic crude, which is understood to behave inside a pipeline like any other crude oil. But the remaining 60 percent (mostly from in situ facilities) is combined with light hydrocarbons known as diluent to create dilbit. In environmentalist circles, as the Keystone XL debate percolated, it became an accepted truth that dilbit was uniquely and catastrophically different in its behaviour inside a pipeline and during a spill. Because it travelled down pipelines at a higher temperature than regular crude and contained residual sand, it was said to be much more corrosive, leading to a much higher likelihood of leaks. And when it spilled, dilbit would be much harder to clean because it sank faster in water. "If it spills in water, you're screwed," was the blunt explanation the Canadian environmental group the Dogwood Initiative offered in a 2015 press release. This was in response to a US National Academy of Sciences study finding that in an ocean spill, the diluent would evaporate within a few days, leaving heavy bitumen behind to sink and disperse and making cleanup much more difficult. In the case of bitumen, the Dogwood release insisted, it would be "nearly impossible to clean up a large spill with current technology."

In truth, there was no conclusive evidence about dilbit's corrosive effects on pipelines or its likely behaviour in various bodies of water. Dilbit is almost exclusively the product of SAGD operations, which have been up and running for less than twenty years, and the use of pipelines as a common method of dilbit transport is younger still. On the pipeline question, a study by Alberta Innovates—the successor to the Alberta Research Council, funded by the Alberta government—found that dilbit was no more corrosive than conventional crude at 65°C but began to grow more corrosive beyond 100 degrees, a temperature rarely reached inside a pipeline. "There is no evidence that dilbit causes more failure than conventional oil," an Alberta Innovates geologist told *Scientific American* magazine in 2013.

The evidence is muddier regarding bitumen spills. A Nova Scotia government laboratory investigating dilbit noted there was "no literature" on dilbit's spill properties when it began its work on the subject in 2013. The lab's own study, still underway, found that dilbit "weathers" faster in ocean conditions than conventional crude does, which is to say it begins to break down as the diluent evaporates, at which point it sinks and disperses. But immediately after a spill, dilbit floats more readily in clumps on the surface, meaning it could be easier to clean up if the emergency response was fast enough. Looking at dilbit's behaviour in freshwater, a federally run lab in Alberta found that in many situations, dilbit sinks slower than conventional oil. Even a coauthor of the National Academy of Sciences study cited widely by industry opponents concedes that dilbit would likely float for up to three weeks after a spill in typical Canadian weather conditions.

So, then: was dilbit in a pipe more dangerous than conventional crude? In some ways, maybe yes; in others, likely not. More study was needed, more time to do the work, better oversight—all common refrains in the Patch. In the meantime, the stuff pumped down pipelines by the hundreds of thousands of barrels, and industry spokespeople would point, when asked, to the one method of transportation they knew for sure posed higher risks to the environment and human health: oil tankers on a train track, like the ones that exploded in Lac Mégantic.

The Patch's impact on the land it stands on and the water it stands beside are well known. To date, oil sands operations have created about 900 square kilometres of "disturbed surface" in the boreal forest of northeastern Alberta—900 square kilometres of cut trees and excavated overburden, open-pit mines and plant sites and well pads. This represents about 0.2 percent of the total area of boreal forest in Alberta (and 0.5 percent of the "area the size of Florida" so often referenced in environmentalist critiques of the industry). Of that terrain, about 220 square kilometres consists of

tailings ponds in various stages of filling or settling, of which about 40 percent is the "liquid surface area" that fools birds into landing on occasion.
Contaminated water from the ponds also seeps steadily into the groundwater around it at a rate of hundreds of thousands of litres per day. The total
amount of disturbed land that has been certified as reclaimed to date is a
little over a square kilometre, or about 0.2 percent.

In addition to the land cleared of vegetation for mining and processing,
SAGD operations require hundreds of kilometres of "line cuts" through
the forest—long, thin ribbons of cleared forest to enable seismic readings
of the bitumen deposits far below the forest floor. The line cuts also provide predators with excellent sight lines on their prey. This has been bad
news for woodland caribou, whose populations in northern Alberta were
already in decline—a process accelerated by the Patch's circuit-board dis-
sections, which have cut 53,000 kilometres of ruler-straight clearing into
the forest.

Oil sands projects draw about 170 million cubic metres of water from
the Athabasca River each year—equal to 1 percent of its average flow—as
part of their everyday operations. The Athabasca's flow is not steady year-
round, however, so the draw rate is sometimes as high as 10 percent of
the total in the drier months. On average, it takes twelve barrels of water
to produce a barrel of bitumen, but more than 70 percent of the water
the industry uses is recycled, so the net ratio is closer to 2.5 to 1. Industry
spokespeople like to point out that the Athabasca is, overall, substantially
less "subscribed" than rivers like the North and South Saskatchewan that
run through prime agricultural land, where 29 percent and 59 percent of
the flow, respectively, is diverted for agricultural, industrial and other uses.

Some unknown volume of contaminants spews from smokestacks and
evaporates off tailings pond surfaces every day in the Patch, dispersing into
the air. It settles in the snow and in the boreal lakes and rivers all around,
and some quantity of it flows away and dissipates to levels beneath measure, and some other quantity accumulates. Processing huge volumes of
bitumen also produces toxic chemicals, and sometimes there are chemical releases of unknown composition whose foul smells drift over nearby

communities and sting eyes and coat throats. Monitoring stations in the Patch sometimes record levels of nitrogen oxides, sulphur dioxide and hydrogen sulphide far exceeding safe levels for human health over brief intervals. In a 2013 study conducted jointly by researchers from Queen's University and Environment Canada, carcinogenic PAHs were found in lake bottoms far from oil sands sites—up to twenty-three times preindustrial levels in lakes thirty-five kilometres away and three times preindustrial levels up to ninety kilometres away. One of the researchers, John Smol of Queen's, told reporters, "Now we have the smoking gun." For at least a hundred kilometres in any direction the wind blows from an oil sands mine, studies were turning up evidence of significant air pollution.

In the pages of an environmental organization's summary report, this all amounts to a powerful litany of abuses. In the rebuttals of industry spokespeople, these are simply challenges to be met in turn. The debate pings back and forth, point by point.

The oil sands are the largest new source of carbon pollution in Canada—but their emissions intensity per barrel has been dropping for years.

The boreal forest is being turned to moonscape under the tracks of monster machines—but it will all be reclaimed, replanted and returned to animal habitat, the same way certain small swaths of it already have. (Plus almost all new operations are SAGD well pads, not mine sites. And seismic lines zigzag now, to aid the caribou.)

It will never again be mature boreal forest and bog—but it can be restored to base conditions for that forest to begin to regenerate.

The tailings are a toxic stew—but never has the industry been closer to finding ways to settle out the mature fine tailings faster and reduce tailings volumes overall.

The air in the Patch is a black cloud of smog and carcinogens—but the industry has steadily improved at reducing its emissions of pollutants like sulphur dioxide and nitrogen oxides, and the air all around is monitored for dangerous chemicals.

The most extensive third-party attempt to provide clarity on these competing claims was an expert review by the Royal Society of Canada (RSC), published in December 2010. The RSC convened a panel of seven experts in geology, biology and environmental health to provide a comprehensive overview of "the environmental and health impacts" of the Patch. Their 440-page report found perhaps unsurprisingly that the enterprise was neither as irredeemable as its critics claimed nor as benign as its boosters insisted. The panel noted "minimal air-quality impacts" in the region and concluded the current level of water use "does not threaten the viability" of the Athabasca River. There was "no credible evidence of environmental contaminant exposures from oil sands developments reaching downstream communities at levels expected to cause elevated cancer cases." And since the oil sands business ranked fourth in Canada among industrial sectors for air pollution, fifth for mercury emissions, and ninth for lead and PAH contamination, it was "not accurate" to describe the Patch as "the most destructive project on earth," or even in Canada. The Patch was, in short, a major source of pollution—but it was very much among its peers in large-scale heavy industry on such measures, not some monstrous outlier.

But even if the extraction of bitumen was less catastrophic than environmental activists had accused it of being, the RSC report also depicted an industry dangerously lacking in the necessary oversight and regulation it claimed to have put in place. The environmental impact assessments of new oil sands projects, the panel said, were "seriously deficient in formal health impact assessments" of the sort required, for example, of World Bank projects. There was "sparse data" on overall water quality and major gaps in other areas of oversight. In general, the "necessary increase in regulatory capacity" that should have accompanied an expansion of the Patch's booming scale was "not evident." If the Patch was not—not yet—a catastrophe, it had done nowhere near enough to ensure that it couldn't soon become one.

This all amplified a message that lurked in the margins of other scientific studies of environmental conditions in the Patch, reports that noted "technical gaps" or "erratic data" and invariably called for further study and better monitoring. And it pointed to the way the extraordinary speed and scale of the Patch's success had taken both the industry and its government minders by surprise, and how poorly they'd adjusted. Critics had long claimed that the oil sands were an underregulated free-for-all, and some of their most outlandish claims about its impact had found an audience in the absence of credible evidence to the contrary. The RSC report concluded that the regulators were asleep at the switch.

Prior to the RSC report, environmental oversight had been provided by a range of one-off and narrow-focused government and nongovernmental organizations. The provincially run Regional Aquatics Monitoring Program (RAMP) kept track of water quality; the independent Fort McMurray–based Wood Buffalo Environmental Association monitored air quality; the stand-alone Alberta Biodiversity Monitoring Institute oversaw wildlife issues. In the wake of a chorus of criticism, from outrage over the dead ducks at Syncrude's tailings pond to the RSC report itself, Alberta's PC government began to talk incessantly of establishing a "world-class" environmental monitoring program, comprehensive in its scope and coordinated across every level and department of government. The result, from 2012 onward, was an organization called the Joint Alberta-Canada Oil Sands Monitoring Program (JOSM), which was set up to coordinate provincial and federal monitoring of the oil sands using a $50-million annual budget provided by the industry. The Alberta government also set up the Alberta Environmental Monitoring, Evaluation and Reporting Agency (AEMERA) to handle its role in the JOSM project.

The early results have failed to live up to the advance billing. Two of Fort Chipewyan's First Nations quit JOSM in frustration barely two years after it launched. Stories of bureaucratic bungling and stagnation soon surfaced in the Alberta press. When the NDP took over from the PCs in 2015, the new government ordered a review of AEMERA. The investigation chronicled "dysfunctional relationships" and poor coordination between its partners in government and industry in an agency that employed one communications staffer for every two scientists. Six years after the RSC report, the "world-class monitoring program" appeared to be a wasteful, ineffectual mess.

In the Patch, meanwhile, violations of the regulations that were in place were on the rise. The single biggest liability dogging the province's most important industry was its environmental record and the growing public dissatisfaction with how it was tracked, and half a decade of world-class posturing had accomplished virtually nothing. At a moment of the highest possible visibility on a global media and political stage, when the thoughtful oversight of a mature industry and its operators was most needed, the provincial and federal governments and their industry allies had produced an ineffectual bureaucratic tangle worthy of a business that still couldn't believe it had gotten that first project off the ground. The energy superpower was being steered by clumsy regulatory hands, it seemed. And yet, still, it grew.

REJECTION SLIP

By 2014, there was very little nuance left in the debate over pipelines and the Patch. In the first weeks of January, rock star Neil Young, who had compared the oil sands landscape to Hiroshima in a visit the previous fall, toured Canada to raise money for the Athabasca Chipewyan First Nation's legal battle against a proposed Shell project. For the rest of the year, the sides only dug in harder, the rhetoric ever escalating. April saw some of the biggest anti-Keystone protests yet in Washington. International celebrities carried on with their helicopter tours and public condemnations—Archbishop Desmond Tutu passed through in May, actor Leonardo DiCaprio and director Darren Aronofsky in August, and Young joined country music legend Willie Nelson for an anti-Keystone concert in Nebraska in September.

A US State Department review of the project in early 2014 acknowledged that bitumen came with a carbon footprint 17 percent greater than conventional crude but did not see it as a significant contributor to climate change, because the oil would be extracted with or without the pipeline. In the backrooms and hallways of the US capital, meanwhile, business-suited armies of lobbyists made their cases for each side. By late 2014, more than a hundred organizations—"from the American Jewish Committee to the League of Women Voters," the *Globe and Mail* noted—had registered lobbyists in the capital at one point or another to argue for or against Keystone XL. TransCanada PipeLines had ten lobbyists working

270

THE PATCH

on the House of Representatives alone and spent nearly $1 million on lobbying in just the first six months of 2014. In the US midterm elections that fall, staunchly pro-Keystone Republicans gained seats on promises to force President Obama to green-light the project. In early January 2015 they tabled the Keystone XL Pipeline Approval Act and passed it in the Republican-controlled House and Senate, obliging the veto everyone knew Obama would exercise, which he did.

Keystone XL became a battle between two entrenched camps, a stark choice between Us and Them. The same division and polarization stalked the Patch everywhere. While Fort Chipewyan's Dene chief, Allan Adam, toured with Neil Young, leaders of the region's Mikisew Cree First Nation petitioned UNESCO to freeze new oil sands developments until there was a review of their impact on Wood Buffalo National Park, a UNESCO World Heritage Site. More than a hundred scientists from around the world, including Nobel laureates and Royal Society fellows, cosigned a letter asking for the same sort of moratorium. Around the same time, Kinder Morgan began preliminary work on its proposed Trans Mountain pipeline expansion just outside Vancouver, in the suburb of Burnaby, and hundreds of protesters descended on Burnaby Mountain to be arrested.

At the Paris climate conference that December, one of the stars of the activist sideshow that accompanied the official negotiations was Ken Smith, a mechanic at Suncor and president of the Fort McMurray chapter of the amalgamated manufacturers' union Unifor. At a forum hosted by Canadian labour and environmental groups, Smith told the crowd, "We hope we're seeing the end of fossil fuels for the good of everybody. But how are we going to provide for our families?. . . We're going to need some kind of transition. We've moved out there, we've invested in that industry—and when it ends, we're going to be left holding the bag."

This was how 2015—and with it, whatever faint vestige of the High Modern definition of progress still lingered in the Patch—came to an end. An oil sands mechanic, in a room full of climate policy advocates and environmentalists, hunting for an escape route.

TWELVE

RECKONING

AFTER THE DROUGHT

In 2015 Fort Chipewyan was a town of a thousand souls surrounded by reserve lands where a few hundred more people lived. The population is almost entirely Indigenous—predominantly Mikisew Cree and Dene, plus a small Metis community. Beyond that, there are a handful of non-Indigenous Parks Canada staffers and Mrs. Mah, whose Chinese-Canadian family has run the only full-service restaurant in town since the 1950s. Fort Chipewyan is a friendly, dishevelled sprawl of a place. New Quonset sheds stand next to abandoned wooden shacks, and there is a broad, empty expanse of waterfront hilltop where the Hudson's Bay Company fort used to be. Old rusted barges lie next to the commercial pier, and a church and ghostly residential school building loom just outside town.

The first trading post was established at Fort Chipewyan by the North West Company in 1788, and it soon became a hub for the fur trade

throughout the vast Northwest. But Fort Chipewyan was not a town in any
real sense for a very long time after that. Until well into the twentieth century, the majority of the Indigenous population continued to live in their
traditional communities, making camp near the fort from time to time.

To the Dene in particular this was still Denendeh, homeland and pro-
vider of all of life's necessities. Smallpox and whooping cough and the
extermination of the bison herds hadn't changed that. Neither had the
miscommunicated, unbalanced Treaty 8 of 1899, nor the loss of hunting and trapping lands to the national park, nor the forced assimilation
of a residential school. The treaty had promised the Indigenous people
of northern Alberta that they could continue to live off their land as long
as the sun still shined and the water still ran. And so they did, for as long
as they could. But then in 1968 a hydroelectric dam at the headwaters of
the Peace River in British Columbia blocked its flow while the reservoir
filled behind it, and for a time the water no longer ran. And that is when
everything changed forever.

The W. A. C. Bennett Dam was, like the Great Canadian Oil Sands
mine opened the year before, a High Modern marvel of its day, a pile of
earth six hundred feet high that would soon churn out hundreds of mega-
watts of hydroelectric power. After its completion, the water level in Lake
Athabasca fell by an average of two and a half feet, and nearly 40 percent
of the Peace-Athabasca Delta's aquatic surface area vanished. Waterways
between lakes and ponds throughout the delta went dry, and entire lakes
disappeared. The waterway networks the Indigenous people relied on
for transport were shattered into isolated pieces, and the muskrats many
trapped for fur declined in total population by more than half because
many marshes were too shallow for them to build winter houses. The Bennett Dam drought lasted three years, after which, a Canadian government
study of the delta noted, "trapping, fishing and subsistence hunting . . .
ceased to be the predominant means of making a living."

The Indigenous people settled permanently in Fort Chipewyan, and
the community was soon ravaged by the many ills visited upon Canada's
First Nations. Poverty was widespread, accompanied by alcoholism and

dysfunction as well as the humiliating reliance on the unpredictable whims of the paternalistic federal government. The occasional government employment scheme changed a few fortunes from time to time—a commercial fishery, sponsored by the provincial government, operated out of Fort Chipewyan for many years before shutting down in 2014—but the best economic opportunities arrived with the expansion of the oil sands industry in the mid-1990s. Most oil sands operators, led by the founding duo of Syncrude and Suncor, introduced Indigenous hiring strategies and procurement quotas for Indigenous-run businesses. In addition to the Fort Chipewyan residents who found direct employment with oil sands companies, the First Nations in the region founded small companies and bid on contracts open only to them. The Athabasca Chipewyan First Nation, for example, launched an operation in 1994 to take care of menial tasks such as hauling garbage. Two decades later, it had expanded into a diversified group of fifteen oil-field companies called Acden, employing 1,400 people in the Fort McMurray area and generating $300 million in revenue. Acden is not obliged to divulge how much of that is profit, but the revenue from Acden and other ACFN enterprises, as well as from similar companies operated by the Mikisew Cree First Nation and other deals with the oil sands, has made Fort Chipewyan a relatively prosperous little township. Unemployment is extremely low, incomes are mostly rising, and the town centre is studded with new health care and seniors' centres, well-equipped schools, a new hockey arena and aquatic centre named for a local hero, and an attached youth recreation centre named for Syncrude.

But the lucrative operations upstream have also transformed Fort Chipewyan into a place where people don't trust the water from their taps, don't like to eat the fish from the lakes and worry about what's in the meat from the moose many still hunt in season. The community is small enough that everyone hears about each new case of some strange cancer. Everyone blames the oil sands.

And any given day in 2015, up the road that runs west out of Fort Chipewyan, past the old Catholic church in a community on the reserve known as Dog Head, you could find a modest suburban-style bungalow belonging to Robert and Barbara Grandjambe. Robert is Mikisew Cree, raised in Fort Chipewyan, and Barbara grew up farther north in Fort Smith. They raised three children in their Dog Head home, and now Robert operates a small business offering delta tours to visitors—by boat in summer, by dogsled in winter. He is also one of the few people left in Fort Chipewyan who engages in traditional trapping and fishing year-round. He maintains a trapline north of Fort Chipewyan in the delta, and in winter he has gill nets stretched below the ice near the mouth of the Slave River. He also does some maintenance and construction work for an Edmonton contractor with projects in Fort Chipewyan.

A path out back of the house meanders through the trees to the paddock where he keeps his sled dogs. At intervals along the way are old vehicles and sheds and cabinetry, which Robert has repurposed for storage and salvage, filling them with gear for his sleds and boats and traplines, fish to feed his dogs—everything he needs to live well in an improvised, ever-changing balance between his Cree heritage and twenty-first-century Canada. Robert speaks Cree, and he can run you deep into the woods on his sled wearing a blue fur-lined parka and bright-red leggings and mukluks all hand-stitched with fine colourful beadwork by his wife, and then he can expound extemporaneously on isostatic rebound, the slow rising of the lands in the boreal forest still underway after spending thousands of years compressed under heavy sheets of ice a mile thick. Everybody in town blames the Patch and BC Hydro's dam for low water levels in Lake Athabasca that never returned to where they were before industry came to Denendeh, but Robert knows some of it is a change in the land itself.

Robert readily acknowledges that the in-between life he's built for himself is very rare in Fort Chipewyan, in any Indigenous community. His family life during his childhood was rough and mean; he never knew his father. He was that rare Cree kid who looked forward to returning to the residential school each fall. Barbara, too, came from a dysfunctional home and sometimes felt suicidal as a teen. After moving to Fort Chipewyan with Robert, she worked for ten years at the local campus of Keyano College, Fort McMurray's community college, as a life skills instructor, teaching

Indigenous kids how to bring stability and basic structure to their lives, from budgeting and food preparation to drug and alcohol counselling.

Together in Fort Chipewyan, the Grandjambes raised their children for the world as it presented itself, pushing them to learn math and English and never teaching them to speak Cree, because who besides Robert would they have to talk to in Cree? "I think we had the responsibility as parents to make sure that we gave them the proper tools," he says. They sent their children to a special Western Arctic Leadership Program at a school in Fort Smith. One of their daughters makes good money in security at a diamond mine in the Northwest Territories, and another is training to be a chef.

You can see their son, Robert Jr., in a National Film Board of Canada short film from 1999. It's called *The Little Trapper*, and Robert Jr. is the eponymous star. He is thirteen years old in the film. In the opening scene, he is at ease behind the wheel of a motorboat, smiling from under the brim of an Adidas baseball cap. In voice-over, Barbara says, "When Robert was born, we put his umbilical cord in a fresh moose track. Tradition I guess has it that he'll grow up to love nature and enjoy the bush and enjoy hunting."

In the next scene, Robert Jr. is in the woods, fashioning a moose call out of birch bark and duct tape. "I was ten years old when I shot my first moose," he says. "I think we're pretty lucky."

The film follows Robert Jr. as he tracks moose, checks his gill nets and sets traps by snowmobile in winter, also as he rides a yellow school bus to class and plays pool with friends in downtown Fort Chipewyan. With the money he made from his furs the previous winter, he explains as he skins this year's catch, he bought hockey gear.

"I teach him everything," Robert Sr. says in the movie. "I teach him how to survive. How to feed himself. You know, he's got two choices in life. He's blessed by having two choices. One is that he can go to school and become a doctor, lawyer, nurse—whatever he wants to be. Or he might just live off the land and wish to be out here. That's his choice."

Fifteen years later, Robert Grandjambe Jr. had, in a sense, chosen both options. He still kept a trapline and sold his furs at auction, still fished and hunted part of the year. He is one of the only Fort Chipewyan kids of his generation fully fluent in all these traditional skills. But he is also a certified millwright, and he has spent several months of the year for the past decade living in work camps north of Fort McMurray, working on oil sands projects.

Robert Jr. had been keenly interested in the trades all through his school years in the Western Arctic Leadership Program, and he jumped at the chance to enroll in an apprenticeship at Syncrude. The millwright trade appealed to him particularly because he knew he would learn skills—things like how to fix motors and gears and pumps—that would serve him as well in his traditional hunting and trapping, where maintaining snowmobiles and motorboats was central to the routine. He had to beat out hundreds of other applicants for the apprenticeship and spent five years learning the trade and working enough hours for certification. If there was a cultural friction between the months he spent each year in an oil sands work camp and those spent maintaining traplines and gill nets in the bush north of Fort Chipewyan, it didn't wear on Robert Jr. much at all. He still considered himself lucky, one of the only people of his generation of Indigenous people in the region who could maintain a trapline, a Ski-Doo, and an oil sands plant's pump with equal ease. He came back to Dog Head often to see his parents, and they still worked together on cleaning and preparing his pelts for sale.

Over the years, Robert Sr. has worked often in environmental monitoring and field research on the delta. When scientific research teams come to Fort Chipewyan to gather samples, Robert Sr. is often their guide and assistant. Many of the deformed fish shown to the news media over the years were caught or collected by him. He was also the Mikisew Cree's environmental liaison officer for five years in the Regional Aquatics Management Program, which was established in the late 1990s as the first effort at stringent monitoring of oil sands impacts on the water downstream from the Patch. The First Nations in the region had been brought together in a regional quasi-governmental organization called the Athabasca Tribal Council. The provincial government and the oil sands industry pooled their monitoring money and distributed it through the council. Robert was the Mikisew Cree's liaison on the project.

"We were that far away from success," he said. "By success, I mean we were starting to gain trust with the people. When they find a deformity or something like that, they bring it to me." Robert would take the deformed fish to be analyzed and share the results with the people who brought them to him. Trust was a rare and sacred thing in Fort Chipewyan at the dark end of decades of indifference, duplicity and mistreatment at the hands of government and industry officials of all kinds. And Robert could feel it building. But then a new chief and band council took over the Mikisew Cree First Nation, and they shifted the monitoring role from the Athabasca Tribal Council to the First Nation itself. That was the end of Robert's tenure.

When Robert and Barbara surveyed Fort Chipewyan from the kitchen table out in Dog Head in 2015, they saw a community carved into factions, divided and subdivided, nursing wounds from decades of abuse and warped by the Patch's easy money. "Shut-up money," Robert called it. It represents, in his estimation, the inverse of a sign of trust.

DUTY TO CONSULT

There are a thousand people in Fort Chipewyan, and it can seem like there are nearly as many claims to authority. The Mikisew Cree and Dene bands—the MCFN and ACFN—each has its own band councils with elected chiefs and councillors, institutions imposed by the federal government's Indian Act. The Fort Chipewyan Metis have their own organization with its own relationship to each level of government. The First Nations also have councils of elders, informal organizations whose membership is nevertheless well understood by the band members themselves. The elders' councils often carry more authority and earn more trust than the elected councils because of their connection to the traditional culture and hierarchy of the bands. The Athabasca Tribal Council lives on with a fuzzy mandate. Each First Nation also has a liaison arm for proceedings with government and industry representatives—the ACFN's Industry Relations Corporation and the MCFN's Government and Industry Relations Department. So there is a GIR and an IRC and the ATC, each sending representatives to RAMP and AEMERA and JOSM and a dozen other committees and consultation groups. All of this to dance around the question of what the industry has done and wants to do, what its activities will do to the water and the air of the region, what governments—provincial, federal, municipal, tribal—intend to do to enable or to stop it.

In Canadian law, when the Crown is contemplating an action that will affect the Treaty rights of Indigenous people—evaluating an application for a new pipeline or oil sands project, for example—it has a legal obligation called a "duty to consult." Over the years, processes and standards and legal precedents have emerged to explain how this duty is fulfilled. But on the ground in Fort Chipewyan, it remains a vague, ever-changing thing. It unfolds as a series of oddly structured engagements with stakeholders, as the band councils and elders take separate meetings with industry representatives. The GIR and IRC officials sometimes preside, and sometimes outside consultants are brought in to explain the hundreds of pages of documentation an oil sands project churns out in its application process. None of it bears much resemblance to proceedings in the distant courtrooms and legislatures where the rules of it all were written.

The duty to consult was enshrined in Canadian law only in a 2004 Supreme Court of Canada decision. Before that, there had been no consultation in Fort Chipewyan—none when the Bennett Dam was built, none when GCOS first started mining bitumen, none when the federal and provincial governments restructured taxes and royalties in the mid-1990s to trigger the great boom in the Patch. When consultation happens now, who knows what it's supposed to mean? When is the duty fulfilled, and by whom? Who gives or denies consent? Which band? On whose authority?

Anyway, there are meetings.

On the road out of town toward Dog Head, there's a Y junction with one branch veering off to the left, toward the Lake Athabasca shore. It leads through the woods to a windswept bluff, on top of which stands a big white house overlooking the confluence of the lake and the mouth of the Slave River. The house was donated to the ACFN by its former owner and has been transformed into the Uncle Fred Youth and Elders Lodge. It hosts courses in moose tanning and traditional drumming and tournaments of Dene hand games—a sort of team sport involving hiding and passing tokens under blankets while distracting opponents with elaborate hand gestures.

One afternoon in September 2015, the Lodge hosted the inaugural Elders and Youth Cultural Gathering. The grounds around the white house were filled with a series of tables and booths, almost like a fairground. Elders sitting in folding chairs, some with Syncrude logos on the back, were teaching moose tanning at one station and wood carving at another. At a long table overlooking the lake, fresh lake whitefish were being cleaned, filleted and hung on racks to dry by neophytes under expert supervision. There was drumming and hand games. A group of enthusiastic young men cleaned ducks and spitted them whole on sticks and roasted them in the big campfire.

For a time, many of the elders sat along a low stone wall near the house in a kind of receiving line, and new arrivals would make their way down the rank, exchanging greetings and offering gifts. A group of oil company representatives in matching nylon windbreakers with "Suncor Aboriginal and Shareholder Relations" stitched on them made its way through the crowd at one point. There was a moose-calling competition, and then teams were formed for the Dene Language Challenge. Each team consisted of a Dene elder, another Dene member, a Dene youth, and one non-Dene guest, almost all of whom were oil company representatives. The Dene elder taught the other three a sentence in Denesuline, and then the rest of the team spoke it before a judging panel of elders. The teams were scored on how comprehensibly they enunciated their sentences.

The Gathering was a convivial affair in a glorious setting, the late summer sun warm and bright, the air thick with smells of roasted duck and drying fish. It stretched on into the evening, everyone trying to reach back to that time before oil sands mines and hydroelectric dams had muddied the water when there was balance here in Denendeh.

The next morning, at the small conference hall across the parking lot from the main lodge, the Dene elders gathered again. It was a less cheerful affair—a meeting with a project team from an oil company that had applied to mine bitumen just north of the spot where the Firebag River flows into the Athabasca. It would be the most northerly lease ever developed, the closest a mine had yet come to Fort Chipewyan. On the way in, elders greeted one another and chitchatted about yesterday's gathering. A Dene elder had died recently in Fort McMurray, and a number of them were flying down afterward to pay their respects. On the way into the conference hall, one elder tried to remember which company would be coming to talk with them. He thought it was Total, the French company. It was actually Teck Resources, Ltd., a conventional mining company that had begun investing in oil sands projects in the last few years and was the lead partner on the Frontier project that the meeting had been called to discuss.

The conference room at the Elders Lodge is about the size of an elementary school classroom. Folding dining tables and conference-hall stacking chairs had been laid out in a squared-off U. Along one wall, there were snacks and coffee in big silver institutional urns. Two of the walls had been covered in poster-sized Post-it note pages dense with questions and comments from a planning session the elders had attended with their IRC colleagues the previous day.

The elders came in by twos and threes and found seats until there were perhaps forty of them in the room and nearly every seat was filled. A white SUV pulled up to the hall while they were settling in and getting coffee, and a five-person team from the mining company came in and started setting up for a presentation. Chairs and tables were moved and rearranged to make space at one end of the room for a screen and digital projector. After introductions and an opening prayer led by one of the elders, an official from the IRC announced that this event was to be characterized as an "information meeting," not a consultation. Then the head of the mining company team set up with a laptop in a seat next to the projector and began a PowerPoint presentation on the new mine and its potential environmental impacts.

For a short while, the Dene elders listened quietly. The mining company representative had a picture of one of the big old iron hooks on the old Hudson's Bay Company fort site they had used long ago to tie up their boats, and he used it as a metaphor for the "trust and respect" that would guide this project. He went on from there about stewardship, speaking mainly about bison populations along the Athabasca, and that's when the elders began to interject. They knew bison, what had happened to bison, two hundred years of all the things settlers had done to bison. They told this mining company rep about declining populations, changes in habitat, all the pressures on the land. One elder spoke with an engineer's level of detail about inflows and outflows at existing oil sands mine sites. You were not going to come into this room and tell these people about taking care of bison. It was amazing, actually, that this mining company representative had tried.

The mining company rep continued his presentation, but he didn't get much further before an elder seated nearest the screen interrupted. The way the room went still, you knew the real authority was speaking up. "People are scared to eat the food they were raised on," he said. He gestured mildly to indicate the Post-it posters all around the room. Why, he asked, hadn't any of these questions been addressed yet? Why didn't this conversation begin there?

The elder's question was directed at the mining company rep, but it reverberated far beyond the conference room that day. There was so much contained in that PowerPoint presentation, in the projector's unblinking eye attempting to show the elders the nature of their place in the world, in the presumption of authority and the temerity to speak of "trust and respect" on Dene land in 2015. To suggest that saying it made it so.

There were so many slides missing from that PowerPoint, so many scenes that needed to come before the picture of bison grazing peacefully beyond the mining company's proposed buffer zone. There was so much unexamined history and so many unanswered questions. They all clouded the room like campfire smoke drying racks of fish no one could say for sure were safe to eat.

There should have been a graph showing smallpox mortality rates among First Nations. A slide with the text of a treaty that was missing a clause, the one that promised the Dene and the Cree freedom to use the land as long as the sun shines. A haunted black-and-white photo of a residential school, a triumphal postcard image of the W. A. C. Bennett Dam, a picture of Dene boats on dry land that used to be waterfront.

Expand the PowerPoint's scope. There could have been a graph of oil prices over the last half century, tracking the shifting priorities of government officials in Ottawa and Edmonton and corporate bosses in Calgary. The famous photo of a bitumen-soaked duck, taken that fateful day in April 2008 when the full cost of the oil sands boom first made the nightly news. Snapshots of protesters holding up handmade anti–oil sands placards in front of the White House in Washington, in front of a megaload shipment in small-town Idaho, on Burnaby Mountain in suburban Vancouver. Graphs showing escalating heavy haul truck sales, oil sands capital investment by year, atmospheric carbon dioxide levels in parts per million by year, cumulative emissions from oil sands production by year. Layer them one on the other, see the lines move in sync. Pictures of Canadian government trade missions to China, stacks of steel pipe awaiting Keystone XL's approval, refineries on the Gulf coast of Texas awaiting shipments of bitumen, cars and trucks in dense traffic, coughing their clouds of exhaust from Calgary to Beijing.

The whole world could have been in that PowerPoint, slide after slide — a visual representation of the ambitions of a would-be energy superpower in the world's biggest industry, with global investment and global consequences. And all of it bearing down on a conference room on the shore of Lake Athabasca, churning the water and clouding the air, as a guy pitched an oil sands mine with talk of trust and respect. Looking for sanction, permission. No one had ever asked the Dene for permission in 250 years. Why would this guy with his projector and his pictures of bison be any different?

It's probably unfair to ask one company to answer for all of that, but it was at least as unfair to think it shouldn't have to answer for some of it. When the elders interrupted the mining company rep to ask when their concerns would be addressed, when they scanned the walls to see their questions written there in thick, black Sharpie, this is what they were all getting at.

Why wasn't the Delta included in the assessments?

How low can oil prices go before you will stop pursuing the project?

Why did you not answer the questions from prior meetings?

Just before the meeting broke for lunch, one of the elders told the mining company rep bluntly, "We know this will go ahead even though we are dead set against it."

After lunch, the mining company people returned to the PowerPoint and tried to get back to their agenda. They talked about the application process and the monitoring programs in place and the natural wonders of the Birch Mountains southwest of Fort Chipewyan. But the interjections became more frequent, and the tension rose, and finally an elder in a broad-brimmed yellow Panama hat and sunglasses like you'd see around the pool at an all-inclusive resort in Mexico began to speak in Denesuline, quiet and firm. After he was done, another elder translated. "The Creator put us here on this land for a reason," the translator said. "The Creator placed us here to look after the land and look after the children."

The meeting carried on, but it didn't get very far after that.

Afterward, some of the Dene elders flew to Fort McMurray to pay their respects to their deceased friend, and the mining company team flew back to Calgary, and the project moved ahead through the application process. The nominal launch date for the construction phase wasn't until 2019 at the earliest, and with oil at less than $50 per barrel, there was, for the first time in many years, no real hurry.

BALANCE SHEETS

In truth, new mining operations north of the Firebag River are rarely front and centre when talk turns to the future in the Patch. "I think the era of big megaprojects up there is really over," the prominent Calgary energy investment analyst Peter Tertzakian told *Alberta Oil* magazine in 2015. "The oil sands has to compete for capital with all the other types of oil projects that are out there. It has to morph into something cleaner, smaller in size and less capital intensive. It's definitely possible to do, but the old paradigm of 4,000-man camps and long construction periods is over."

Imperial's Kearl mine and Suncor's Fort Hills mine, then, might be the last of the giants. Notwithstanding the economic downturn and the tireless pursuit of megaload protesters in the Pacific Northwest, construction finished on Kearl in mid-2015. And all through the dismal months of the oil-price crash, thousands of construction workers continued work on the Fort Hills plant, ninety kilometres north of Fort McMurray, which is set to begin delivering 180,000 barrels of bitumen per day by the end of 2017. Fort Hills has been in the works since the early days of the boom but finally began construction in 2013 with an estimated $13.5-billion price tag. In the end, it will end up costing Suncor about $15 billion. The plant is intended to run for fifty years, and in order to achieve the return on investment that initially attracted all that capital, Fort Hills requires an average oil price of $95 per barrel for WTI.

Long-serving oil executives typically say they are optimists, and oil sands bosses in particular consider it an essential skill. The future has looked grim for the oil sands for most of its hundred-year history, with the exception of one wild, glorious decade or so of the long boom—though even those years were plagued by skyrocketing costs and punctuated by the global economy's biggest failure since the Great Depression. And so the Patch's sunny-minded companies push on with the grand project of growing production beyond 2.4 million barrels per day. With Fort Hills and an expansion at CNRL's Horizon and a handful of SAGD projects that were too far along to shut down during the downturn all set to begin pumping oil into the marketplace, the Patch will add another 500,000 barrels to its daily ration by 2018. It's anyone's guess whether the market price will make any of it profitable out of the gate.

The entire oil sands business was predicated on rising prices and relentlessly expanding demand. But in the age of climate change, the reality looks more like a time of volatility, price shocks, ferocious competition and a demand plateau the whole industry now dances across, hoping there is no cliff's edge just ahead. Analysts estimate the overwhelming majority of new oil projects developed by non-OPEC countries in recent years were launched in anticipation of $80 oil. That once seemed like a certainty but now looks like an optimist's dicey bet.

In the Patch, the older projects are generally able to weather the worst of the price shocks. The industry-wide average break-even point in 2015 was estimated at around $47, and Syncrude claims operating costs at its mines are around $37. Cenovus, meanwhile, is chasing a break-even point of $40. Presuming the swoon of 2015 and 2016 was an anomalous phenomenon, the industry will soldier on, continuing to grow past the three-million-barrels-per-day mark, though it will almost certainly do so at a pace nothing like the long boom's giddy speed.

Cheap oil and rising costs and competition from faster, cheaper rivals like the American shale plays begin to raise a question that grows steadily harder to answer: What is the oil sands for? Add in the necessity of reducing greenhouse gas emissions, and the question becomes an existential one.

Wonky studies of projected carbon dioxide emissions and proven fossil fuel reserves inevitably come to the same conclusion again and again: the most expensive, most carbon-intensive fuel sources will be the first to go. Coal is always at the top of the list, already being phased out of electricity grids across Canada, in numerous US states, and in many European countries. But the next item on the list is usually unconventional oil. And although those wonky studies tend to make their case on climate policy grounds — these are the dirtiest barrels — the bigger and nearer threat to the Patch's future might be on the cost side. What if bitumen becomes *unprofitable* long before anyone has the temerity to shut down the oil sands on climate grounds? What if bitumen reserves are "stranded assets" caught in a global "carbon bubble"?

For Mark Carnavale, a British investment fund manager, the notion of "unburnable carbon" first began to worry his analyst's mind in the wake of the global financial crisis of 2008. He'd taken notice of a string of extremely lucrative debuts on the London Stock Exchange by coal-mining companies promising big returns on newly unlocked reserves. China, India and other emerging economies had been stoking their fast-growing economic engines with insatiable demand for coal, and the future-tense curves sloped ever upward. Carnavale, who'd become a major investor in low-carbon clean technologies, couldn't square those rosy demand scenarios with what he knew about the urgent need for emissions reductions to combat climate change. He used to grouse about these overoptimistic IPOs with a colleague at Deutsche Bank, Mark Fulton, who specialized in studying climate change impacts on long-term investments. They decided to hire a researcher named James Leaton to investigate it. Leaton was an environmentalist with a financial bent who'd done oil and gas policy analysis for the World Wildlife Fund and financial consulting for PricewaterhouseCoopers. They called their team the Carbon Tracker Initiative (CTI); Carnavale anticipated that it would last six months, just long enough for Leaton to complete and publish his report.

The report, *Unburnable Carbon*, was published in the fall of 2011. It introduced the terms "carbon bubble" and "stranded assets" to a wider audience. And more important, it attached hard numbers to the concepts. It noted that the industrial world had already burned 886 gigatons of carbon dioxide and had a remaining budget of 565 gigatons left if it was to stay under the 2°C global warming threshold. The world's two hundred largest fossil fuel companies, meanwhile, controlled proven reserves capable of releasing 745 gigatons. The implication was clear: if catastrophic climate change was to be avoided, huge amounts of those reserves had to remain in the ground unburned.

Carnavale decided to have a hundred copies printed for whatever small crowd of climate-obsessed financial analyst types turned out for the launch. How big a crowd could that possibly be in money-mad London, where the focus was always on the latest IPO, not a wonky emissions report? CTI's report was well but modestly received in those limited wonky circles. But then its numbers turned up as the backbone of Bill McKibben's *Rolling Stone* article, "Global Warming's Terrifying New Math," in the summer of 2012. Suddenly CTI was at the centre of a global debate about climate change action—and a growing movement against the expansion of the oil sands. The six-month side project turned into a full-time gig, as CTI transformed from a one-off project into a think tank publishing a series of reports on the profitability of the fossil fuel industries in a lower-emissions world.

As their first order of business, Carnavale and his colleagues started recruiting financial industry heavyweights to give their work heft among bankers as well as climate policy obsessives. Among these was Paul Spedding, the global head of oil and gas analysis at HSBC, who had read and responded with interest to *Unburnable Carbon*. Spedding saw the biggest risk for oil companies not in the sheer volume of their stranded-asset reserves but in the chaos that those assets might create for oil prices as an industry built on the assumption of perpetual growth came reluctantly to grips with declining demand.

"My feeling is that if you're going to engage anybody in the investment world, it helps to have a financial argument," Spedding said. "Obviously, a lot of institutions were getting pressure from groups who were concerned about the environment. But quite often the argument was, 'Morally you can't produce this.' Unfortunately, oil companies do what the market lets them do, normally." With Spedding's help, CTI developed ways to measure the carbon bubble on an oil company's balance sheets. Spedding knew that when you said to an analyst, "Plug these numbers into your spreadsheets and see what happens," that's when you got the financial world's attention.

By 2013, CTI's reports had made their way onto the financial pages of the newspapers. In a 2014 feature on CTI's "stranded asset" argument, the *Economist* noted that a group of institutional investors controlling more than $3 trillion in assets had quizzed the forty-five largest oil companies on whether they believed any of the reserves on their books were at risk of being stranded. The companies that responded were dismissive of the risk, citing persistent demand—ExxonMobil, for example, operated under the assumption that 75 percent of the world's energy in 2040 would still come from fossil fuels—and the unwillingness of governments around the world to take even the first fledgling steps down a path that would lead to a 2°C world. "We do not believe that any of our proven reserves will become 'stranded,'" Shell wrote in response.

At the time of the report, oil had rebounded from its financial-crisis trough and vaulted back above $90 per barrel, and oil companies were pouring money into projects in the Patch and everywhere else with re- newed zeal. Just a couple of years later, as prices sank below anyone's expectations, Spedding wondered if they might answer that question dif- ferently. Shell, for example, had abandoned its Carmon Creek SAGD development in the fall of 2015—a project it had funded lavishly in the heady days of 2013 and now wrote down at a $2-billion loss. Shell claimed it had planned for $70 to $110 oil, Spedding said, but the decision on Car- mon Creek made him suspect it wasn't ever going to be profitable at $70. A future in which fossil fuel companies were under mounting pressure due to climate impacts and competition for shares of a shrinking market wasn't going to look like that rosier scenario of ever-increasing demand that companies like Exxon had been banking on. It was more likely to resemble the chaos unleashed by Saudi Arabia's decision to let prices col- lapse. In which case the financial argument for the Patch began to look dubious even before talk turns to its carbon footprint. This is the caveat, the crux of the Patch's conundrum at the end of the High Modern era.

FUTURE PERFECT TENSE

The Patch's corporate optimists have answers for all of this. They might be fractured, partial answers, future-tense and even verging on absurd in some cases, but they are answers. In an October 2015 story on the oil sands bust, the *New York Times* spoke to an "executive and investor"—remaining anonymous perhaps to avoid attaching his company to uncharacteristic pessimism—who admitted the Patch had lost the environmental debate. "I don't know how the issue got away, but it's obvious now that it did," he said.

Few oil sands bosses would concede the point for the record with their names attached, but the loss of control had been widely felt, and many oil sands companies were starting to accept the fact that they would have to fully embrace action on climate change in order to keep doing business and see new pipelines built and new projects approved. When Alberta's NDP premier, Rachel Notley, rolled out her climate policy package for the press in November 2015, she was joined at the podium by CEOs from Suncor, Shell, Cenovus and even CNRL's Murray Edwards, who was historically no fan of left-leaning anything.

"This plan will position Alberta, one of the world's largest oil and gas producing jurisdictions, as a climate leader and will allow for ongoing innovation and technology in the oil and gas sector," Edwards told the press.

The celebration of "innovation and technology" was the Patch's back door into the climate camp. The industry may have had little time for debating the size of its carbon bomb, but it had been pouring money into R&D departments for years to improve efficiency, clean up tailings ponds faster and reclaim mine sites after the bitumen had all been hauled away. The Patch was willing to bring its zealous optimism to bear on technological fixes for its carbon footprint. The industry could even get high-minded about it.

"I looked at the oil sands, and I thought, You know what? This is North America's insurance policy for bridging to future high-density, non-carbon energy sources," geologist Maggie Hanna told an interviewer in 2013. Hanna was then working as a consultant for Suncor, brought in to help figure out how to rethink its old industrial technology for the twenty-first century. "Your upgraders are 1940s technology with a little 1960s sprinkled in for good measure and some 1980s instrumentation, and SAGD is 1980s," she told her Suncor colleagues. "We've got to do better, and there are a lot of things out there that I know about that can help this." Hanna went on to work with two start-up companies developing new efficiency technologies for the Patch.

Hanna's framing of the issue was typical of the newly enlightened oil sands business. There was a low-carbon future out there, a world where electricity came from renewable energy and cars were all electric, but it was a half century or more away. The task for the oil sands was to continue to make money and keep the nation's economic engine humming along while shrinking its environmental footprint by increments. The Patch was the bridge to that future. It was part of the solution. It was still *necessary*.

Lorraine Mitchelmore, the president of Shell Canada, was onstage with Notley when she introduced Alberta's climate plan, which included an absolute cap on greenhouse gas emissions from the Patch. It would be one of Mitchelmore's last public acts before resigning, and she used the press around her exit to tout the industry's environmental bona fides.

"As an oil sands producer, I believe that the limit set on carbon emissions will provide the incentive needed to put Canadian oil on the path to becoming the world's most environmentally and economically competitive," she wrote in a *Globe and Mail* op-ed. Shell had recently inaugurated a carbon capture and storage project at its bitumen upgrader near Edmonton, she noted, which would reduce emissions by a million tons per year. And the industry was just getting started. Like many oil sands executives, Mitchelmore pointed to the "groundbreaking" Canada's Oil Sands Innovation Alliance (COSIA) as the standard-bearer when she discussed green-minded innovation.

Oil companies, as a rule, do not like to share. They guard intellectual property and strategic plans doggedly from competitors and view R&D projects not as efforts to improve the industry as a whole but as levers through which to gain competitive advantage. By 2010, however, a handful of oil majors active in the Patch decided the environmental challenges they all faced could be solved better through collaboration. The six companies, which included Suncor and Shell, formed a partnership called the Oil Sands Leadership Initiative to pool research resources and share new technologies. Two years later, the group of six expanded to thirteen and became COSIA. By 2016, the organization's constituents had together invested more than $1 billion in collaborative work on reducing water use, reclaiming land, remediating tailings ponds and reducing greenhouse gases. COSIA innovations have already produced a 36 percent reduction in the amount of water needed per barrel of bitumen, and six member companies are working together to replant trees along seismic line cuts. COSIA member CNRL, meanwhile, has launched a pilot "biorefinery" project that uses algae to convert carbon dioxide emissions into fuel at one of its in situ facilities. Industry boosters suggest CNRL's waste might one day be jet fuel.

COSIA's marquee initiative is the Carbon XPrize. Modelled on the XPrize for space exploration, the Carbon XPrize will give awards of $10 million each to the two research teams that come up with the best technologies to turn carbon dioxide into a usable product. The competition attracted twenty-seven competitors—advanced research labs and entrepreneurial ventures from around the world that are working on ideas to turn carbon dioxide emissions into everything from biofuel to fish food and concrete. (The prizes will be awarded in 2020.)

There is a whole cluster of research and test-project work beyond COSIA that is aimed at reducing the industry's footprint and refurbishing its public image. CNRL CEO Murray Edwards invested his own money in Carbon Engineering, a start-up whose technology promises to capture carbon dioxide directly from the air; Bill Gates is also an investor. Oil sands companies have invested in technologies to take water out of tailings before they even reach ponds, and they are testing the use of solvents instead of steam in SAGD projects, which would greatly reduce the emissions per in situ barrel; a pilot project at Imperial's Cold Lake in situ site used the technology to reduce carbon dioxide emissions by 25 percent per barrel. What if bitumen were converted into a buoyant solid and transported to market in a shipping container instead of a pipe? What if zeppelins could be used to ship equipment to oil sands sites? Research and development is ongoing in both areas, and many more.

When the industry speaks of its bright future, this is what it imagines: an oil patch that's more Silicon Valley than Saudi Arabia, with a range of technological breakthroughs and processing innovations that make bitumen cleaner to produce than Saudi crude and create spin-off products to help reduce carbon footprints beyond the oil business. This, they insist, is that fabled bridge to the low-carbon economy. Construction is underway. And if the need for this future-tense technology once seemed decades distant, the price shocks of 2014 have convinced many in the Patch that it's urgently needed now.

Jim Gray, who was a leader in Alberta's conventional oil industry in the 1970s and 1980s, surveys the landscape and sees a "new normal" of $50 to $60 oil in an industry no longer driven by discoveries but by technology. "Nowadays it's technology that is generating the discoveries," he says. "What's a discovery? A discovery means you've found some oil that you have the technology to get it out at a profit."

In that landscape, Gray argues, technological innovation in the oil sands industry is necessary not only to shrink its carbon footprint but also to ensure its survival in an energy world changing faster than it has at any point since the first days of the gushers. "We run the risk of these becoming marginalized," he says. "We have to have all hands on deck. We have to have an urgent level of research and innovation and technology. We have to recognize that we are in a fight for our life up here."

In the meantime, the dark clouds gathered in the Patch month by month throughout 2015 and 2016. No sector of the global oil industry was hit harder by the price shock. By the end of 2015, eighteen oil sands projects representing eight hundred thousand barrels per day of new production were cancelled or on hold, thirty-six thousand jobs had been cut, and annual capital investment levels declined more than $20 billion from the peak investment year of 2013.

Bakken shale companies, their operations growing more efficient and more automated throughout the downturn, were claiming to be profitable at $30 per barrel, while the oil sands struggled to get to $40. The real action in new energy technology was in renewable energy, smart grids, electric cars, industrial scale batteries. Studious oil analysts now spoke openly of a "Kodak moment" for the whole industry, by which they meant not a pretty snapshot but a shift in the energy industry not unlike the switch from film to digital photography that left a once-mighty company in ruin. If the Patch ran on optimism, it seemed to get harder by the day to justify.

"It's the only place in Canada where you can look and see fifty years ahead of you." You only had to rewind to January 2014 to find workers in the Patch expressing this kind of amazement at the intensity of the construction boom then underway. A year later, there was much less to marvel at, and less still a year after that. But there was still 2.4 million barrels per day, and soon it would be 3 million or more. And so the Diversified buses went out to site and back twice a day, and Raheel Joseph's cricket team practiced in the evening sun. The haul trucks went to the mine face, received their four-hundred-ton scoops from the shovel and drove back to the hopper in orderly lines down good mine roads like the ones Dee Parkinson-Marcoux built. Earth still needed moving, and so Marvin L'Hommecourt worked his ten-and-ten driving a Caterpillar D11 bulldozer at Imperial Kearl.

And the flights still came in at Fort McMurray's big new airport from Edmonton and Calgary and Toronto, and the bleary-eyed Patch workers piled off. One night near midnight in August 2015, Nick Martell was among them, thankful still to have plenty of work for his giant crane. He'd heard about that green energy stuff; they even put wind turbines up on the coast of PEI. That might sound like the kind of work that could use a crane operator like Martell, but he wasn't going to be able to pay off the debt on his lobster fleet at PEI wages. And so he turned in at his buddy's house and got some sleep, and the next morning at dawn, he was headed out to site.

OIL PATCH IDYLL

Robert Grandjambe Jr. came home to Fort Chipewyan in February 2016 after a stretch of work at Syncrude. The morning after he returned to his parents' house in Dog Head, he set out on his snowmobile to set the traps on his trapline. He was baiting them for wolves. They didn't fetch the greatest prices in the fur market, but he had to thin out their populations along his trapline from time to time or they would slaughter the smaller fur-bearing animals that earned the best money. He returned to the traps a few days later and came back to his parents' house with three wolves and a lynx. He set up in his father's backyard shed that evening to skin them.

The wood stove warmed up the place against the boreal cold, and Robert stripped down to the T-shirt he was wearing under rust-coloured overalls. He wore purple surgical gloves and used a small, sharp knife to cut the pelts away from the carcasses. He worked in a fast, practiced way that wasn't anything like a hurry. An uncle showed up, and then his grandfather, and they sat drinking Coors Light from cans and trading news and stories while Robert worked on the wolves. His uncle explained he was heading to Fort Smith soon to get a motor fixed. His grandfather told a story about a funny thing that happened on a hunt long ago. Robert said he had trapped twenty-six wolves this winter, a personal record. And he reckoned the bears would be rising soon—they'd be up early this spring because there had been fewer berries than usual last fall.

Easy balances are hard to strike in the Patch, but on one peaceful winter evening in Fort Chipewyan, one oil sands millwright and his kin had found one, swapping stories of old traditions and new developments around the wood stove while three wolves and a prized lynx were readied for market.

Maryellen Fenech was shocked at how quickly she fell in love with Fort McMurray. She was a city girl, raised in Toronto, the daughter of Maltese immigrants. When she first moved to Edmonton with her husband, she found it too small and too cold. When they decided to relocate to Fort Mc-Murray to open up a new John Deere dealership, she reluctantly agreed to stay for at least two years, five at most. Six months in, she didn't want to leave. Almost everyone, it seemed, was from somewhere else, and they formed quick friendships that felt like family. Fenech had been there for eighteen years by June 2015, and she had no plans to leave any time soon.

When Fenech first arrived in Fort McMurray, she and her husband had settled in Beacon Hill, a quiet suburb up on the ridge across Highway

63 from downtown Fort McMurray. The husband was gone, but Fenech had stayed in Beacon Hill, remarried, and started raising a family there. Her new husband, Dan MacDonald, was from Antigonish, Nova Scotia, and his parents came out and worked in the Patch. They went home to Nova Scotia after the 2008 crash but then returned when the money to be made in the rebooted boom was too sweet to pass up. They moved back into Beacon Hill, just up the block. It was a quiet street, in a quiet neighbourhood, never much through traffic. Fenech and her husband had two kids, and they could pop over to their grandparents' house whenever they wanted. Fenech's house backed on a narrow stretch of woods that buffered the backyards on her street from the ones the next street over, and there was a path there. In the morning, she could walk her daughters to the gate, say good-bye, and watch them walk in the shade of the trees all the way to the school grounds.

Fenech's husband worked at Syncrude, putting in eighteen-and-threes in the summer of 2015. She had found part-time work awhile back with the United Way, and at some point it became full-time. Now she was fourteen years into a career as the finance and operations manager of the United Way branch that led the nation in per capita donations. It had done so for eight years straight. People made good money in Fort McMurray, and they were happy to give back.

The Feneches lived well, owned everything they had outright except for a manageable mortgage on the house, didn't need to work overtime to pay for it all. They even had a big pickup truck with a lift kit. "I have a lifted truck," she said. "For a girl from Toronto, that's a pretty funny thing."

In the summer, they loaded their quads onto their lifted truck, filled it with camping gear and launched off into the vast boreal wilderness. "Just go drive," she said. "Go somewhere and take it for a couple of rips." Her daughters loved bombing through the woods with them on the quads.

On lazy summer mornings, Fenech liked to sit with a coffee at a picnic table in her breezeway—a cozy spot, well shaded, with a view of the woods. Neighbours dropped in from time to time. In the quiet of a Fort McMurray weekday morning at the start of summer in 2015, with the sun shining on the trees, Fenech sat at her picnic table and radiated the ease of a person who has found the place she wants to be in the world.

Eleven months later, it all burned to the ground.

THE BEAST

For Raheel Joseph, the morning of Tuesday, May 3, 2016, started out like most others. He headed to work not long after five o'clock, off to the Diversified bus dispatch shed in the industrial park on the northern fringe of Fort McMurray for the usual safety briefing and maintenance checks. Then he made the pickups on his route and was on Highway 63 northbound well before seven, driving day-shift workers to the Suncor base site under a daybreak sky of clear, gleaming blue.

It was one of those things everyone remembered vividly later on—what a lovely spring day it was. Until it wasn't at all.

When Joseph returned home after his morning route, planning to take a nap, his wife was worried. A wildfire had broken out east of Fort McMurray a couple of days earlier, and it was moving steadily closer to town. She had opened the kitchen window while she was doing the breakfast dishes, and now they were covered with a thin layer of ash. Joseph reassured her it wouldn't reach the city and went for his nap. His wife started cooking—if they needed to leave, they would have provisions for the trip.

Maryellen Fenech's office at the United Way is in the MacDonald Island administrative building. Her office window offers a clear view up the Athabasca River westward, with the Fort McMurray Golf Club on one bank and the tip of the Abasand Heights neighbourhood on the other. Fenech spent the morning of May 3 engrossed in the usual office routine. But then around noon, she looked up and saw puffs of dark smoke just beyond Abasand. And then she saw mean orange flames leap skyward around the same spot.

She didn't believe her eyes at first. She called in a couple of coworkers, and they stood in her window and watched. And after they'd all seen it, she called home to see what was happening in Beacon Hill.

Fenech's husband, Dan, had the day off. She would be so grateful later that in the midst of it all, he wasn't up at site, that she hadn't had to manage it all alone.

"Hon, it's still nice up here," he told her. But she told him about the view from her office window, the flames shooting up, the billowing smoke. Someone from Fenech's daughter's school was calling on the other line, so she got off the phone with Dan and learned the folks at the school were making arrangements to get kids picked up early. When she got back on the line with Dan after that, he said, "Actually, hon, you need to come home now."

Fenech closed up her computer, went and put away files and told her boss what was happening, that she was leaving for the day. On her way out, people were coming up to tell her they were evacuating all of Beacon Hill. And not a half hour later she was in the house she'd come to love on the quiet curving street with the path along the edge of the woods out back leading to the school, and she was trying in a frenzy to decide what to bring with her as she and her family fled.

It was a little after one o'clock. An hour earlier, it'd been another day at the office. That was how fast the wildfire the firefighters would name "the Beast" descended on Fort McMurray.

There can be pockets of surreal calm in the midst of disaster, and Maryellen Fenech and her two daughters—Gabbi, who was eight years old, and Olivia, who was six—found one as they packed up their emergency supplies and drove off to a friend's house in Timberlea. There was no thought—not yet—of leaving town entirely. They were going to stay with friends for a couple of days, that's all. They left Dan at the house, to close the place up and check in on a few neighbours who might need a hand, and then they drove the fifteen kilometres from Beacon Hill to Timberlea without incident. In Timberlea, it was a still a sunny spring day, and Dan and his parents soon joined them at the friend's house. They all went out on the patio to watch the smoke to the southwest, and they laughed in that stressed-out tension-breaking way people do in the midst of shrieking uncertainty, because surely this would all be over in a day or two.

Fenech thought she'd been calm and clearheaded as she packed and fled. She'd gathered the essential papers, passports and insurance and ownership documents, and she'd packed bags for the four of them, rounded up the supplies they needed for their dog. Only later would she discover she'd tossed eight pairs of pyjamas in a bag for one of her daughters but just a single pair of shorts, that she'd forgotten to pack any underwear for Dan. That she was in a panic in the midst of a catastrophe.

At the friend's house in Timberlea, watching a wall of smoke rise on the horizon and the bright day turn the sickly orange of sun refracted through forest-fire haze, Dan was calm and reassuring. He said nothing about what had happened after Fenech and the kids left.

He'd gone to check on the neighbours, to help a couple of the young mothers on the block load up their trucks and make sure no one was still sleeping off a night shift. It all went very fast. Dan was only twenty minutes behind Fenech and the girls, but by the time he got back to his truck the traffic was slow and heavy on the only road out of Beacon Hill down to the highway.

The next day, in a hotel room in Edmonton, Fenech and her husband watched the news coverage of the Beast on the TV in horrified shock. The fire was an international story by then, and every network seemed to be showing a smartphone video shot from the dashboard of somebody's vehicle as it navigated Beacon Hill Drive down the hill toward the highway. The sky all around was black, and the vehicles and trees were inky silhouettes through smoke that made a sunny afternoon look like the dead of night. The electric red of the blaze hung low on every horizon, and as the truck inched along, great burning cinders fell down all around, as if it were raining fire. Many McMurrayites said afterward that the evacuation felt like a scene in a postapocalyptic movie, and this was the video clip that captured that terrible mood best.

"Oh my God," Fenech said to her husband, "I'm so grateful we didn't drive through that."

She said it more than once, how grateful she was. And finally Dan turned to her and in a quiet voice he said, "Hon, that's what I left in." The

video had been shot by their neighbour's son, a young guy who'd been home sleeping after a night shift, probably awakened by the firefighters Dan had seen going door to door as he pulled out of their driveway. The kid would have been just a couple of minutes behind Dan on Beacon Hill Drive. And they were all just ahead of the fire that would devour forty-four of the fifty-five houses on their tranquil suburban street before nightfall.

Raheel Joseph awoke from his nap in the middle of the afternoon and started preparing for his evening shift. His wife continued to prepare food and pack for a possible departure, and the radio was playing nothing but automated Emergency Response messages. But Joseph was a dutiful employee in a job he cherished, and his home in Timberlea was not far from the dispatch shed, and as a bus driver he knew the fastest shortcuts, so he decided to check in at work. He arrived around three o'clock, and the dispatcher told him Diversified was still running as many of its routes as it could, but any employee who needed to go home to take care of family and prepare for evacuation could do so.

Joseph went home, and he strapped his nineteen-month-old daughter into their car and they loaded it with all the provisions and supplies his wife had prepared, and they evacuated. Traffic was heavy on Confederation Way, but they made it to the highway junction. Almost everyone was going north—the oil sands work camps and aerodromes had all offered their space and supplies to evacuees by then—but Joseph spoke to the police officer directing traffic and learned the highway was open to the south as well. He headed that way, thinking of Edmonton four hundred kilometres down the road, with its larger airport and ample amenities, his brother living in the city and dear friends farther along in Red Deer to stay with.

Kiran Malik-Khan put in a full day at work. She had moved on from the United Way to take a job as the communications coordinator for the Fort McMurray school district the previous summer, and on the day the Beast roared into the city, the school district office was pure chaos. From

lunchtime on, she and her colleagues hustled to coordinate early dismiss-
als, notify worried parents, somehow move all the city's schoolchildren
safely home in the midst of rapidly deepening crisis. She knew her husband was at home with her two boys, so she could focus on this work that
so badly needed doing. She left the office at half past four, thinking she
was heading home to a quiet dinner with her family after a long, wild day.

Malik-Khan's commute usually takes fifteen minutes; on May 3, 2016,
in an eerie echo of the crazy traffic of the Patch's boom years, it took two
hours. Coming up Confederation Way, she saw a woman on the side of
the road, leading horses in the other direction. But her husband was calling over and over as she inched along, checking in, saying everyone was
fine at home.

When she finally arrived, her husband greeted her at the door. "We
have to leave in ten minutes," he told her. She stared back at him, dumb-
struck. "What did you just say?" she asked.

"We have to leave in ten minutes," he repeated. "The entire city is now
being evacuated."

It was one of those moments you imagine yourself in when you're
watching a disaster movie. You might even think to yourself, *This is what
I'd do, what I would take with me.* But in the moment, Malik-Khan went
numb. She had ten minutes to choose the things most important to her
in her whole ordered Fort McMurray world. Like many evacuees, she
thought of practicalities—passports, paperwork, proof of the existence of
that ordered world, in case it didn't survive the calamity.

Her husband had made plans with the close family friends they did
everything else with, holiday barbecues and kids' birthdays and *iftar* meals.
They would meet and go north in a convoy. But when they arrived at their
friends' house, plans had changed. Their cars loaded with food and water
and whatever keepsakes everyone had grabbed in their ten numb minutes
of panicked packing, they went south on Highway 63 instead.

Through the late afternoon and into the evening, the Beast devoured
homes and everything in them, block after block in Beacon Hill and

Abasand Heights. The city built to mine bitumen was forever altered, and the people of Fort McMurray poured out onto the roads in their cars and SUVs and pickup trucks. The entire city evacuated, slow and steady and mostly calm, like some final apocalyptic commute. White work trucks with their buggy whips flapping overhead, lifted F-150s and Chevy Silverados, all the same truck-dominated traffic of the Patch's daily routine—all of it was out on Confederation Way and Thickwood Boulevard and Franklin Avenue, up and down Highway 63, fleeing the city.

Maryellen Fenech and her convoy of friends started their evacuation inching down Confederation Way, but they barely moved in an hour and a half. Dan was monitoring the radio and the internet. The RCMP had closed the highway south of downtown Fort McMurray for a time as the roaring fire jumped across it to burn through Waterways and out toward the airport, but Dan heard it had been reopened, so their convoy managed a U-turn and headed back around the loop and down Thickwood Boulevard to the highway.

The ones who went south all remembered passing the Super 8 Hotel, which stood on the west side of the highway just south of the intersection with Beacon Hill Drive. It burned to the ground in a ferocious sea of flames that evening. The enormity of it all hit Maryellen Fenech's kids hard as they passed; Kiran Malik-Khan's twelve-year-old son started to cry as he watched the hotel burn.

Thousands and thousands of the evacuees went north. They bunked in work camps, which were emptier than normal because of the oil-price doldrums. They were evacuated to Edmonton and Lac La Biche and Red Deer and Calgary on commercial and charter airplanes that took off from the Patch's many aerodromes. More than six thousand people had been airlifted to safety on sixty-six flights from Shell's Albian Sands airstrip alone by May 6. A warehouse at one of those aerodromes was converted into a makeshift field hospital as Fort McMurray's entire hospitalized population was evacuated north. The boom's largesse found a strange, redemptive purpose in the flight from the Beast.

A city of eighty thousand emptied entirely in a single afternoon. It did so in terror and in panic, but also with calm and kindness and order. There were virtually no stories of greed or grotesque selfishness, no roadside jousts over the order in the line of escape. Instead, there were extraordinary stories of bravery and generosity and inventive problem solving. The firefighters battling the Beast were superhuman in their selflessness and resolve; the city's fire chief, Darby Allen, became a national hero overnight. A sixteen-year-old girl rode her beloved horse down the highway's shoulder because her family's trailer had room for only two of their three horses. A school principal loaded a yellow bus with all the children whose parents hadn't managed to find a way to pick them up, and she picked up other stranded McMurrayites along the way, and then she drove for fifteen hours straight— first to a rendezvous at a work camp north of the city, then back through the fire's path to towns south of Fort McMurray where the last anxious parents waited—to get all her kids safely reunited with their families.

Eighty thousand people and only one highway out of town, the mean-est, fastest wildfire the boreal forest of northeastern Alberta had ever seen, and not one person lost their lives in the conflagration. (Two teenagers perished in a highway crash as they fled a small community south of the city.) Afterward, some folks wondered how much the orderly evacuation owed to the Patch's obsession with safety. Few other cities of such size could boast of a population as thoroughly trained in emergency proce-dures. Maybe this was what all those tedious daily safety briefings had been for. Fort McMurray evacuated like a company town, and who knows how many lives that saved.

Robert Grandjambe Jr. had left his work site north of Fort McMurray a week before the fire broke out. In spring, the ice road to Fort Chipewyan is impassable, and the river, still choked with slabs of ice, can't be navigated by boat. So Robert Jr. took the long way around, a broad semicircle south of Fort McMurray and then west and north around the delta to Fort Smith, Northwest Territories, where a rough little year-round road allows him ac-cess to his winter hunting grounds from the north.

Robert Jr. knew nothing of the fire until he emerged from the bush days later, southbound by snowmobile for his parents' house in Fort Chipewyan, towing the haul from his hunt on a sled behind him. Once he was back in cellular range, his phone exploded with the news. Dozens of evacuees had been airlifted to Fort Chipewyan, he learned, and now the community was running short on basic supplies. There had only ever been the one small grocery store, and its stock always ran short in the spring, when neither truck nor barge could reach Fort Chipewyan from the south.

Robert Jr. posted messages on social media saying he was coming into town with hundreds of geese and ducks—"country food," he called it. The game was distributed through the community's efficient informal networks to those who most needed it. In the Patch's darkest hour, one sliver of its population came to rely, as trappers had centuries before, on the bush skills of its Indigenous inhabitants.

The Beast obliged the largest wildfire evacuation in Alberta's history. Harrowing images of the fire and accounts of escape appeared in media outlets worldwide. The fire cut a mean scar across the cityscape from the edges of Timberlea and Thickwood in the northwest down to the airport in the southeast. Along the way it destroyed huge swaths of the residential neighbourhoods of Abasand Heights and Beacon Hill, the Gregoire industrial area south of downtown, and the original rail and steamship hub of Waterways. More than 2,400 structures in the city were destroyed, leading to approximately $3.6 billion in insurance claims, the largest payout in Canadian history. Had the prevailing winds not pushed the inferno southeast out of the city—had it turned instead northward, through the heart of downtown, leaping across the Athabasca to the most populous suburbs—it is hard to imagine what would have been left of Fort McMurray after that.

Two thousand firefighters spent sixty days containing the Beast. Residents began to return to the city in early June, once the blaze had moved far enough away into the vast boreal forest to make it safe to do so. The Patch's oil sands operations endured weeks of shutdowns—not because the fire threatened their operations but because staffing them was impossible. Roughly a million barrels of the industry's daily output had to shut down for the month, but by early June work schedules and production levels escalated rapidly back to normal.

Along with forty thousand other evacuees, Kiran Malik-Khan and her family went to Edmonton. They found an apartment, and Malik-Khan was back at work from a temporary office there within ten days, helping with the recovery. Maryellen Fenech and her family stayed a few nights in an Edmonton hotel. A few days after they arrived, a friend texted with a picture of their street, confirming what they had assumed but hoped wasn't true, which was that their house was gone. They flew back to Dan's hometown of Antigonish, Nova Scotia, and by the week after the fire, her kids were in school there. They left the kids with their grandparents and returned to work, and by the end of July, the whole family was back in Fort McMurray, living in a rental in Timberlea and beginning the process of building a new house on the site where the one they adored had stood. Raheel Joseph and his wife and daughter stayed with his brother in Edmonton until Joseph could return to work in early June. He left his family there the rest of the summer—his wife was having considerable anxiety about the fire and worried about the impact on their daughter's health from the lingering smoke—but eventually they returned. They returned, like eighty thousand other evacuees, because Fort McMurray was not a work camp or busted boomtown. It was their home.

"You couldn't pay me a million dollars to live anywhere else," Kiran Malik-Khan said after she'd returned to her house in Timberlea. "I love Fort McMurray."

Such sentiments surprised the world beyond the Patch, because the boomtown hype had been mistaken for the city's true face. The fire unmasked Fort McMurray. Those who saw the place as a font of easy money or the root of all climate evil saw it for the first time as it actually was. The old stereotypes fell quickly away in the relentless press coverage of the Beast. Observers across the country and around the world could see themselves, finally, in the horror and desperate flight and gritty, aching labour of survival. Fort McMurray was a model of calm resolve, and the outsized High Modern trappings of the oil sands business were central to its salvation.

Perhaps this is why, when some commentators attempted to overlay a climate change narrative on the disaster, it mostly wouldn't take. Not because a wildfire of such magnitude had nothing to do with a global climate more prone to extremes of heat and drought—those were certainly factors in the Beast's awesome power—but because this was so clearly a human tragedy before it could be anything else. It was too much to ask one vulnerable little city in the woods of northern Alberta to pay for the emissions sins of the whole overheated, oil-addicted world.

Not quite everyone returned to the Patch after the fire. The mobile workforce, already declining in response to month after month of sub-$50 oil, thinned even further. Some small portion of those who lost everything decided not to rebuild. Maryellen Fenech's in-laws were among them; they had already tried to retire to Antigonish once before, and this time they went back to Nova Scotia for good.

Robert Grandjambe Jr. went back to the Patch for a few months after the fire, and he was in line for a full-time millwright job with Enbridge when he decided to devote himself instead to his traditional skills and way of life—and to teaching those skills to the vast majority of Indigenous youth who had no other way to learn. He didn't regret his work in the Patch, but he felt it was time to do more to respect the land and the deep knowledge of it that he'd acquired.

"I believe in the fur industry and I believe it's important to maintain and sustain that livelihood," he said. "So there's no better time to be the example and stand above and say, No, I don't need oil and gas to feed my family or to have a brand-new truck or to buy something."

Robert Jr. had managed a tricky balance between two very different worlds all his life. But now he was ready to move on, to immerse himself entirely in the one he thought would best sustain him in an uncertain and tumultuous age.

THIRTEEN

COMPLICITY

I was born on an air force base on the Canadian prairie the summer of the OPEC embargo. My father flew fighter jets for a living, flew them nearly every day of the working week for years at a stretch, burning jet fuel to roar through the sky faster than the speed of sound. And so if the sins of the father are visited on the son, then my carbon budget was surely blown before I could walk.

I spent my adolescence at CFB Cold Lake on the southern rim of the McMurray Formation in the mid-1980s, just after Imperial Oil began developing in situ deposits in the area. At my brother's high school, off-base in the nearby town of Grand Centre, it was a common path for a teenage boy struggling in school to quit and go off to work as a rig pig, an unskilled labourer on an oil drilling site. Sometimes it was said on the school grounds they'd gone off to the tar sands, which was the only term anyone used for the industry in Cold Lake in those days.

When I was in grade 9, there was a guy a couple years older than me who liked two of the girls I hung around with, and he and his buddy would come by our junior high school at lunch, his buddy driving the brand-new Chevy Camaro he'd bought with the money he made working on the rigs. The three of us would pile in the back of that Camaro and go roaring around the back roads through the forest or into town to get McDonald's takeout. They would often blast "Cadillac Ranch" by Bruce Springsteen on the car's booming stereo. *Open up your engines, let 'em roar / Tearin' up the highway like a big ole dinosaur. . . .*

I attended high school in North Bay, a small city four hours north of Toronto on the southern edge of Ontario's boreal forest. North Bay was a sprawled-out little burgh, and the bus routes were infrequent, the waits at the bus stops bone-chilling several months of the year, and so like every other able-bodied kid in North Bay, I took my driver's test within days of my sixteenth birthday. And then I was free. On winter nights when there was fresh snow, my friends and I would celebrate our liberation by driving to the empty shopping mall parking lot and doing donuts and figure eights in the snow, spinning out and laughing at the centrifugal thrill. It was a ritual that felt like a birthright in northern Ontario in the 1980s.

My father was posted to Germany while I was in university, so the trip home for the holidays was a transatlantic flight. My parents bought a stylish vintage BMW 520 from a fellow Canadian heading home, and I drove it every chance I got when I was in Germany for work in the summers. Sometimes I'd drive aimlessly through the Black Forest, stopping at castle ruins. Or I'd take it out on the autobahn and push the needle as far as I dared. I flirted with 200 km/h once. The highway gets narrower and longer at that speed, like a tunnel.

A significant part of my job as an adult has always been to travel to places and see things most people don't and then tell stories about them. I have circled the globe on planes several times over. I rode motorbike taxis across Bangkok and autorickshaws, with their filthy growling two-stroke diesel engines, throughout Delhi and Hyderabad. I drove rental cars from North Carolina to Florida and Colorado to New Mexico at the end of continent-wide flights. I flew to Copenhagen more than once and rode a bicycle all over town. All of this travel, just to tell stories about solutions to the climate change crisis.

I live in Calgary, the corporate capital of the Patch. My wife grew up in the city and my two children have known no other home. When my daughter was born, the congratulatory package of health-care brochures and baby-product samples handed out on departure from the hospital included an invitation to plant a tree in her name in a grove maintained by BP. She attended the city's lycée for a time, and one September we arrived to drop her off for the first day of school to find that a new sign with the Total logo on it over the entrance; the company had recently made major oil sands investments, and the lycée had made a deal to guarantee spots in the school for the children of Total employees. I ran for Parliament once, as a Green Party candidate in a 2012 by-election, and came surprisingly close to winning through the efforts of a volunteer team thick with oil-and-gas sector employees.

I am dug in, is what I mean. I sit in a house warmed by natural gas to tap at a petrochemical polymer keyboard. I might prefer walking and trains to cars and airplanes, but I'm as fully complicit in the long rule of oil as anyone. As everyone. This is our world, and it is caught between one age and another, the fossil-fuelled High Modern and whatever comes after it in a world shaken by climate change. The only difference between the Patch and anywhere else is that its complicity is so much more prominent on the landscape.

When I was planning my first visit to Fort McMurray and the oil sands mines, I didn't want to think of Mordor or the moon, some easy other-worldly resonance with no connection to my life or my country or the civilization that sustains me. I didn't want to be summarily absolved of my connection to it and my complicity in it all. So I made a trip to the Grand Coulee Dam, that megalith of the High Modern in the mountains of eastern Washington state. It is one of the largest concrete structures on earth, built in the 1930s as part of Franklin D. Roosevelt's visionary New Deal. It was a wonder of the world on completion and still significant enough—and widely enough celebrated—in the 1970s that an elaborate visitors' centre was added to the complex. More recently, the dam's minders introduced a laser light show, projected onto the massive concrete face of the dam nightly in the summer months.

I also paid a visit to Port Arthur, the Texas city not far from the site of the Spindletop oil strike on the Gulf of Mexico where millions of the world's barrels of crude are refined into products we use every day. The south side of Port Arthur is a cluster of refineries, a vast maze of pipe and smokestack and hydrocarbon processing, the reeking guts of the continent's energy business.

I made these pilgrimages as inoculations, so that the scale of the oil sands—its most arresting feature—would have analogues in my memory. Suncor offers a tour of its base site through the Oil Sands Discovery Centre in Fort McMurray, and when my tour bus turned the same corner Raheel Joseph's Diversified coach does every day, just past the plant's main gate, and unveiled a broad, rolling landscape of pipe and smokestack and open-pit mines, I was ready for it. It felt not like some alien intrusion on the pristine boreal landscape but like an extension of a long progressive tradition and an outpost of a global energy regime.

I knew the industry's critics all too well. After a decade tracking the progress made on building an industrial order free of fossil fuels, I understood intimately why bitumen had been cast as the last fuel source the world needs now. What I needed was to connect the Patch to my colleagues and the other parents on my daughter's baseball team back in Calgary, to the thoughtful progressives I met in Calgary politics who turn out to be Syncrude engineers or Suncor lawyers or sustainability managers for Cenovus. The Patch, after all, is a Canadian institution, an industrial cluster built by the collective will of several levels of government across many generations. It is a place where Canadians live their lives in a Canadian city like any other. The Patch is us.

We could begin there, on that middle ground, but for the trenches to either side. The Patch has become a battlefield, in some sense literal but primarily ideological, and our way forward runs through it. The battle that began there will come everywhere, if it hasn't arrived already, because it's a battle over how anyone who relies on fossil fuel—which is virtually everyone—will restructure their lives for a world with much less fossil fuel in it.

The early reports from the Patch, frankly, aren't promising. It is either Hiroshima or a wonder of the world, a vital economic engine or the most destructive project on earth, an essential commodity or dirty oil, Mordor or Fort McMoney. There is no nuance in this rhetoric, no room for compromise. These are ideological weapons in a zero-sum fight over complicity. The Patch's opponents say all the complicity rests on the other side of the battlefield, with the corporate exploiters making billions by destroying the planet. Its defenders say there is no crime to be complicit in, or else that the crime is all the world's.

How could someone justify what this is doing to the land, the water, the air, the whole planet's climate?

How could it be wrong to deliver people the fuel they need every day of their lives?

There is no common ground. And that is how both sides lose.

As a nation, Canada aims for placid civility. It is polite and dull in the stereotypical version of the story. If its sociopolitical culture has a bias, it is toward mushy middle ground.

There is a way to summarize the long arc of Canadian history as a series of opt-outs, concessions and compromises. Like any overly tidy historical device, this one hacks away some inconvenient underbrush and prunes any number of significant but tangential branches. But it's a plausible through-line all the same: the transactional collaboration between voyageurs and Indigenous peoples. The influx of British Loyalists unwilling to embrace the American Revolution. Robert Baldwin's invitation to Louis-Hippolyte LaFontaine to run for a seat in Upper Canada after being bullied into withdrawing by rebellious mobs in Lower Canada—the first real political collaboration between French and English Canadians, which enshrined phrases like "historic compromise" and "moderate reformer" in Canada's political lexicon. A Confederation deal that only went halfway, under duress, for fear of American encroachment. Middle-power status and the Quiet Revolution and official multiculturalism. The notwithstanding clause in the nation's Constitution—a deeply compromised founding document more than a century in the making, delivered nevertheless with a Charter of Rights and Freedoms that became a model copied around the world.

This arc has a dark shadow. The unsettled legacy of the Royal Proclamation and the Quebec Act, which enshrined English conquest but left room for the French to endure. The institutionalized hypocrisy of the Indian Act and the numbered treaties that annexed half a continent from Indigenous peoples who had no written legal tradition of land rights or private property. A nation whose economic foundations were built almost entirely on resource extraction but whose self-image would come to be coloured by pride in its tradition of conservation and stewardship in a vast hinterland.

Canada's political culture is, in any case, cautious and consensus seeking. It was not designed for radical change or rapid transformation. It doesn't do revolution. In many ways, it seems a poor fit to respond to the extraordinary challenge to the status quo posed by climate change, ill-suited to the total reimagination of the very foundations of modern civilization the crisis obliges. But perhaps Canada's mushy middle is the best place to build the kind of broad, lurching, jerry-built consensus that long-term action on climate change requires. A mining operation in the remote Canadian wilderness became the front line of this century's energy and climate debate by a sort of accident of American politics. But what if Canada's placid civility is the best way to bring together all the disparate factions and interests that must come on board to meet this challenge?

There is a paradox in Canada's relationship with its natural spaces that is older than the country itself, an awkward two-step attempting to balance the national economy's deeply exploitive disposition toward resource development with a civil society increasingly oriented toward a gentler and more custodial role of sound environmental stewardship. This is the core contradiction between the High Modern and Anthropocene definitions of progress, and it has been embedded deeply in the national character. Or to put it less charitably, Canada has always tried to have it both ways. The tension between the two understandings—the presumption of balance—snapped under the pressure of the Patch's long boom.

For the first three centuries or more of European settlement in Canada, there was nothing understood to be contradictory in these custodial and exploitative roles. The idea of nature as a storehouse to feed human needs and a treasure trove to feed human ambitions was a pillar of Western civilization. If not for fur and fish and logs, gold and wheat and nickel and uranium and oil—if not for *commodities*, why would anyone have established a colony or founded a nation here?

Even Canada's first national parks—beginning with Banff, established in the Rocky Mountains of Alberta in 1885—reflected this dual role. It was understood by the government of the day that parkland was being set aside both for its aesthetic and ecological merits and for its natural resource value. Until the 1920s, the shores of Lake Minnewanka in Banff National Park were home to a thriving coal-mining camp. Only with the National Parks Act of 1930 did resource development begin to be restricted in Canada's national parks.

In the years after the Second World War, Canada found a tenuous but manageable balance between its resource extraction economy and its increasingly stewardship-minded civil society. Guided by a series of broadly liberal governments and managed by a professional, evidence-driven bureaucracy, Canada's resource economy girded itself with environmental assessments and regulations understood to be as smart and stringent as any in the world. What's more, Canada came to be seen as a leader in the emerging political art of reining in an industrial economy's environmental oversights and excesses, a place eager to sponsor the kind of research that drove international regulatory initiatives to reduce water pollution from phosphates and the air pollution causing acid rain. When scientists discovered a huge and growing hole in the earth's ozone layer, Canadian

researchers and bureaucrats were so central to the response that the ensuing global ban in the manufacture of ozone-depleting chemicals would
be named the Montreal Protocol. And in civil society, the global environmental movement traces its origins in significant measure to a small
crew of Vancouver activists whose "Don't Make a Wave" campaign against
nuclear weapons tests in the Pacific Ocean morphed into Greenpeace,
one of the first environmental groups with truly worldwide scope.

When climate change began to emerge as a substantial environmental
issue in the late 1980s, Canada's initial response was to extend its emerging expertise in environmental research and stewardship to the newest
challenge of the day. The first major international meeting of climate scientists was hosted by the Mulroney government in Toronto in 1988, which
begat the Rio Summit in 1992 and the Kyoto Protocol in 1997. Canada
prided itself on its climate leadership, ratifying the Kyoto treaty with much
fanfare.

Climate change, however, is not a hole in the ozone layer, and carbon dioxide is not analogous to the chlorofluorocarbons that punched that
hole. The problem was not the product of a refrigerant manufactured by
a handful of chemical companies. Climate change is pervasive, universal
and ongoing, emergent everywhere and visible nowhere, at least at first. It
is caused—day by greenhouse-gas-emitting day—by almost every single
thing citizens of an industrial economy like Canada do from the moment
they drive to work in the morning until they settle back in at night, warm
in homes heated by natural gas and lit by lamps still sometimes powered
by coal. And Canada, it turns out, is one of a handful of the most egregious
contributors to the great emissions bonfire, our carbon budgets swelled by
homes in need of heat, great distances in need of crossing and fossil fuels
in search of profit. Our national carbon footprint is among the half-dozen
largest on earth in per capita terms.

Climate change has called into question the very foundations of
Canada's economy, spilled sand in the prosperous lubricant of its placid
civil society, distorted the historic good-guy image in the national mirror.
In response, Canada has grandstanded, backtracked, equivocated and

dissembled. Only once the Patch became a global smear on the nation's reputation did Canadians attempt to stare themselves full in the face of climate reality's mirror for the first time. It was not a pretty image. But then, in the Anthropocene, whose is?

Maybe because the deep contradictions between the High Modern and Anthropocene definitions of progress have come into their highest relief to date in Canada—in the Patch—Canadians have begun to see more clearly than most how complex the process of reconciling those definitions will be. This is the Patch's great lesson: The climate crisis took generations to create. It will take a generation or more to solve. It was unintentional, arising from what was understood to be the most vital job of a modern industrial society—fuelling its engines. It won't be solved in a campaign, and the solutions aren't anywhere near simple enough to fit on a protest placard or a billboard.

At the end of November 2016, Justin Trudeau stepped up to a podium in Ottawa and announced that his government was approving two major oil pipeline projects and rejecting a third. All three were intended to carry bitumen from the Patch to tidewater ports and international markets. One of the approved projects was the expansion of Kinder Morgan's Trans Mountain pipeline, the twinning of the company's existing pipe from Edmonton to the port of Vancouver. Nine months earlier, Trudeau had worked with provincial governments across the country to agree on a coordinated national climate plan, which would include a binding price on carbon dioxide emissions and the phasing out of coal-fired power plants nationwide. In the circles most excited by the climate plan, the pipeline approvals were seen as a betrayal.

I'd spent more than a decade at that point reporting on climate change solutions. I understood exactly how urgent our shift away from fossil fuels was, and I knew what the world on the other side of the transition might look like. In a way, I've already been there. I've toured wind farms in Denmark and solar-powered villages in Thailand. I've seen wondrously efficient architectural marvels in India and wholly self-sufficient zero-emissions communities on the coast of Scotland and in the New Mexican desert. I've interviewed brilliant engineers and tireless entrepreneurs and crafty old politicians working on the design of that low-carbon world. In the south of Germany, I once sat with an architect in a townhouse that generated more energy than it used from nothing but the sun, and I heard about how he had built it, how he'd built a whole community of them. Then I thanked him for his time and walked the streets between the rows of the townhouses he'd designed and wondered why houses were still being built any other way.

I'd seen that new world emerging, liberated from fossil fuels and the scourge of climate change. In recent years, a slogan has emerged, popular among renewable energy advocates and climate change campaigners: *100% Possible*. An entire modern society, running exclusively on emissions-free energy—this is the rallying cry. I'd been chanting my own version of the same mantra for years. I'd been to an island in Denmark called Samsø that was maybe the first jurisdiction on earth to actually pursue that goal and achieve it in a systemic way. I knew the tune well.

I had once been convinced that the mounting evidence and compelling case studies could win the day pretty much on their own. The concepts had been proven. They could be copied—would be copied—and achieve the same successes. So it would go, on and on, project by project and policy by policy, energy and then transportation and then urban design, until the whole impossibly scaled mess of climate change was surmounted. Now that people knew what was possible, we would hit critical mass and the tide would shift. Any day now.

In retrospect, I made a single monumental mistake: I'd discounted politics. It's an error I still see in the circles where the *100% Possible* slogan and others like it—*Keep It in the Ground*, for example—hold sway. Politics, with whatever ugly baggage comes attached to it, is the necessary vehicle for collective action in democratic societies. Politics is how Karl Clark funded research to develop hot water separation process for bitumen; the way Howard Pew was convinced to invest millions of dollars of Sun Oil's money in a bitumen mine; the way Syncrude found funding after its financing nearly collapsed; the means by which a tax and royalty regime was installed to trigger the long boom. And now politics must find its way to a middle ground, a plateau and long fade in the Patch as the technology and economics and political will come together to build that low-carbon world. And it must do so, alas, with a battleground as its starting point.

There is no set of policies so flawless and no social movement of such undeniable force that the industrial order that spent two hundred years building a system to justify and replicate itself will simply crumble away to usher in a new system boasting the perfect political efficiency that would be needed to make *100% Possible* manifest the world over in a decade. Climate politics is already more muddled than most kinds, and energy policy is a morass of vested interests. The transition from one energy regime to another will be managed by the same tangled nest of hypocritical, compromised, self-interested politics that runs the enormous machine today. And so, here in Canada, there are both carbon prices and pipeline approvals—messy Canadian compromises, the best we can manage to date.

In the spring of 2006, early in my hunt for climate change solutions, I received an invitation to a symposium at a country estate in northern Germany. One of the other guests was a British campaigner named George Marshall, obsessed with what he was then calling "the psychology of denial." Marshall wanted to know why he and other climate change advocates perceived such an urgent threat when the general public did not. He also wondered why the public response to climate change had not followed the orderly march from alarm call to advocacy to action that was seen with other environmental issues, such as ozone depletion.

In 2014 Marshall published a book on the subject called *Don't Even Think About It: Why Our Brains Are Wired to Ignore Climate Change*. He'd spent the years since I'd met him in Germany talking to social anthropologists and behavioural psychologists, as well as activists for and against action on climate change, and he'd uncovered a cognitive tic that he was convinced explained our conflicted, counterproductive collective response.

"The things that we pay immediate attention to are things that are here and now," Marshall said in an interview. "Things where there is a certainty of imminent threat, especially those that are caused by an identifiable enemy with the intention to cause us harm. And the problem is climate change has none of these qualities. Climate change appears to be in the future, uncertain, distant in both time and place. And possibly, above all, it suffers from the fact that there is no clear enemy with the intention to cause us harm. In fact, if anyone is responsible, it is ourselves. And that generates another level of anxiety and moral challenge for us that makes us want to push this issue even further away into the far distance, and not to deal with it."

There is an entire niche in the scientific literature alongside Marshall's book. There are studies looking at the cognitive biases at work, polemics on how to "reframe" climate change as a more positive or more immediate or more conservative issue. In social psychology, there is a concept known as a normative threat: a perceived challenge to a social group's moral order seen as so dangerous that it triggers something like an all-out-war response. Under a normative threat, a social group will lurch away from new ideas and open dialogue, demanding total and forceful rejection. This is the result of the moral challenge Marshall talks about. Action on climate change commensurate with the scale of the problem promises to change how we light and heat our houses, how we travel daily to work, what kind of things we can buy and eat and what they cost. For a significant portion of the general public in Canada or anywhere else, action on climate change is a normative threat. In the Patch, beyond the necessary PR-minded compromise stances of the executives at some of the biggest companies, it is most certainly seen this way: the climate activists would take away everything they cherish—their jobs, their community, their industry—if they could.

Climate change, again, is not a campaign. It won't be beaten. We won't "win." We will either change our daily lives and the industrial basis of our societies, or we won't, over years and decades. In mean little increments. Through fleeting elation and hard compromise. Or I'll be proven wrong, and change will come suddenly, and I will be delighted to have misjudged the situation so thoroughly.

I once attended a presentation given by renowned broadcaster and environmental activist David Suzuki at a church in downtown Calgary. Suzuki narrated a slideshow about his life and work, lingering on his time in Haida Gwaii, the majestic island chain off the coast of northwestern British Columbia. In the early 1980s, he'd done a story on his CBC program *The Nature of Things* about a growing movement among the Haida people and environmental activists to stop logging in the pristine Sitka spruce rainforest on one of the islands. The broadcast triggered a wave of support, and Suzuki joined the protest. They stopped the logging company. In his presentation, Suzuki showed a picture of the victory celebration on some remote beach after the battle had been won.

I sat in the audience wondering if climate change would ever see a moment of triumph as clear as that. Or if I would. Who would even gather on the beach? What beach, even?

When the Patch's boosters say they are simply supplying a product everyone uses every single day, they are not wrong. When the prime minister says, "No country would find 173 billion barrels of oil in the ground and just leave them there," he's not wrong. When antipipeline protesters say some of that oil has to stay in the ground, they're not wrong. When Indigenous people say they've never been properly consulted about what those pipelines and bitumen mines are doing to their land, they're not wrong.

There's more to the debate, though, more to the way forward, than being right. A thing of such scope and power and wealth as the Patch doesn't go away overnight or in a few years. Building the entire industrial basis of modern society on a new energy regime does not happen overnight or in a few years. We will have the Patch for decades. It is a fixture on the Canadian landscape. It employs tens of thousands. It is a truly national project, or else the term has no meaning.

We have all benefited. We are all stakeholders. We are all complicit.

ACKNOWLEDGMENTS

I would first like to extend my deepest thanks to the Canada Council for the Arts, the Alberta Foundation for the Arts and the Chawkers Foundation for their generous financial support of the research and writing of this book. A writer's finances are never pretty, and the intensive field research required for a project like this simply could not be undertaken without such vital funding.

I also owe a deep debt of gratitude to the Calgary-based Petroleum History Society and the Glenbow Museum. The Society's "Oil Sands Oral History Project," archived at the Glenbow, was an invaluable gift to my research. The hundred-plus interviews with oil sands industry pioneers, leaders, workers and critics in the collection saved me countless hours of digging and research. This book's historical depth is in large measure thanks to those interviews.

I would like to extend my deepest thanks as well to the many friends and colleagues in Calgary and beyond who generously shared their knowledge of the Patch and their contacts in it. My thanks to Todd Babiak,

Cody Battershill, Kim Blomme, Catherine Brownlee, Ken Chapman, Heather Douglas, Petra Dolata, Max Fawcett, David Finch, Dan Furst, Paul Haavardsrud, Terrance Houle, Bruce Manning, Emma Grace May, Bob Mitchell, Naheed Nenshi, Eric Newell, Adrienne Nickerson and Leor Rotchild.

My thanks to Peter MacConnachie at Suncor, Brett Harris and Sonja Franklin at Cenovus, Brad Bellows at MEG Energy, and Jason Kielau at ATCO for their assistance with gathering background information on the oil sands industry. In addition to those cited by name in the text, thanks to Melissa Blake, Kyle Harrietha, Daniel Stuckless, James Teasdale, Justin VannPashak and Paul Spring for their time and guidance on the ground in Fort McMurray and Fort McKay. Thanks to Stuart Macmillan of the Peace-Athabasca Delta Environmental Monitoring Program for essential help with my research on the environmental science of the region. Thanks to Dene elder Fred Djiskili, Lisa King of the Athabasca Chipewyan First Nation Industry Relations Corporation, and Meghan Dalrymple for vital assistance with field research in Fort Chipewyan. John Phyne and Lynda Harling Stalker of St. Francis Xavier University lent their expertise to my research on the Patch's Atlantic Canadian labour force. Sean Mahoney of the Conservation Law Foundation was a helpful guide to the antipipeline protests in South Portland, Maine.

I owe a huge debt to Andrew Leach of the University of Alberta, who not only made sure I didn't embarrass myself too badly on the subject of oil sands economics but brought his knowledge to bear on my many other questions about the industry. James Daschuk of the University of Regina reviewed the sections of this book dealing with the history of Indigenous peoples on the Canadian prairie with great care and critical insight. Any errors that remain in the text on these and all other topics are mine alone.

This book would never have come to be without the generosity of my brilliant writer friends Sheila Heti and Will Ferguson. My agent, Sam Hiyate, at the Rights Factory, was a dogged champion of this project from start to finish. At Simon & Schuster Canada, Kevin Hanson had as much to do with conceiving this book as I did and went above and beyond to turn it from concept into reality. Brendan May has been a thoughtful and patient editor. To the entire team at S&S, my eternal gratitude for your hard work.

I owe the usual inadequate thanks for the usual extraordinary support of my family. My parents, John and Margo Turner, and my father-in-law, Bruce Bristowe, continue to be steadfast in their support of this writer's long and uneven career. As ever, my wife, Ashley Bristowe, provided editorial advice, strategic counsel, research design and more good ideas than I could fit into this book. She is the Calgary-bred reason I made a home and a life in Canada's oil capital and the primary source of the joy I've found here. My children, Sloane and Alexander, delight me daily and provide the motive force for all my work.

A final note on the research: when I began work on *The Patch*, I anticipated that some of the best sources would be reluctant to speak publicly about it. I was surprised and deeply disappointed to discover that many of the industry's key players and some of its most vocal critics proved not just reluctant but completely unwilling to speak to me for this book. The list of names at the other end of denied interview requests and unreturned email and voice mail messages could fill several pages. It would include virtually every major corporate name associated with the oil sands, with the partial exceptions of Suncor, MEG Energy and Cenovus, whose media representatives were willing to entertain informal conversations and carefully controlled interviews in Calgary but refused to allow me to see any aspect of their field operations (aside from the public tours of the Suncor base site the company sometimes offers through the Oil Sands Discovery Centre in Fort McMurray) or speak to anyone employed by them on site. On one hand I can understand the reticence to go on record about a story that neither boosters nor critics believe has ever been told fairly, but I would argue that no agenda is well served by refusing to allow more light in; it only amplifies the distortions. The Patch's story is an important one, and it is still being written, and it should be shared.

GLOSSARY

BITUMEN: A sticky, black, tar-like mixture of *hydrocarbons*.

BOREAL FOREST: The northernmost forest zone in the northern hemisphere. The boreal forest stretches in a belt across North America, Europe and Asia.

COLLOIDAL SUSPENSION: A phenomenon in which a solid substance is permanently suspended in a liquid without being dissolved into it.

CRUDE OIL: Raw, unrefined *petroleum*.

DILBIT: Diluted bitumen; a blend of bitumen and petroleum products such as naphtha to lower the viscosity for long-distance transport.

FINES: The slurry of 15 percent to 30 percent clay particles and other solids suspended in the water in tailings ponds. Has a viscosity and texture similar to yogurt. Also known as "mature fine tailings" or "fluid fine tailings."

FOSSIL FUEL: Term referring to any natural fuel that is formed from the remains of living organisms. Includes petroleum, coal and natural gas.

GCOS (GREAT CANADIAN OIL SANDS): Founded by J. Howard Pew in 1967,

GCOS was the first company to begin mining bitumen at a commercial scale in the oil sands.

HYDROCARBON: An energy-dense organic compound consisting entirely of hydrogen and carbon. Hydrocarbons are typically created by decomposed organic matter, and they are the main constituent in petroleum and natural gas.

HYDROTRANSPORT: The transportation of ore from collection drums to a main processing plant. Hydrotransport is also the first stage in the bitumen separation process.

IN SITU OPERATIONS: Mining operations that extract bitumen using drilling rigs and horizontal wells. (See *SAGD*.) Contrasts with *open-pit mining*.

KEYSTONE PIPELINE: Oil pipeline system that runs from the Western Canada Sedimentary Basin in Alberta to refineries in Illinois and Texas, as well as to oil distribution centres in Oklahoma. A planned fourth phase for the pipeline, Keystone XL, became a symbol of the battle over climate change and was rejected by US President Barack Obama in 2015.

KINDER MORGAN TRANS MOUNTAIN PIPELINE: Oil pipeline system that runs from Edmonton, Alberta, to Burnaby, British Columbia. It is the only oil pipeline in North America that transports both crude oil and refined oil products to the West Coast.

OPEN-PIT MINING: Mining operations that extract bitumen by digging it up from the earth using massive truck-and-shovel technology. Contrasts with *in situ operations*.

PETROLEUM: A naturally occurring liquid oil that can be refined into numerous types of fuel. Petroleum is composed of *hydrocarbons* and other organic compounds.

SAGD (STEAM-ASSISTED GRAVITY DRAINAGE): A mining technology for producing heavy crude oil and bitumen. Two horizontal wells are drilled into a deposit several metres apart. The upper well injects steam into the deposit, liquefying the bitumen, which drips into the lower well. The lower well then collects the bitumen and pumps it to the surface for processing.

TAILINGS POND: A large pool into which the crushed stone and other waste (tailings) produced from mining and drilling are drained. Also known as a settling basin.

UPGRADING: The process by which bitumen is transformed into a higher-quality synthetic crude oil prior to shipping to refineries for further processing. Upgrading involves either removing carbon or adding hydrogen to bitumen, removing sulphur and nitrogen, and breaking the more complex heavy oil molecules into simpler, lighter ones.

WCS (WESTERN CANADIAN SELECT): A grade of crude oil made of low-grade heavy oils. Typically sells at prices well below *WTI*.

WTI (WEST TEXAS INTERMEDIATE): A grade of crude oil used as an international benchmark in oil pricing. Also known as "Texas light sweet."

For a bibliography of major works consulted for this book and full chapter-by-chapter source notes, please visit ChrisTurnerWorks.com.

INDEX

Unifor, 270
United Nations:
climate change conferences, 23, 213,
226–28, 231, 251
Permanent Forum on Indigenous Issues,
208
University College London, 260
University of Alberta, 37, 167
University of Calgary, 258
University of Waterloo, 210, 211, 218
upgrading, 18, 75–77
upstream, defined, 75
Upton, 45
uranium, 212

van der Veer, Jeroen, 14, 15
Vancouver, 114, 115, 118, 270, 282, 314,
315
Venezuela, 11, 44, 257
very large crude carriers (VLCCs), 145

W. A. C. Bennett Dam, 210, 220, 272, 278,
282
Wapasu Creek Lodge, 20, 22
Wapisiw Lookout, 170, 171
Waterways, 8, 37, 301, 303
Waydowntown (film), 93
Weaver, Andrew, 257
West Texas Intermediate (WTI), 100, 112,
115, 284
Western Arctic Leadership Program, 275,
276
Western Canadian Sedimentary Basin, 76,
141
Western Canadian Select (WCS), 100, 115,
139
WestJet, 136

whaling, 230, 231
Wichita, Kansas, 142
Wild Idaho Rising Tide, 245–46
Wildlife Rehabilitation Society of
Edmonton, xxi
Wilfrid Laurier University, 210, 211
Williams Brothers, 68
Wilson, Chris, 203
Winter Olympics (1988), 122
Wisconsin, 116, 117, 120, 140–42
Wolfe, Brent, 211, 218–23
Wood Buffalo Environmental Association,
204, 268
Wood Buffalo National Park, 210, 214, 219,
270
work camps, 19–23, 72, 135, 137
work uniform, 18–19, 93–94
World Bank, 267
World Economic Forum (2008), 15
World Economic Summit (2013), 253
World Heavy Oil Congress (2015),
117–19
Woynillowicz, Dan, 195

Yarega oil field, 68–70
Yasuni National Park, Ecuador, 13
Yellowknife, 211, 222
Yergin, Daniel, 51
Yes Men, 233
Yom Kippur War, 177
York Factory, 28, 29
Yost, Helen, 245–46
Young, Neil, 214, 269, 270
Youth Climate Coalition, 233
Yukon, 27, 32

zero emissions, 122, 260, 316